BELFAST BOYS

Belfast Boys

How Unionists and Nationalists
Fought and Died Together in
the First World War

Richard S. Grayson

continuum

Continuum
Continuum UK, The Tower Building, 11 York Road, London SE1 7NX
Continuum US, 80 Maiden Lane, Suite 704, New York, NY 10038

www.continuumbooks.com

First published 2009

British Library Cataloguing-in-Publication Data
A catalogue record for this book is available from the British Library.

ISBN 978 1 84725 008 7

Typeset by Pindar NZ, Auckland, New Zealand
Printed and bound by MPG Books Ltd, Cornwall, Great Britain

Contents

Abbreviations

ANZAC	Australian and New Zealand Army Corps
BET	*Belfast Evening Telegraph*
BNL	*Belfast News Letter*
BT	*Belfast Telegraph*
BWN	*Belfast Weekly News*
BWT	*Belfast Weekly Telegraph*
CO	Colonial Office (used in notes only)
CO	Commanding Officer
Cpl	Corporal
CWGC	Commonwealth War Graves Commission
DCM	Distinguished Conduct Medal
DoW	Died of Wounds
DSM	Distinguished Service Medal
Inniskillings	Royal Inniskilling Fusiliers
IN	*Irish News*
INV	Irish National Volunteers
INVA	Irish Nationalist Veterans' Association
IRA	Irish Republican Army
IRB	Irish Republican Brotherhood
IV	Irish Volunteers
IWM	Imperial War Museum
KIA	Killed in Action
L/Cpl	Lance Corporal
MM	Military Medal
NA	The National Archive, Kew
NAM	National Army Museum
NCO	Non-Commissioned Officer
NLI	National Library of Ireland
NW	*Northern Whig*
OR	Other Ranks
PoW	Prisoner of War
PRONI	Public Record Office, Northern Ireland
Pte	Private
RAMC	Royal Army Medical Corps
RFA	Royal Field Artillery
RIC	Royal Irish Constabulary

RNAS	Royal Naval Air Service
RIRifles	Royal Irish Rifles
RUC	Royal Ulster Constabulary
SDGW	Soldiers Died in the Great War
SHC	Somme Heritage Centre
Sgt	Sergeant
UUC	Ulster Unionist Council
UVF	Ulster Volunteer Force
WO	War Office
YCV	Young Citizens Volunteers

TERMINOLOGY

'Unionist'/'Nationalist' (upper case) indicates a member of the Ulster Unionist Party or Irish Parliamentary Party, whereas 'unionist'/'nationalist' (lower case) is used for a member of the wider community, which generally supported the party. Neither 'republican' nor 'loyalist' were widely used terms in 1914–18, with 'nationalist'/'unionist' covering most people, but where they are used here, an upper case initial indicates a formal party association rather than broad support. As was common among all people in 1914–18, Derry is used for the city and Londonderry for the county. Unless in a direct quotation, the following terms are used: Ulster denotes the nine-county province; Northern Ireland refers to the six counties of the state established under the Government of Ireland Act (1920); Irish Free State is used for the other 26 counties of the island of Ireland from 1920 to 1949, after which Republic of Ireland is used.

In references, place of publication is London unless otherwise stated.

PERMISSIONS

Material from private archives has been reproduced by kind permission as follows: J. H. M. Staniforth (Rosamund Du Cane); H. Gill (Fr Fergus O' Donoghue SJ, Irish Jesuit Archives); S. Matier, A. Milne and War Diary of Walter Collins (Somme Heritage Centre); H. F. N. Jourdain and D. McWeeney (National Army Museum); F. W. S. Jourdain and W. Collins interviews (Imperial War Museum Sound Archive). As regards W. A. Lyon and J. F. B. O'Sullivan (held at the Imperial War Museum), every effort has been made to trace copyright holders; the author and the IWM would be grateful for any information which might help to trace those whose identities or addresses that are not currently known. I am grateful to the *Belfast Telegraph*, Somme Heritage Centre, and Royal Ulster Rifles Museum for permission to reproduce photos without charge, as credited at individual items. Pardons for executed soldiers are reproduced by permission of the National Archive, Kew. Material from the letters of W. A. Montgomery is quoted by permission of the Deputy Keeper of the Records, Public Record Office of Northern Ireland.

Illustrations

Maps

Tables

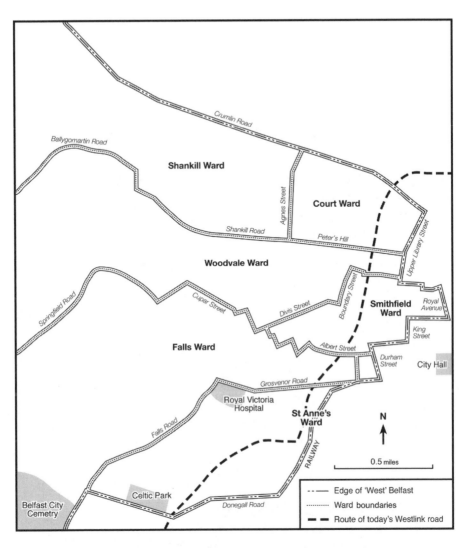

Map 1 Boundaries of 'West' Belfast as defined by author
Note: The area defined as 'West' Belfast in this book also includes Andersonstown and Ligoniel, just off the western edge of this map.

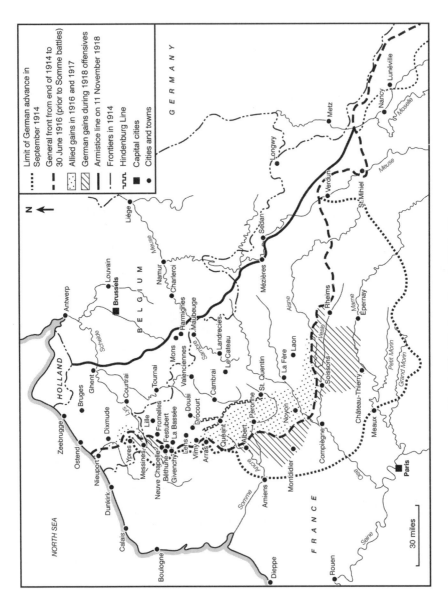

Map 2 The Western Front, 1914–18

Legend:

Limit of German advance in September 1914

General front from end of 1914 to 30 June 1916 (prior to Somme battles)

Allied gains in 1916 and 1917

German gains during 1918 offensives

Armistice line on 11 November 1918

Frontiers in 1914

Hindenburg Line

Capital cities

Cities and towns

N

NORTH SEA

GERMANY

HOLLAND

BELGIUM

FRANCE

Calais
Boulogne
Dieppe
Dunkirk
Zeebrugge
Ostend
Nieuport
Dixmude
Ypres
Bruges
Ghent
Courtrai
Messines
Neuve Chapelle
Béthune
Givenchy
Lille
Fromelles
Festubert
La Bassée
Tournai
Lens
Vimy
Arras
Quéant
Drocourt
Douai
Cambrai
Valenciennes
Mons
Le Cateau
Landrecies
Maubeuge
Harmignies
Charleroi
Namur
Brussels
Louvain
Antwerp
Liège
Albert
Péronne
St. Quentin
Noyon
La Fère
Laon
Compiègne
Montdidier
Amiens
Rouen
Meaux
Paris
Château-Thierry
Soissons
Rheims
Epernay
Mézières
Sedan
Verdun
St. Mihiel
Longwy
Metz
Nancy
Lunéville

Schelde
Meuse
Sambre
Somme
Ancre
Oise
Seine
Aisne
Vesle
Marne
Petit Morin
Grand Morin
Moselle
Meuse

30 miles

Preface

This book offers a new approach to the study of the First World War. It challenges simplicities and myths that surround the memory of the war in Ulster by focusing on one of its most divided areas: West Belfast. It tells the story of men from both sides of the religious and political divide as they enlisted for war. It describes how men from different backgrounds sometimes went to war together, side-by-side in the same battalion. It tells how men could fight in the same army against a common foe, but hold different views about how Ireland should be governed after the war. The book explores how other men volunteered regardless of their religion or politics simply because they needed a job.

It is important to tell this story because the historical memory of Belfast's service in 1914–18 is a simplistic one. Service by unionists has been celebrated by their unionist and loyalist descendants. It is a central element of their British identity. Conversely, service by nationalists has been written out of contemporary nationalist and republican narratives. Both sides of the divide have heroes from 1916. For unionists and loyalists they are the men who fought on the Somme, but for nationalists and republicans they are the leaders of the Easter Rising. Meanwhile, where either community has been aware of its forebears' service, it has tended to assume that the men fought in different parts of the army. As a result, the war has influenced contemporary identities by helping to define them narrowly. Yet in 1914–18 there was a strong element of Irishness among unionists, who found themselves in 'Irish' regiments and marked St Patrick's Day; similarly, nationalists were comfortable with membership of the British Empire, seeking devolution, not independence, from Westminster.

Consequently, this book tells a nuanced and interwoven story. It brings together the stories of Protestants from the Shankill and Catholics from the Falls to show where they shared experiences – and just as importantly, where they differed. It tackles the extent of sacrifice, showing that more men from the area were killed than was previously imagined, but also that more men survived: mortality rates were not as high as the public today tends to imagine.

The book is able to tell this new story by using a new method for studying the First World War. The author has researched sources that have never been used in this way before. Military historians often neglect newspapers, yet for Belfast they contain a wealth of contemporary detail on men of all ranks that simply cannot be found in any other place. Meanwhile, in addition to sources such as church memorial rolls and wills the author has analysed over 14,000 individual pensions and service records, which, when combined with other sources, have resulted in as many as 8,484 servicemen being identified from the west of the city, of whom at least 1,990 lost their lives. The pensions and service records became searchable online over 2007–9, and that has enabled searches for a particular place name, which can then be refined to specific streets. This development has made local studies possible in a way that they never were before, allowing street-by-street recording of those from a specific area who served. That allows the writing of a socio-military history that begins in the street rather than the trench or the training ground. Such a detailed study of individuals from a local area has never been published before.

A brief survey of previous literature demonstrates how unique this approach is. There are plenty of books that deal with the story of individual units of the British army in the First World War: stories of battalions, regiments and divisions. Many deal specifically with Irish units in the British army.[1] Others cover the Irish war experience more generally.[2] The specific issue of recruitment has a huge literature.[3] There are also studies focused on parts of Great Britain, which place units in their local context, linking one or two battalions, sometimes Pals' battalions, to an area.[4] But beyond some valuable 'Book of Honour' projects, nobody has told a story that represents the experiences of all the men from a town or city who can be found in all the sources, regardless of the units in which they served.[5] Yet if we are fully to understand recent debates on the impact of the war on Ireland, such as those relating to casualty figures, local studies are essential.[6]

This book focuses on 'West' Belfast. Today, as in 1914–18, it is one of the most divided parts of any city in Europe. It is essentially the areas widely known as the Falls and the Shankill, but also draws in outlying areas such as Ligoniel and Andersonstown, along with areas that might now be – but were not in 1914–18 – considered part of the city centre or of south Belfast. At the core of this study are units of the 36th (Ulster) and 16th (Irish) divisions, parts of which are well known to have been linked to the Shankill and the Falls. In particular, the book considers the 9th Royal Irish Rifles formed from the West Belfast Ulster Volunteer Force, and the 6th Connaught Rangers and the 7th Leinsters comprising many Belfast nationalists. However, these volunteer battalions only arrived on the Western Front in late 1915, so this book draws in men serving in other units, in every major theatre of war, from the retreat at Mons to the final victory. Consequently, it includes the regulars of the 2nd Royal Irish Rifles in action from early in the war, men of the 6th Royal Irish Rifles who served at Gallipoli, and those of the 1st Royal Inniskilling Fusiliers who went from action at Gallipoli to the Somme. It considers the war at sea and in the air as it involved men from West Belfast, and some of the ways that war affected the men, women and children who remained at home. It also examines what happened to the men who returned, including some who joined the Irish Republican Army to fight against the British. The book explores the lives of the men when they returned home. It concludes with an exploration of why remembrance of the war plays such a controversial role in Belfast's politics today.

In so doing, this book tells a different story from those that dominate the public imagination in Belfast. These focus on the 36th (Ulster) Division with the 16th (Irish) Division as an aside. While much attention is paid to both divisions, their men were a minority of those who served. Unionists and nationalists were serving side by side in regular battalions from the start of the war, while many others served in far-flung parts of the British military, often distant from their fellow Belfast men.

The nature of the sources, and the inherent bias of some, means that I am sceptical about efforts to reach a final total for the number of men from West Belfast who served in 1914–18. It is particularly difficult to compare levels of service among Protestants and Catholics. Despite this, by using sources that have not been used in this way before, we can be clear that many more served than has been imagined, and that many more were killed than was previously thought. But these numbers also mean that the overall fatality rate was lower than the public tends to assume because the number who returned alive is not widely known by a public which assumes that most on the front line were killed.

The patterns in these statistics are explored at the end, after the story has been told. This is a military history that begins in the street rather than the trench, so the story begins in 1912. In that year, the streets of Belfast were threatened with war, not because of the shooting of an Archduke in Sarajevo, but because of politics far closer to home.

Civil War?

... the people of Ulster will resist, and I think they will be right ...

ANDREW BONAR LAW MP, UNIONIST LEADER

*... there were no people in the whole of Ireland who were more ready to
fight and, if need be, to die, in defence of the liberty of their country than
the Nationalists of Belfast.*

JOSEPH DEVLIN, NATIONALIST MP FOR WEST BELFAST

In the summer of 1914 many people in Britain feared that their soldiers were
about to be plunged into bitter conflict. Yet it was not the threat of a war on the
Continent which caused so much alarm, but the possibility of civil war in Ireland.
After decades of parliamentary struggle, Home Rule for Ireland was about to pass
as the will of parliament, and it looked as if the Liberal government would not
turn back on its intention to give Ireland significant self-government within the
British Empire. Home Rule would not formally end the union between Britain
and Ireland as MPs would still be sent from Ireland to London and the Crowns
would be one. Yet Unionists had no desire for domestic Irish matters to be
resolved by a Catholic-dominated Dublin parliament and strongly opposed these
plans. Their Ulster Volunteer Force, in the north-eastern counties of Ireland,
recruited 100,000 men, armed and in uniform, ready to resist any attempt to force
Ulster into a self-governing Ireland. They faced the Irish Volunteers, a force at
least as large across Ireland, including as many as 40,000 recruits in Ulster, formed
with the aim of defending Home Rule. By late July 1914 these two private armies
were armed and drilled. In Belfast they paraded at relatively close proximity.
Most observers feared a bitter civil war. Instead, the war in Europe saved Ireland
from that fate.

By 1912 West Belfast was a potential tinderbox. It contained geographically
separate communities distinguished from each other by religion, politics and
tradition, with Catholics (approximately 24 per cent of the population of Belfast)
generally poorer and in lower skilled jobs than Protestants.[1] Many of the major
events of the Home Rule crisis took place in central Belfast and other parts of the
city, such as James Craig's house Craigavon and the Balmoral Showgrounds of
the Agricultural Society. But West Belfast, especially Celtic Park, played its part.
One of the earliest incidents came on 8 February 1912 when Winston Churchill,
then First Lord of the Admiralty in Asquith's Liberal government, came to Belfast
to speak in favour of Home Rule. Churchill's visit was big news.[2] On his arrival,

Churchill found hostile demonstrators at the Grand Central Hotel, along with both infantry and cavalry on the streets to protect him. Meanwhile, soldiers positioned themselves in 'boundary' areas such as Cupar Street. The streets were decorated by both communities – in the Catholic Falls with flags and bunting and in the Protestant Shankill with effigies of Churchill and the Nationalist leader, John Redmond MP.[3]

In Celtic Park itself, around 7,000 people crammed into a huge marquee lashed to the Grand Stand. They heard Churchill on fine oratorical form. He made an impassioned plea for Home Rule to ensure harmony between Britain and Ireland and as the surest way to secure a strong Irish voice within the British Empire. He told the audience that Home Rule would 'Meet the grievance, heal the quarrel, bury the hatred, link the interests, conciliate, consolidate the Empire'.[4] Redmond followed, endorsing Churchill's imperialist sentiments, stating that Home Rule would allow Ireland to 'come at last into our rightful place in the Empire'. A key figure at the meeting was the leader of Belfast Nationalism, Joseph Devlin, the Nationalist MP for West Belfast from 1906 to 1922. Devlin was born in the Falls in 1871 into a working-class family. He had strong support from the *Irish News*, for which he had once been a journalist, and a powerbase in the Ancient Order of Hibernians, a Catholic equivalent of the Orange Order.[5] Devlin made a speech tailored, like Redmond's, to allaying Unionist fears, talking about his record in campaigning for better working conditions for Protestant factory workers, and saying that in an Irish parliament, 'I will find myself in closer touch with the Protestant artisans of Belfast and Ulster than I would with the Catholic farmers of Munster and Connaught.'[6] Nationalists took the meeting as a sure sign that Home Rule would come soon. Aside from some demonstrations in central Belfast, and a few wandering gangs of youths in the evening, there was no sign of a major uprising against the First Lord of the Admiralty.[7]

Home Rule had been debated in parliament regularly since 1886. But it had never been anything more than a theory, because whenever the Liberal government managed to take a bill through the House of Commons, the Conservative-dominated Lords blocked it. But the Lords' powers were greatly weakened in 1911 by the Parliament Act. Those who opposed Home Rule were looking down the barrel of a gun and altered their behaviour accordingly.

Leadership of Unionism rested on two men. One was Andrew Bonar Law MP, the Conservative and Unionist leader in parliament who had Ulster Presbyterian family connections. The other was Edward Carson MP, who although from Dublin, had emerged as the leader of Unionists in Ireland as a whole. Both were willing to resist the law of the land with force if necessary. At Balmoral Showgrounds in Belfast on 9 April 1912, up to 200,000 marched in opposition to Home Rule. They were rallied both by Carson and by Bonar Law, who claimed the backing of many in Great Britain. That meeting initiated a mass campaign of opposition to Home Rule culminating in 'Ulster Day' on 28 September 1912.

Meanwhile, the summer of 1912 was tense in Belfast. There was sectarian rioting partly in response to an attack by drunken members of the Ancient Order of Hibernians on a Protestant Sunday School outing at Castledawson.[8] Though many miles from Belfast, the attack inflamed tensions so much that many Catholic workers were expelled from shipyards. On 14 September there was a football match at Celtic Park between Linfield and Belfast Celtic. As an understated police report said, 'Supporters of these two clubs belong to different parties': they meant Unionist in the case of Linfield, and Nationalist for Celtic. Trouble between the two clubs eventually forced Celtic out of the league altogether in 1949, and 1912 was a precursor of things to come. Prior to the game tensions were high, and 60 people ended up in hospital after a half-time battle between supporters, followed by a police baton charge and further trouble outside the ground. Displays of different flags prompted the fighting and the end result had been a street battle with crowds throwing stones at each other, interspersed by occasional gunshots.[9] Later in the year there was a boycott of Catholic publicans in the city by Unionist Clubs which took six months to peter out.[10]

Ulster Day took place in this tense atmosphere. Heeding Carson's call, 237,368 men and 234,046 women publicly declared their opposition to Home Rule, mainly across Ulster, but with signatories throughout other parts of the UK. Asserting loyalty to the King, male signatories pledged to use 'all means which may be found necessary' to defeat Home Rule and to boycott any Home Rule parliament. Women signed a declaration of their 'desire to associate ourselves with the men of Ulster in their uncompromising opposition to the Home Rule Bill now before parliament'.[11] Throughout Ulster Day, shipyards and factories in Belfast were closed to support the campaign. Thousands of people signed the Covenant at Belfast City Hall, and there were sites for signing across Belfast and the rest of Ulster. In the West Belfast parliamentary division, there were four sites in the Shankill district alone: Albert Hall, Bellevue Street Mission Hall, Shankill Road Orange Hall and Woodvale Presbyterian Church Lecture Hall. In the rest of the division, further venues were used in the Falls, Smithfield and Woodvale districts.

The nationalist *Irish News* described the day as a 'silly masquerade'.[12] However, there has never been any such example of mass public support for a political campaign in any part of the UK before or since. It also dramatically shifted political debate. From then on, much of the debate revolved around whether Ulster might be excluded from the Home Rule settlement. This was formally proposed by Carson in January 1913, although at that point, he was using exclusion as a weapon against the Home Rule movement because he did not believe that the British government would countenance partition.[13]

On 16 January 1913 the Home Rule Bill passed its third and final reading in the Commons with a majority of over one hundred. Redmond said that 'the star of Ireland is mounted in the heavens'. This Bill did not allow for the exclusion of Ulster, so Bonar Law threatened, 'the people of Ulster will resist, and I think they will be right'. He added that 'If you shot down a hundred of them in Belfast to-morrow a thousand would be ready the next day to share the same fate.'[14] The Bill could not be passed finally until it had been through the Commons twice more. After that, the Lords would not be able to overturn the settled will of the MPs. Even though there was to be a delay, Bonar Law's words showed that violent resistance was now firmly on the agenda.

Lines were further drawn at the annual meeting of the Ulster Unionist Council (UUC) on 31 January. Two momentous decisions were taken. A scheme was approved for a 'provisional government' to govern Ulster in the event of the final passage of Home Rule.[15] Meanwhile, the Council established a military arm: the Ulster Volunteer Force, which built on informal drilling already taking place by Orangemen and Unionist clubs. In Belfast, UVF regiments matched parliamentary constituencies. Within these regiments there were battalions, formed from companies with sections beneath them. At first, sections were linked to workplaces, but later organized by streets in which members lived.[16]

By the end of February 1914 the UVF claimed to have recruited around 90,000 men, one-third of them in Belfast. In May 1914 the police believed that the Belfast figure was as high as 24,509. There is a debate about whether the UVF was a credibly organized and armed force, but many of the men were in uniform and regiments steadily went about acquiring the trappings and trimmings of a regular army such as regimental colours.[17] There was potential for full mobilization of the UVF over the weekend of 21 and 22 March 1914. A rumour spread that the Unionist leaders were to be arrested. Two light cruisers were moved by the Royal Navy into Belfast Lough, bringing with them troops to add to those already stationed in Belfast, but no move was made to arrest Carson or his supporters. However, the tensions of the time had informed the so-called 'Curragh Mutiny' of 20 March, when 60 British cavalry officers at the Curragh camp near Kildare tried to resign their commissions (although the resignations were not accepted). The officers feared that the army was about to be used to enforce Home Rule and their actions undermined any chance that the government had of relying on the army in Ireland to impose Home Rule on Ulster. A month later, tensions grew with a full mobilization of the entire Belfast UVF on the night of 24 April 1914. Although this mobilization helped to test the effectiveness of the UVF's organization it was largely a bluff to cover the landing of around 20,000 rifles at Larne from the a boat named the *Mountjoy*, after the ship that had lifted the siege of Derry in 1689 and relieved the Protestants defending the city. That evening, the West Belfast UVF's Special Service Section guarded the Old Town Hall in Belfast which was the headquarters of the organization as a whole.[18]

Throughout this time, the UVF drew on the military expertise of former soldiers. From early 1914, men in the West Belfast UVF were often taking part in daily drills. Average attendance was no more than 50 men, although as many as 350 attended the 'Divine Service Parade'. They also regularly trained on a regimental basis in places such as Fernhill House, north of the Shankill, and Glencairn, the house of James Cunningham, off the Ballygomartin Road. One company drilling in Stewart's Yard in the Shankill Road benefited from the instruction of two former members of the Royal Irish (RI) Rifles, Sergeant Major W. J. Brannigan (of Springfield Road) and Sergeant Samuel Roberts. In

Andersonstown, one of the West Belfast companies was drilled by Charles Bell (of Upton Cottages) and his brother Francis, both formerly of the Royal Irish Fusiliers and both reservists. Men from Springfield Road were trained by George Roberts, another former RIRifles Sergeant, and Alex Perryman, a former Private in the Royal Inniskilling Fusiliers. By April 1914, the West Belfast UVF mustered up to 400 men for almost daily route marches, under the command of a former lance-sergeant in the King's Royal Rifles, Matthew Glover.[19]

Meanwhile, Nationalists were actively campaigning in favour of Home Rule. Throughout 1912 and 1913, Devlin spoke at public meetings in Belfast, more widely across Ireland, and on any Liberal platform in Great Britain which would

L/Cpl Charles Bell, 1st Royal Irish Fusiliers, Upton Cottages, Glen Road, reservist and UVF organizer, KIA 25 April 1915 (*Belfast Evening Telegraph*, 4 June 1915, p. 6)

host him. Devlin and his supporters were convinced that an Irish parliament was imminent, and many of his activities involved trying to reassure Protestants that this posed them no threat. Meanwhile, Devlin told a Liberal audience in Scotland that talk of civil war was 'arrant humbug and bluff'.[20] Yet there was a more militant response from nationalism through the formation of the Irish Volunteers in November 1913. Overtly, the Irish Volunteers used conciliatory language, aided by the fact that if Home Rule was passed they would be upholding the will of the British parliament. At their founding meeting in Dublin on 25 November, several thousand people heard their aims decreed as being 'to secure and maintain the rights and liberties common to all the people of Ireland without distinction of creed, class or politics'. The inspiration behind the movement was Eoin MacNeill, a professor at University College, Dublin. MacNeill had no close connection with the Irish Parliamentary Party. The Irish Volunteers drew in members or future members of the Irish Republican Brotherhood such as Pádraig Pearse who would play a central role in the Easter Rising in 1916.[21] Consequently, by the end of 1913, two rival citizens' armies existed in Ireland, and if the Irish Volunteers managed to recruit in Ulster, that could only add to the likelihood of civil war.

Redmond and the Irish Parliamentary Party were alarmed by the potential for radical action which existed in the Irish Volunteers. When a branch was formed in Belfast in March 1914, they kept their distance. Yet in May, the Belfast corps held a parade of around 1,500 men in Belfast, beginning in the Falls Road and marching to Hannahstown to the north-west of the city.[22] By the end of the month there were public signs of the Nationalist Party in Belfast realizing that the Volunteers were a force to be reckoned with and even welcomed, with an *Irish News* headline reporting the 'Gratifying Progress of National Muster'. The entire Belfast regiment used Shaun's (now McRory) Park, on the western edge of the city, for weekly training. This was also the venue for drills by the West Belfast unit, which were attended by an average of 60 men every two or three days, under the command of John Magee, a former colour sergeant in the Royal Irish Fusiliers.[23]

At the end of the May 1914, the Commons passed the Home Rule Bill for a third time. The Lords could now do nothing to defeat the measure. On the streets of Belfast the UVF mobilized in case there should be any move by the British government against their leaders or resources. On the afternoon of Saturday 6 June, the rival volunteer groups drilled in Belfast. Carson reviewed the West Belfast Regiment at Glencairn. The Special Service Corps of that regiment were by this time fully armed with the rifles from the *Mountjoy*. Carson captured the sentiment of the moment as he proclaimed, 'now, men, that you have got your arms, no matter what happens, I rely upon every man to fight for those arms to the end.' Meanwhile, the rapprochement between parliamentary Nationalism and the Irish Volunteers was marked by Joseph Devlin inspecting 1,500 men at Shaun's Park.[24] Ironically, given their professions of loyalty, it was the Unionists who would have been the rebels had they violently opposed Home Rule, the will of the British government.

Devlin's embrace of the Belfast IV came as Redmond steadily gained formal control of the IV across Ireland. Following Redmond's sanctioning of the movement, membership across Ireland rose to 129,000 by May.[25] A key task for the new regime in command of the Volunteers was to equip the men with arms and uniforms. In early July the 'Defence of Ireland Fund' was launched to raise funds for the purchase of arms and ammunition. In the middle of that month the Belfast Regiment of the Irish Volunteers, now numbering around 2,000, acquired the trappings of military ceremony in the same way as the UVF when they were presented with regimental colours at one of their now weekly parades in Shaun's Park. Their flag was of St Patrick's blue, and incorporated Ulster's red hand and a burst of sunlight around the word 'Eire', along with the regiment's name. Soon after, the Volunteers secured more practical equipment with the landing of 50,000 rifles at five different points on the Irish coast. On 26 July there was a mass meeting in the Clonard Picture House in the Falls Road to raise further funds. Devlin was stuck in London, but sent a letter to be read out. In it, hidden amidst his usual conciliatory rhetoric, was a more steely message: 'if the call came to them, there were no people in the whole of Ireland who were more ready to fight and, if need be, to die, in defence of the liberty of their country than the Nationalists of Belfast'.[26]

The existence of the two volunteer forces made Ulster a tinderbox. In Belfast, the rival private armies drilled at least once a week, often in neighbouring parts of the city. Tens of thousands of rifles had found their way in the hands of these volunteers and the two communities had a relatively recent history of sectarian conflict. That made even an accidental outbreak of fighting a real possibility.

In an attempt to dampen the potential for violence, the British government continued to seek a solution to the Ulster question based around partition. Ideas considered included 'six-county exclusion' (comprising the counties of today's Northern Ireland) and options for individual counties to withdraw from Home Rule for a limited period. The latter had support from Nationalist leaders, but they would not support the more radical options which were starting to find favour with Carson.[27] All such efforts came to naught at the Buckingham Palace Conference in July. With Home Rule about to reach the statute book, it looked as if the outbreak of a war was only a matter of time. On 4 August, it happened, not in Ireland but on the Continent, and not over Home Rule but the issue of Belgian neutrality.

2

Volunteers and Reserves

We intend . . . to claim a full and an increasing share in the work and the glory of the Empire, which the blood and brains of Irishmen have done so much to create.

JOSEPH DEVLIN, NATIONALIST MP FOR WEST BELFAST

Only about a week before the outbreak of the war in Europe did the general public start to think it possible. Even then, in Ireland, Home Rule still dominated the news. On 27 July 1914, the *Irish News* focused on a 'Battle on the Streets of Dublin' that followed the landing at Howth of 3,000 guns for the Irish Volunteers. Yet it carried one ominous headline to a smaller story: 'Great European War Threatened'. That story reported Serbia's reply to the Austro-Hungarian ultimatum, which had followed the assassination in Sarajevo a month before of Archduke Franz Ferdinand, the heir to the Austrian throne. The network of alliances and pledges of mutual support between countries in 1914 ensured that when Austria-Hungary declared war on Serbia on 28 July, Russia and Germany were drawn in on opposite sides. Meanwhile, Germany turned its attention to Russia's ally, France. When Belgium was attacked as a way in, the UK was dragged in, due to its pledge to protect Belgian neutrality.

The outbreak of war for the UK on 4 August 1914 had immediate consequences for the situation in Ireland. Both volunteer armies were forced to examine whether they would assist the war effort. Many Volunteers were reservists, whether in the Army Reserve of former soldiers, or as Special Reservists, who were not necessarily former soldiers but had undergone formal military training. Men of the Special Reserve had to report to their battalions as soon as war broke out. Other reserves were mobilized and sent wherever they were needed, often their former regiments. They included brothers, Charles and Francis Bell, who had led UVF drills in Andersonstown, and returned to the Royal Irish Fusiliers.[1] On 6 August, the *Irish News* reported the departure on the previous day of 600 reservists from the Irish Volunteers and 'a quota of the Ulster Volunteers'. At the outbreak of war, the police believed that there were 3,250 men in the Belfast Irish Volunteers, of whom 1,200 were reservists.[2] Victoria Barracks in Belfast was a hive of activity, especially for men who were in reserve for the RIRifles – 250 of them left their barracks on the evening of 6 August, marching to fife and drums through city centre crowds to embark on the Heysham boat, *en route* for Tidworth Camp in Hampshire.[3] In Omagh there were unprecedented scenes as the Irish Volunteers and UVF, joined by the Irish Volunters' brass and pipe band along with the pipe band of a local

Orange Lodge, formed a joint guard of honour to send off reservists of the Royal Inniskilling Fusiliers. There were no scenes to match that in Belfast, although the UVF there formed a guard to send off the 1st Norfolk Regiment, which had been stationed in the city prior to the war.[4]

Choices available to non-reservist Volunteers were more open. Speaking in parliament the day before war broke out, the Foreign Secretary, Sir Edward Grey, said that 'The one bright spot in the whole of this terrible situation is Ireland.' That was informed by Redmond's pledge of Nationalist support for the British government, including offering the Irish Volunteers for the defence of Ireland, so that British troops could leave Ireland for the front. Redmond comfortably supported a government that was about to grant nationalists Home Rule, and it was easy for Nationalist Ireland to support the defence of plucky little *Catholic* Belgium. Furthermore, it had long been a core part of the nationalist case that Protestants should not equate Home Rule with 'Rome Rule'. Redmond thus asked, 'Is it too much to hope that out of this situation there may spring a result which will be good not merely for the Empire, but good for the future welfare and integrity of the Irish nation?'[5] In the past, there had been a saying that 'England's difficulty is Ireland's opportunity.' Redmond's approach shows that the Nationalist leadership in 1914 saw England's difficulty as an opportunity again, but this time best exploited by holding out the hand of friendship.

Carson had also offered the UVF for home defence before war broke out. Meanwhile, the Unionist stress on service to King and Country made it inevitable that many Unionists would enlist. Any who harboured doubts were encouraged by Carson who sent a telegram to UVF battalion commanding officers, instructing reservists to join their regiments immediately. The day after war began, Carson was in consultation with the War Office over how best to deploy the UVF.[6] However, many UVF men enthusiastically enlisted without waiting for any direction to do so from the Unionist leadership.[7]

Regardless of politics, there were also practical reasons for enlistment such as unemployment and low pay. Linen production, a major source of employment in Belfast, was affected by the loss of some continental markets on the outbreak of war. On 7 August, the members of the Power Loom Manufacturers' Association reduced working hours to 28 per week, which greatly reduced workers' incomes. The next week, other sectors felt the pinch. Combe Barbour's Falls Foundry closed on 11 August, with 1,800 workers laid off. Mackie's Albert Foundry closed most of its departments a few days before. Within a month, many of the workers were taken back as orders recovered from the initial shock of war (and Mackie's later became a munitions factory, which produced an estimated 75 million shells),[8] but the lay-offs had already boosted recruitment.[9] So whether from desperation or enthusiasm, many UVF members enlisted before the organization was recruited *systematically*. This reduced the numbers able to join up in later weeks with the West Belfast UVF, when it looked as if its members joined up in smaller numbers than in other parts of the city. Yet the reality was that many had enlisted in preference to unemployment and all that meant for their families.[10]

Meanwhile, in Westminster, Home Rule's future was uncertain. As the European crisis deepened in July, Prime Minister Asquith postponed discussion of an Amending Bill, even though he had concluded that permanent exclusion of counties Antrim, Armagh, Down and Londonderry from Home Rule was the only way forward. Asquith was hardened in that resolve by the enthusiasm with which the UVF was enlisting. He believed this made coercion of Ulster into Home Rule impossible. Thus, on 18 September, Home Rule finally became law with two caveats: implementation was suspended for the duration of the war and there would be special (although as yet undefined) provision for Ulster. This angered Unionists, who believed that advantage had been taken of their goodwill. Nationalists celebrated, but as the war dragged on, they found it ever harder to use the indefinite promise of Home Rule to restrain more radical elements in their ranks.[11]

All eyes now turned to winning the war in Europe. The UVF was in some senses a ready-made army, and Lord Kitchener was keen to secure its men. Carson wanted their special identity to be recognized and won a pledge from the War Office that if enough men were recruited from the Ulster Volunteer Force then they could be part of at least one Ulster division, although a plan to have the division wear special insignia was later dropped in favour of purely regimental badges.[12] To form one whole division, at least 16,000 recruits would be needed, plus men to stay in Ireland in reserve battalions. A division consisted of three infantry brigades, each containing four battalions. These 12 battalions could include 1,000 men each. As many as 4,000 others served in a division in the Royal Army Medical Corps, Army Service Corps, Royal Field Artillery and Royal Engineers. A small number would join the division in specialist roles such as vets and chaplains.

Armed with the War Office's pledge and challenge to Carson, the leading Unionist MP James Craig ordered 10,000 uniforms at Moss Bros in London. Carson returned to Belfast to obtain approval from the Ulster Unionist Council for the effective transfer of much of the UVF into the British army. This was enthusiastically given, yet it did not mean the end of the UVF. Carson stressed to the UUC that it [the UVF] would remain in existence, with all the weapons and uniforms it had held before. Those who were too old or too young for the front could swell UVF ranks at home to ensure that Ulster was ready to resist Home Rule at the end of hostilities. Meanwhile, the UVF could serve as a feeder for the army.[13]

Carson's deal with the War Office meant that the UVF could join the army by regiment, with a guarantee that they would be kept together and that the UVF's officers would, where possible, become the officers of the new British army battalions formed as part of the 36th (Ulster) Division. The North Belfast Regiment of the UVF started proceedings on Friday 4 September, followed on subsequent days by East, West and South Belfast.[14] Consequently, membership of a UVF regiment had a significant impact on the battalion into which its members went, although lines were blurred in the Shankill area, which was split between the North and West Belfast parliamentary constituencies. When the UVF was formed, it was influenced by parliamentary boundaries, so men from Shankill and Court wards generally went into the North Belfast unit rather than the West Belfast unit. That pattern continued to exert some influence on UVF entry to the Ulster Division, although men from the Shankill area appear to have been more likely to join the 9th RIRifles than any other unit, regardless of their UVF affiliation. However, some did go into the 15th RIRifles and that may have been partly due to established UVF patterns. The men enlisted at the Old Town Hall, where the UVF had its headquarters. On arrival, each man signed an attestation form, recording personal details such as age, height, hair colour, religion and next-of-kin. Following a medical examination, if he passed, the new recruit swore an oath of allegiance to the king. On Saturday 5 September, the first batch of 360 men from North Belfast left by train for Ballykinlar Camp in County Down, a short way from Belfast. They were designated as the 7th Battalion of the RIRifles, although by the time they went to the front they had been renumbered as the 15th.[15]

On the first day of enlistment for the West Belfast UVF, volunteers assembled at Stewart's Yard in the Shankill Road. They were addressed by Colonel T. E. Hickman, the Conservative MP for Wolverhampton and a senior UVF figure who had become the Recruiting Officer for the whole of Ulster. Joining Hickman were James Craig MP, plus Stewart Blacker Quin, who was the Unionist candidate for West Belfast and the commander of the 1st Battalion West Belfast UVF. Quin himself was too old to enlist, but having heard him say that 'at his desire his son-in-law joined them that day', 400 men from the West Belfast UVF marched down the Shankill Road to the Old Town Hall. This was considerably fewer than other units. The *Belfast News Letter* reported the reason as being job losses a few weeks before had led many men to enlist, and that reservists had further depleted the potential West Belfast regiment. It is also worth noting that the West Belfast UVF was smaller than units in other parts of the city, comprising just two battalions (from which was drawn the Special Service Section).[16] In comparison, the South Belfast UVF contained seven battalions.

The day after enlistment, the *Northern Whig* described 360 West Belfast Volunteers assembling at 2 p.m., again in Stewart's Yard, where each man was presented with a box of cigarettes. Their march to the city's County Down railway station was accompanied by crowds and scenes that were rich with unionist symbolism. Men entered the Shankill Road from Stewart's yard by marching under the two name-plates of the *Mountjoy* (the ship used for UVF gun-running) held aloft by bayonets. At their head, the regiment's bugle and fife band was preceded by 'a bulldog bedecked in a Union Jack'. On reaching the station, the men boarded trains for a new camp at Donard Lodge near Newcastle, County Down, as Ballykinlar was temporarily full. Once there, they formed the core of the new 9th Battalion of the RIRifles, and over the next two days they were joined by the South Belfast UVF, forming the 10th Battalion, and another 128 men from the West Belfast UVF.[17] Little more than a week after Carson's call, around 500 men from the West Belfast UVF had joined the army, in addition to 300–400 already in the army as reservists or unemployed volunteers. In Belfast as a whole, when the bulk of recruiting was over, the UVF announced that 6,700 of its members had joined, but there was still a steady flow of UVF recruits even after then, rising to 7,031 between 4 August and 6 October. This was short of its 8,000 target and meant that, instead of providing two brigades, the Belfast battalions were grouped together in the 107th Brigade, which by the end of September was entirely based at Ballykinlar under canvas. The rest of Ulster provided enough men for the two further brigades, 108th and 109th, which joined the 107th to comprise the 36th (Ulster) Division.[18] The 109th Brigade included another Belfast-based unit, the 14th RIRifles recruited from the Young Citizens' Volunteers, an initially non-political body, which had become aligned with Unionism.

While the UVF enlisted, there were developments in nationalist ranks. The politics of the Ulster Division made it unionist and Protestant. It is almost impossible to find Catholics in its ranks in the early days, except for a few in the 14th RIRifles.[19] So where could Catholic nationalist volunteers go? Redmond's offer of the Irish Volunteers for home defence was not problematic for the bulk of the membership, and there is some evidence to suggest that even the Sinn Féin supporters among the Volunteers did not balk at that.[20] Indeed, the offer gave them ample excuse to show their strength, and on Saturday 5 September, almost 3,000 of the Belfast regiment paraded in front of Joseph Devlin 'for the first time in public fully armed'. Arms had arrived in the city earlier that week and 'caused the liveliest satisfaction' among the Volunteers.[21] But nationalists were wounded by unionist accusations that Roman Catholics were not joining the military in substantial numbers, despite claims in the *Irish News* that Catholics were joining in much larger numbers than their share of the UK's population would require for simple equity. The newspaper drew particular attention to West Belfast, saying that simply on the basis of which Catholic families had applied for relief due to men serving, 'In the district of St Peter's alone, the most exclusively Catholic district of Belfast, it is reckoned at a low estimate that 800 men have been called up or have recently enlisted.' The *Irish News* went on to estimate that in addition to regulars, 3,000 Catholics had left the whole of Belfast to serve.[22]

The Nationalists were losing the public relations war over recruitment because, unlike the unionists, they were not collectively enlisting in one division. So Redmond announced in mid-September that he wanted Irish soldiers kept together in an 'Irish Brigade', a phrase that was redolent of previous Irish service in war.[23] When Home Rule was finally placed on the statute book, Redmond was emboldened to take further steps in support of the government. On 20 September, his speech at Woodenbridge, County Wicklow, marked a shift in the Nationalist attitude to military service. Redmond told the Irish Volunteers assembled (the East Wicklow Brigade), that they had a 'two-fold duty' to defend Ireland's shores but also to fight 'wherever the firing line extends in defence of the right of freedom and religion in this war'.[24]

This call was not well received by the more militant sections of the IV. In

Dublin, Eoin MacNeill and his supporters issued a statement announcing the removal of Redmond's nominees from the Volunteers' Provisional Committee because Redmond had, they said, violated the founding principles of the IV by advising them 'to take foreign service under a Government which is not Irish'.[25] That sparked meetings throughout Ireland organized by Redmond's supporters to pass votes of confidence in the leader. Across the whole island, approximately 93 per cent of the Volunteers backed Redmond.[26] In Belfast, up to 300 Volunteers, described by the police as 'The Sinn Fein and I.R.B. sections, together with the extreme labour party', opposed Redmond's position on the war, and backed MacNeill. Yet even that was not enough to turn the Belfast Regiment against Redmond as it was rallied by Joseph Devlin. As many as 2,000 pro-Redmond men remained in the city having not yet joined up, and he also implicitly had the support of the 1,000 or so Volunteers who had already departed. At a meeting in St Mary's Hall on 4 October, Devlin called on the Volunteers to 'take their stand behind Mr Redmond'. The event was full of mixed symbolism, with 'God Save Ireland', 'A Nation One Again' and even 'God Save the King' all sung by the crowd. By mid-October, Redmond had reaffirmed his control of the Irish Volunteers, renamed as the Irish National Volunteers (INV) and was putting his line out to them through a weekly newspaper, the *National Volunteer*.[27]

Redmond now turned to ensuring that enough Volunteers joined the British army to make real the idea of an Irish brigade. The potential for this had been signalled by Kitchener's decision on 12 September to form the 16th (Irish) Division from troops recruited in Ireland. That was then enhanced by Kitchener's instruction to its Commanding Officer to clear space in a brigade (47th Brigade was eventually agreed) for men from the INV to be drafted into battalions together.[28] At a mass meeting in Belfast's Clonard Picture House on 25 October, Redmond turned up the heat on those still undecided about joining up. How humiliated Irishmen would feel, Redmond said, 'if when this war was over, they had to admit that their rights and liberties had been saved by the sacrifices of other men, while the Irishmen remained safe at home and took no risks'.[29] Meanwhile, the *National Volunteer* stressed the Irishness of the 16th Division, even telling the Volunteers that it was 'being equipped entirely from Irish-manufactured goods'.[30] Such sentiments amounted to the same kind of collective pressure being put on communities in England to form Pals Battalions. The strength of attachments to both Volunteer movements in Ulster is believed to have been a significant factor resulting in higher levels of recruitment among both Catholics and Protestants in Ulster compared to the rest of Ireland.[31]

A week and a half into November, Redmond's pressure was making an impact on the numbers of INV men enrolling. On 12 November, even the *Belfast Evening Telegraph* (usually as grudging about nationalist efforts as the *Irish News* was about unionist ones) admitted that 'during the week efforts have been made by some local Nationalists to get their men to join the army'. By that day, 300 had indicated their willingness to join up. The first batch of 60 mustered at Berry Street's National Club and then enlisted at Clifton Street. Many were followers of

Redmond, like brothers Robert and Michael Brennan. Both staunch nationalists, Michael would say in later years that he had joined up to fight for the freedom of small nations such as Belgium.[32]

A steady flow continued from the INV to Clifton Street (which was replaced in February 1915 as the Irish Brigade's recruiting office by 47 Mill Street). This all played into a running debate within unionist and nationalist newspapers about service levels, with each side making bold claims. As early as September 1914, the *Irish News* had claimed that 'there are at the present moment "in active service", and in proportion to the Irish nationalist population and the population of other areas, at least five times more [Irishmen] than there are Englishmen and twelve times more than there are martial representatives of Ulster Unionism.'[33] By February 1915, the same newspaper was arguing that if nationalists were

Pte Michael Brennan, 6th Connaught Rangers, Alton Street

not getting credit for high levels of recruitment it was because many soldiers who wanted to enlist in the Irish Brigade were being sent elsewhere under false pretences.[34] Throughout the war, newspapers regularly disputed claims made by politicians and journalists from the other side. However, on 19 November 1914 both the *Belfast News Letter* and the *Irish News* agreed that 700 men had enlisted in the Irish Brigade and would begin to depart for the training camp at Fermoy in County Cork the next day. Speaking at a mass meeting in St Mary's Hall on 18 November to send them off, Devlin linked their joining the army to the existence of Home Rule on the Statute Book. The willingness of the INV to enrol showed that Ireland would keep its pledges, he said. The symbolism of the meeting showed how far Redmond and his party were taking a political risk. The colours of all the Allied nations were part of the décor, and on the platform the

Pte Robert Brennan, 4th Connaught Rangers, and family, Alton Street

Union flag and green flag with harp were intertwined, but at the centrepiece of decorations on the balcony was a large Union flag.[35] So long as Home Rule remained the limit of nationalist ambitions, such symbolism could continue. But if they should ever want more, then Redmond and Devlin, prominent cheerleaders for recruitment into the British army, were in a vulnerable position.

Amid all the bluster of recruiting, the work of women was crucial. The events at St Mary's Hall had largely been organized by the Irish Women's Council of Belfast. The INV's Nursing Corps paraded to the Hall before the event, from the Falls Road and into Divis Street in 'neat white uniforms with the red Cross and pretty rosettes of orange and green ... with the splendid Craobh Ruadh pipers at their head'.[36] Elsewhere in the city, women made their contribution to the war effort in a variety of ways. On 11 August, the Women's Ulster Unionist Council offered the services of the UVF Nursing Corps and its dressing stations throughout Ulster. The Council also volunteered to help distribute food and clothing, and to help take care of families and dependants who had joined the services. There was fundraising for motor ambulances to be presented to the Ulster Division. But there was also help for those left at home. In Divis Street, the Babies' Club was used by women with children below the age of 2, whose husbands were at the front.[37]

As nationalist recruits left Belfast, there were enthusiastic street scenes on 19 November when most (600) of the INV recruits departed for Fermoy. They were all initially attached to the 6th Battalion of the Connaught Rangers, though many later went into the 7th Battalion of the Leinster Regiment (formally the 'Prince of Wales's Leinster Regiment (Royal Canadians)' although it had by now no connection with either Wales or Canada). Both battalions became part of the 47th Brigade of the 16th (Irish) Division. Though not as numerous as the Ulster Division that had departed for training in County Down not long before, the INV had their own enthusiastic parade through Belfast, watched by thousands. They marched behind 'pipers in Gaelic costume, flourishing banners emblazoned with the Red Hand of the O'Neill and distinctively Irish National devices and mottoes', singing Irish military songs. As they reached the Great Northern station, further Irish songs were sung, plus 'God Save the King' and the Belfast Celtic 'war song'. Joseph Devlin bade farewell to each recruit individually on the train, which then set off for Dublin. There was no parade in Dublin, merely tea and cigarettes, but having taken another train to Fermoy, the men were greeted by an enthusiastic reception from local bands. At the Volunteer Drill Hall they paraded with volunteers from the surrounding area, who accompanied them to their camp.[38]

Once at the camp, they followed a standard routine. It involved rising at 6 a.m., with the first parade an hour later, followed by exercises and an obstacle course. At 8 a.m. breakfast consisted of bread, butter and tea, with variable extras such as sardines, cheese or tinned salmon. The longest parade of the day lasted from 9 a.m. until 12.30. At 1 p.m., lunch (usually soup, beef and potatoes) was served, with a further parade from 2 p.m. to 4.30 p.m. After tea the men's time was their own. Interspersed between parades and meals were snatched moments of rest, plus the all-important cleaning of uniforms and equipment in advance of parades. That pattern continued until May 1915 when 47th Brigade carried out mock battles in the area around Fermoy, until their departure to Aldershot in September when musketry became the focus of training.[39]

After the first batch of men went to Fermoy, they were periodically joined by other recruits. On 25 November, 350 more INV members departed Belfast for Fermoy. This comprised 100 of the first batch of 700 recruited, plus another 250 who had enlisted later. The night before their departure, another evening event was held at St Mary's Hall, and the men marched through the city centre the next day through a crowd that almost matched the size of the one that had seen off the first contingent. This time, the men were sent to the 7th Leinsters rather than the Connaughts, but when they reached Fermoy they were met by many Belfast friends. The *Irish News* noted that 'Everywhere the sharp Northern accent was heard.' It also reckoned that by this point about 80 per cent of the Belfast INV was in the army.[40] General Sir Lawrence Parsons, commanding the 16th (Irish) Division, wrote to Redmond saying, 'We are getting good batches of I.N.V. from Ulster & have already filled the 6th Connaught Rangers.'[41] When a further 100 nationalists departed in January and February, Devlin could claim that through military service, 'We intend not only to maintain our national rights, but to claim a full and an increasing share in the work and the glory of the Empire, which the blood and brains of Irishmen have done so much to create.'[42] His message was clear: you can trust us with Home Rule for we are loyal members of the empire.

Of course, much enlisting was regardless of the rhetoric of political leaders. Even among UVF men, volunteering was not always influenced by a desire to serve King and Country, or political motives. Jack Christie, a Shankill man and UVF member who went into the Ulster Division, recalled: 'when the War came, it wasn't a challenge or anything to do with patriotism, it was simple: here's an escape route to get out of the mill, for surely life holds more than what this mill can offer?'[43] Many others were also joining up independently of any political effort at recruitment. One old soldier was John McManus of Majorca Street. Originally from the Ballynahinch area in County Down, he had first joined the British army in 1868, from Leitrim, County Down, and served until 1901. He saw much of the world, mainly in the Essex Regiment: Hong Kong, Malta, the Straits Settlements (now Singapore and parts of Malaya), Gibraltar and Hong Kong. Aged 62 in 1914, his military experience made him an ideal choice as a company sergeant-major in the 18th RIRifles, a reserve battalion.[44] Daniel McKeown, had enlisted in the Royal Irish Fusiliers in 1889 as a regular soldier at the age of 19 and was stationed in both Dublin and Armagh. By the time of his discharge in 1910 as a sergeant, after 21 years, including service in the Boer War and in India, he and his family were living in Bantry Street, off the Springfield Road in West Belfast. A shoemaker by trade, he re-enlisted on 3 September 1914, and was exactly the kind of experienced soldier the army needed. His initial role, until

Sgt Daniel McKeown, 5th Royal Irish Fusiliers, 37 Forfar Street

September 1915, was to train soldiers of the 5th Royal Irish Fusiliers in the 10th (Irish) Division, a non-political formation that recruited throughout Ireland.[45] Men such as McKeown would continue to heed the call for volunteers, if not in 1914, then in 1915. Another Boer War veteran who joined up from the Falls area was Francis McCann of McDonnell Street, who had fought in the Boer War at Ladysmith and Tegula Heights where he was wounded. Joining up in 1915, aged 38, he found his experience put to use in the 8th Royal Irish Fusiliers in the 16th Division.[46]

An unknown number of men did not pass the basic medical at the recruiting office, while others who enlisted did not last more than a few months before being discharged, with a batch leaving the 6th Connaughts in February 1915. John Cummins of Albert Street in the Falls was judged to be medically unfit, although that did not stop him reapplying, unsuccessfully, for the 4th Connaught Rangers only months later. In some cases, longstanding medical conditions were overcome or covered up by enlisted men and took several months to become apparent. One example is Robert Webster of Disraeli Street in the Shankill. He was discharged from the 9th RIRifles in June 1915 after nine months of service due to cataracts he had had since childhood. The service record of Robert Brennan, who had enlisted with his brother Michael, suggests that he may also have had an underlying condition. He had tried to join the 6th Connaughts and was typical of many men who enlisted but did not reach the front, serving instead in the regiment's 4th Battalion on the stores and provisions side of operations in

Bere Island, County Cork, before discharge through ill health in June 1916.[47]

Poor discipline also led to discharge, as officers decided that some men were just more trouble than they were worth. Patrick Quinn of Wall Street in the Shankill lasted three months in the 7th Leinsters before being discharged for misconduct in February 1915, including threatening a sergeant-major with a bayonet. Charles Mervyn of Slate Street in the Falls was out by the end of March for his 'leading' role in a riot of 17 February. Another Falls man, Robert Marshall of Sultan Street, was regularly absent from training between February and May 1915 and was discharged as 'a degenerate of the worst type'.[48] The 6th Connaughts were especially disorderly. There were two drink-inspired disturbances in October 1914 and another on either Christmas Eve or Christmas Day. Of the second incident, a sergeant in the battalion, J. H. M. Staniforth, wrote, 'We had a fearful mutiny last week.' He described how 50 drunken prisoners had taken over their prison. As a result of the violence, two men died of wounds in hospital.[49]

Among attempted enlisters were many who were underage and were turned away. David Starrett, who was from York Street in the city centre, was refused when he told the recruiting sergeant that he was 16. A few days later, he claimed to be 19 and was passed A1 after giving a hearty cough. He was drafted into the 9th RIRifles and soon became the battalion Commanding Officer's batman.[50] Another underage enlister who got away with it was James Colville, who was the last Shankill veteran of the Ulster Division to die in 1989, aged 92. He was slightly under 17 when he enlisted in December 1914.[51] Others could not brazen it out. Louis Cohen of Bristol Street in the Shankill and a member of Belfast's small Jewish community, lasted only two weeks in the Ulster Divisional Train of the Army Service Corps before his father, Hyman Cohen, claimed him out. Esther Sherlock of Cyprus Street in the Falls claimed her son back from the 3rd Inniskillings. He was 16 and had been serving for eight months, but his mother wrote 'I have got none at home as his father is also serving in the colours. I do feel so lonely at home without someone.' At the other end of the age range, Peter Murphy of Ton Street enlisted in the 7th Leinsters in mid-May 1915. He was out a month later having been found to be 49 years old and unfit.[52]

That did not mean that there was no work for older volunteers, especially if they were ex-soldiers. John McManus, aged 62, was mentioned earlier. John McMullen of Irwin Street had first enlisted in 1884, serving until 1901 in the 1st and 2nd Inniskillings. He saw action on the Indian North West Frontier in 1897–98 and in South Africa during the Boer War. He became a sergeant on enlisting in the 6th Connaughts in November 1914, aged 39, and served with them until September 1916 when he was sent back to Ireland for less demanding service. Meanwhile, William Robinson of Benares Street enlisted in September 1915 aged 58 and served until July 1918, mainly with the 4th Royal Irish Fusiliers in County Cavan.[53]

Some of those discharged refused to take no for an answer. David Boyd of Ligoniel Road was discharged from the 15th RIRifles for unspecified misconduct, but re-enlisted in the Royal Engineers in February 1915. A month later, his past was discovered and he was 'discharged with ignominy'. Alexander McErlean of Wilton Square South joined the 9th RIRifles in September 1914, underage, and was only discharged in May 1915. In October 1916 he legally joined the Royal Flying Corps. Thomas Allen of Fleming Street enlisted in September 1914 and was discharged in June 1915. Defective eyesight was the overt cause, but he also had a poor disciplinary record, being absent from parades on five occasions between January and May 1915. However, he re-enlisted in August 1917 and served six months in the Inland Water Transport section of the Royal Engineers. Hamilton Quee of Conlon Street made three attempts to enlist in 1914–16, never staying in more than three months. He enlisted in the 6th RIRifles, the 122nd Royal Engineers and the 3rd Royal Irish Fusiliers. But each time his hammer toes, varicose veins and middle-ear disease led to his discharge. More successful at staying in was Richard Mussen of Dundee Street who enlisted in the 9th RIRifles in September 1914 and was discharged in June 1915 with defective vision and chronic middle-ear disease. However, somehow he re-enlisted, only to be killed in battle as a member of the 1st RIRifles on 21 March 1918.[54]

There is evidence of the authorities taking mental health problems seriously where there was a risk to others if the soldier was sent into action. A common diagnosis was 'melancholia'. Robert Briggs of Elizabeth Street and the 19th RIRifles was diagnosed and discharged in September 1916, having been depressed since he enlisted, which he ascribed to the death of his mother, sister and brother. Frank Malone of Hanover Street and the Royal Army Medical Corps was discharged with melancholia in December 1915. He was depressed because he believed he had heart disease and doctors also noted that 'he is alone and wants to get married to save his soul, as if he died as he is, he fears he would never see the face of God'. John McIlwaine of Palmer Street was discharged in December 1914 from the Army Service Corps' Ulster Divisional Train for being 'densely stupid'. He was back again six months later in the 17th RIRifles, being dismissed a year on with melancholia. John Rice of Sidney Street was discharged in February 1916 from the same battalion for 'melancholia & suicidal tendency'. He had attempted to take his own life. One member of the 6th Connaughts, Alexander McCartney of Crane Court, was discharged in September 1915 for 'insanity' and being 'delusional'. He apparently believed himself to be a wealthy man who was to buy a butcher's shop on discharge, and regularly said that pigs were outside his hospital waiting to be slaughtered.[55]

Discharge rates may well have been high in Belfast. Official figures from October 1915 suggested a UK-wide rejection rate of 25 per cent. Relatively high rates of dental problems made the figure 42 per cent for Ireland as a whole.[56] It is difficult to be clear what the figure was for Belfast, but of the 2,692 individuals whose service or pensions records survive, and who therefore actually enlisted, 662 (24.6 per cent) were discharged before completing three months of service, mostly for medical problems.

Those from the Belfast INV who did enlist successfully were soon at Fermoy, far from their loved ones. The Ulster Division was closer to home: in the case of the 9th RIRifles at Newcastle on the County Down coast. From November 1914, a special train departed Belfast at 9.30 a.m. on Sundays, calling at Ballykinlar camp before making its way to Newcastle and then beginning its return journey at 6.30 p.m., with return tickets sold for the price of a single fare. Families were not the only visitors. Both Carson and Bonar Law visited the soldiers in camp, maintaining the link between Unionism and the Ulster Division.[57]

The Ulster Division remained close to Belfast through the winter and spring of 1915. Basic training was not entirely hazard-free: two members of the 9th RIRifles died in training, although it is not clear what the cause was.[58] During this time, the 9th RIRifles also celebrated St Patrick's Day, being presented with shamrock by the wife of 107th Brigade's then Commander, G. H. H. Couchman.[59] The day was marked to some extent in all Irish regiments, regardless of their political composition. Such commemoration points to a degree of 'Irishness' among unionists that might surprise some today.

When training was complete, 17,000 men of the division marched into the city on the afternoon of Friday 7 May; the next morning, they assembled in their respective districts at points where they had left their arms the night before. For the 9th RIRifles that meant the West Belfast Orange Hall in the Shankill Road, before marching southwards along the Lisburn Road to a review by Carson at Malone. The event was partially designed as a recruiting device. As the *Belfast News Letter* said, the Division had been filled, but the War Office was now requesting a further 6,000–7,000 recruits from Ulster for reserve battalions before the division could go to the front. Posters lining the route asked 'Wouldn't you rather be marching with your pals to-day than looking on?' and 'Is the Ulster Division to be kept at home because you hesitate?' The parade route was decked with Union flags, and pictures of the street scenes show the centre of the city as cramped as could be. Following the review, the non-Belfast battalions left the city as soon as possible, but the four battalions of the 107th Brigade remained over the weekend, when they had a chance to say farewell to their families.[60]

So often the Belfast newspapers seem to inhabit parallel worlds and the *Irish News* did not cover this massive parade. Instead, it commented on the simultaneous departure of the INV's Belfast Commanding Officer, Hugh McNally, a qualified doctor who had enlisted and was taking up a medical position in the Royal Navy. He was seen off by the remnants of the Belfast INV at the Brigade Hall in the Falls Road on the day after the Ulster Division's city parade.[61] Within two months, the Ulster Division left its camps to depart for Seaford in Sussex, for further training before departure for the front. The 16th Division set off for Aldershot in September. Here they made temporary homes as they carried out their final training before their departure for the Continent and the front line.

3

The British Expeditionary Force, 1914–15

*My regiment is going forward to attack the Hun to-morrow . . . at dawn,
and, if possible, give him about turn to Berlin. Now, by the time you
receive this I will be lying in a soldier's grave somewhere in France.*

SERGEANT WILLIAM SHEARER, 2ND ROYAL IRISH RIFLES,
WRITING TO HIS WIFE

While the men of the Ulster and Irish divisions volunteered and trained, West
Belfast men were already at the front in other units. Indeed, by the time those
two divisions arrived in France in late 1915, unionists and nationalists of West
Belfast had been at the front for well over a year in battalions with no link to
the politics of their home. Some men were reservists of different types. Others
were former soldiers who re-enlisted while being under no obligation to do so
and found that their experience was valuable at the front. In 1914 alone, West
Belfast men were killed in the 4th (Queen's Own) Hussars, 1st Cheshires (which
had been stationed in Belfast), Army Service Corps, 2nd Connaught Rangers,
1st Royal Irish Fusiliers, Highland Light Infantry, Royal Field Artillery, 2nd
Royal Sussex Regiment, 1st Royal Scots Fusiliers, and six different ships of the
Royal Navy. There were also clusters of West Belfast fatalities in other battalions:
four in the 2nd South Lancashires and 13 in the 1st Irish Guards. Among the
South Lancashire deaths was Samuel Quinn, whose brother Robert, in the same
battalion, was captured by the Germans and died in captivity in May 1915. The
family had lost another son in the Boer War. Two other brothers appear to have
served in 1914–18 and survived.[1]

Beyond such clusters, the largest numbers of men who died in 1914–15
were in three infantry units: the 1st and 2nd RIRifles and the 2nd Royal
Inniskilling Fusiliers. These regular battalions were in the 120,000-strong British
Expeditionary Force (BEF) which crossed the Channel over ten days from
12 August 1914. Although wars are never won by retreats, the part they played
in the 'Retreat from Mons' was crucial in bringing the initial German advance
to a halt.

The 2nd Inniskillings joined the battle in a wave of reinforcements on
26 August at Le Cateau, south of Mons, as part of 12th Brigade, 4th Division.[2]
Among the battalion's regulars were reservists like Private Andrew McCormick
of Emerson Street in the Shankill. He had joined up in 1897, serving in the
Boer War with the 1st Inniskillings, and later in Crete, Malta and North China
before discharge in 1909. He was a repeatedly brave soldier, ending the war as a

company sergeant-major with the Russian Medal of St George (third class) and the Distinguished Conduct Medal.[3]

With a mix of old soldiers, reservists and regulars, the 4th Division at Le Cateau was on the extreme left of the British line. They thus faced strong pressure from the Germans, who were following the Schlieffen Plan, which focused on trying to swing around the end of the Allied line, threatening the BEF with encirclement and capture. Early on the morning of 26 August, General Sir Horace Smith-Dorrien decided that II Corps (consisting of the 3rd and 5th divisions) plus the 4th Division would stand and fight before he carried out a general order to retreat. From 8.05 until 10.45 a.m. and then again from 2.15 to 4.30 p.m., companies of the 2nd Inniskillings engaged with the Germans and did not retreat until 11.30 p.m.

The confrontation, which began in mist after a night of rain,[4] came at a time of open warfare, with armies moving rapidly and the cavalry charge still a part of battle. Moreover, the landscape was largely undamaged, with fighting in and around villages in which buildings still stood and civilians sought shelter. There was also an atmosphere of chaos, with British lines sometimes cut by columns of retreating French soldiers.[5]

In this environment, Private Robert Scott of the 2nd Inniskillings was one of the first three West Belfast fatalities of the war. Scott, in his mid-thirties, was from Oregon Street in the Shankill, a general labourer and a member of the Church of Ireland. He and his wife Margaret had at least four children. Although an early fatality, Scott's death was typical of many, as it took nearly two years to be confirmed. In retreats, bodies remained where they fell. More than one year after his death, the *Belfast News Letter* could only say that he had last been seen wounded in August 1914. Only in July 1916 was an announcement made that Scott was now presumed dead. His body was never found.[6] His name, like many others of the 2nd Inniskillings, is simply recorded on the La Ferte-sous-Jouarre Memorial, which commemorates nearly 4,000 officers and men of the BEF who died between August and October 1914 and have no known grave.

On the same memorial are another two West Belfast men killed at Le Cateau that day. One was twenty-year-old Gunner John McGrogan, of the Royal Field Artillery's 124th Battery. A warehouse porter before joining up in January 1913 as a regular soldier, he was a Catholic from Stanhope Street off Peter's Hill.

Private James Templeton was the third fatality on 26 August at Le Cateau. Another man of that name, from Enfield Street, was later shot for desertion, and there will be more on that soldier later. However, the first West Belfast James Templeton to die in the war was from Cupar Street. Templeton was a Presbyterian. His case illustrates that West Belfast men came from communities that were more denominationally mixed than is the case today. Cupar Street is between the Falls and the Shankill, and is now one of those roads divided by a 'peace line'. It was not until the Troubles of the early 1920s and from 1969 that the starkest divides grew up, but even in 1911 when the census was carried out, the road had ends that were more Catholic or Protestant. However, the Templetons lived at 156 with Methodists and Church of Ireland either side, and Catholics only two doors down at 160. Declared missing on 3 October 1914, confirmation of his death did not come through to his wife Susan until September 1915.[7] For such families, the short battle of Le Cateau was unresolved for well over a year.

Following Le Cateau, on 15 September, the 2nd Inniskillings took up defensive positions at the village of St Marguerite, holding the area for three weeks until 7 October under regular and heavy shell-fire. The trenches that would shape the battles fought over the next four years had begun to develop, but there was one last German rush for the channel ports and the 4th Division was moved south of Ypres as part of the defence of the coast. During this time there were continued West Belfast fatalities in the 2nd Inniskillings. However, because the line was more stable, news reached home relatively quickly: the names of three of the five killed on the night of 20/21 October had reached families and appeared in newspapers by 18 November.[8] The remainder of the year was comparatively peaceful for the 2nd Inniskillings. On 20 November, the men enjoyed the 4th Division's baths at Nieppe, the first divisional baths on the Western Front. At the baths, soldiers not only washed but were given clean underclothes and had lice removed from their uniforms. Throughout the war, this should have happened weekly and when it did so, was a source of comfort and relief to soldiers.[9]

Although the 2nd Inniskillings had suffered the first West Belfast fatalities, theirs had not been the first news of fatalities to reach home. The first to make the newspapers was Corporal Arthur Doran of the 2nd RIRifles, a resident of Merkland Street. Like many volunteers he was a political activist. Although a member of the Church of Ireland, his politics were nationalist and he had stood in local elections. As a trade unionist he was secretary of the Irish Operative Butchers' and Fleshers' Association and an active member of the Independent Labour Party. A memoriam notice placed in the *Belfast Evening Telegraph* by the Belfast City ILP paid tribute to 'Comrade Corporal Arthur Doran'.[10]

Doran is interesting for reasons other than being the first West Belfast casualty publicly reported. First, there is some confusion over his actual date of death, with 26 or 27 August, and 15 or 18 September all possibilities.[11] Such confusion was common. Second, more men in Doran's battalion can be identified as having West Belfast links than in any other battalion except the 9th and 14th RIRifles. 332 men in the 2nd RIRifles can be positively identified as being from West Belfast. Indeed, more 2nd Battalion men with a confirmed West Belfast address died in 1914–15 as died on the Somme in the 9th in July 1916 (102 in the 2nd RIRifles and 61 in the 9th) although, of course, these losses in the 2nd were not concentrated on just a few days.

So in 1914–15, the label of 'West Belfast Battalion' belongs to the 2nd RIRifles. Yet that battalion was markedly different to the 'political' volunteer battalions as it contained men from across the religious and political divides of the Falls and the Shankill. The battalion had a Jesuit chaplain, Father Henry Vincent Gill, who was a native of Dublin and in the course of the war received both the Military Cross and the Distinguished Service Order.[12] In his postwar memoirs, Gill said that 'About 70% of the men of the 2nd R. Irish Rifles were Catholics, chiefly from the North of Ireland, but with a large sprinkling from the other parts of the Provinces.'[13] However, as we shall see later, there are striking examples of the battalion being politically mixed, in the figures of Michael McGivern and William Shearer.

At the outbreak of war, the 500 or so regulars in the battalion were supplemented by a similar number of reservists. They travelled from Belfast to join the regulars already based at Tidworth, near Salisbury. One of those regulars, Corporal John Lucy, described the new recruits thus:

> Our reservists came streaming in to make up our war strength; cheerful, careless fellows of all types, some in bowler hats and smart suitings, others in descending scale down to the garb of tramps . . . Smart sergeants and corporals and beribboned veterans of the South African war hatched out of that crowd of nondescript civilians, and took their place and duties as if they had never left the army.[14]

The battalion was among the first of the BEF to arrive in France, early on 14 August 1914, as part of 7th Brigade, 3rd Division. By 23 August they were at Harmignes and facing enemy artillery fire.[15] In their first engagement with the Germans their machine guns inflicted heavy casualties,[16] yet they soon retreated with the rest of the British army. The weather did not help: it was consistently hot in late August and early September, which could sap the energy of men in retreat, while in late September there were regular heavy storms which posed different problems. The retreat was also hampered by the army's own efforts to delay the Germans. On 14 September, near Braine, the battalion had to cross a river by planks because a railway bridge had been recently blown up.[17] By the end of the month, 70 men from the battalion had been killed, but this was only a prelude to the nearly 200 fatalities in October at Neuve Chapelle in an operation that became known as the Battle of La Bassée.

The battle began at a time when the Allies had stopped retreating and started probing German lines attempting to break through. This was mainly through mobile warfare rather than the advances from trenches that were to mark later encounters. The attack at La Bassée began on 12 October, with the 2nd RIRifles playing a small part on the next day. Their main role in the operation began on 22 October when they arrived at Neuve Chapelle, by which time the task was to hold ground rather than gain it, faced as the British were with strong German opposition. Finding front-line trenches already prepared, the battalion dug reserve and communication trenches. The first casualties at Neuve Chapelle came on 23 October, not from German guns but from 'friendly fire': night patrols were fired on by men from the 8th Brigade and there were some fatalities.

The fighting over the next two days at Neuve Chapelle was bloody and chaotic. At one point, when the 2nd RIRifles had driven the Germans from a trench which the latter had taken after heavy bombardment of British lines, the 2nd came under further friendly fire, this time from the artillery. This could only be stopped by word of mouth as the telephone wire back to HQ had been cut by shelling. On the night of 24/25 October, the battalion repelled a German attack with bayonets in 'a hand-to-hand struggle'.[18] By the end of 25 October, the battalion's war diary (a daily record of activity) noted that the battalion was 'practically without officers'. By the time it was ordered behind lines, the fighting strength of the battalion was only about 200 men, down from about 700 when it reached Neuve Chapelle. It was no wonder that Corporal John Lucy later described Neuve Chapelle as 'the place of our destruction'.[19] At least 26 of the 2nd RIRifles' West Belfast men had been killed in the battle. They included Riflemen Patrick Partridge and Thomas Quail, both of whom left widows with five children.[20] Such was the chaos of the battlefield that none of the bodies of these 26 were ever identified, and the men are simply commemorated among the 13,000 names on the Le Touret memorial.

Following La Bassée, although supplemented by a draft of four officers and 80 men, the battalion was well below full strength, and in early November contained only 351 men and 12 officers.[21] Despite this, over November and December it was circulated between the front (at Hooge, Locre, Kemmel or Westoutre) and the reserve trenches. This rotation of battalions is rather at odds with the popular myth, reinforced by modern portrayals such as *Blackadder Goes Forth*, of men joining up in 1914 and spending four years in a hole in the ground, unless they faced slaughter by going over the top in a 'big push'. On average, from 1915, battalions spent ten days a month in the trenches, with no more than half of those days in the firing-line.[22] When not at the front, time was spent on menial and strenuous tasks. Although the main form of transport was the horse, the men carried rations and ammunition to the front line themselves. Charles Brett, an officer with the 6th Connaughts, later recalled how 'The soldier . . . spent much of his resting time as a beast of burden.'[23]

During this time, the 2nd RIRifles developed a reputation as one of the worst disciplined battlions in the army. This was not related to fighting spirit or effectiveness, but due rather to offences committed by the men. In December, a sergeant was shot by his own men while distributing the rum ration. Alcohol was a persistent cause of disorder throughout the war, although there is no evidence that Irish regiments were generally more disorderly than the rest of the army. However, a perception of how to deal with 'the Irish' meant that men in such units were often more likely to be punished harshly than those in other battalions.[24] Such sanctions often involved different types of 'field punishment', which could include loss of pay, extra duties, being confined to a diet of biscuits and water, or being chained to a wagon wheel for two hours a day.

It was during the days in the firing-line that most casualties occurred, often due to shell-fire, but snipers also took their toll. One of those who lost his life was Corporal Michael McGivern, a pre-war reservist. Before the war he was poised to fight for Home Rule as a member of the Irish Volunteers. McGivern's death was one that could be put down to nothing other than being unfortunate enough to be in the wrong part of the trench at the wrong time, and to be hit by whatever the Germans happened to throw in the direction of the battalion. He was one of two men killed on 17 December while the battalion was rooted in the trenches at Kemmel, no man ever quite knowing when death might call. McGivern, who had been employed at Greeves's flax-spinning mill, close to the Falls Road, left his widow, Mary Ann, with four children in Merrion Street. He had arrived in France less than a fortnight before he was killed.[25]

By the time news of McGivern's death reached home, the first winter of the war was biting hard. In the 2nd RIRifles, Captain Gerald Burgoyne noted how swollen feet due to 'standing in icy cold mud and water' were common.[26] Meanwhile, the first wartime Christmas arrived. In Belfast, the season was marked in the usual ways, although the *Telegraph*'s annual children's Christmas drawing competition had a military theme. Children were asked to draw pictures of soldiers, sailors or nurses.[27] The 2nd Inniskillings spent Christmas behind the lines. Their experiences may have been similar to those of Driver Fred Thomas of the Royal Field Artillery. He was from the edge of the West Belfast area, Roden Street, and had been a member of the South Belfast UVF. He wrote home of beer, plum-pudding, tobacco and a sing-song around the camp fire. In a reference to the pre-war private armies he also said that he 'had come across large numbers of Sir Edward's army' and 'some of John Redmond's', adding, 'We are all doing our best for the flag.'[28]

Christmas was different for the 1st RIRifles who were at the front and took part in one of the most remarkable events of the entire war: the Christmas truce. Their war began rather differently from the other battalions discussed here in that they were already abroad, in Aden, at the outbreak of hostilities.[29] But by November they were in France as part of 25th Brigade, 8th Division (with the

Cpl Michael McGivern, 2nd Royal Irish Rifles, 38 Merrion Street, KIA 17 December 1914
(*Belfast Evening Telegraph* 15 January 1915, p. 6)

2nd Lincolnshires, 2nd Royal Berkshires and 2nd Rifle Brigade). Their journey via England gave men the chance to go home on leave. Lance-Corporal Rex Ross visited his parents, Robert and Julia, in Linview Street, while Rifleman John Blair visited his mother in Wilton Street. It was the last time either man was home as they were both killed in action just four months later.[30]

When the battalion reached the front at Laventie on the evening of 15 November, the heaviest fighting of 1914 was over and their casualties were relatively light for the remainder of the year. One stretch at the front began on 23 December. The battalion war diary of this time was compiled by Captain Alan O'Halloran Wright. Originally from Adelaide, he had been a boy soldier in the Boer War, aged just 14, serving with the South Australian Mounted Rifles. It is not clear how he came to be in the RIRifles, but his mother, who was living in England by 1915, had given her Irish maiden name, O'Halloran, to her son.[31] In the war diary, Wright noted that on Christmas Eve, 'Nothing of importance occurred until 8 p.m., when heralded by various jovialities from the trenches the Germans placed lamps on their parapets and commenced singing.' The Germans said that if their opponents would meet them in the middle, they would not fire, and this offer was taken up. Wright's impression of their foes was that many spoke English well, were well clothed, clean-shaven and had 'good physique' though 'rather inclining to extremes of age'. At 8.30 p.m. a report was sent back to brigade headquarters, explaining that there was a truce but that 'all military precautions' were being taken. Close to midnight the battalion then reported to brigade HQ that they had met with Germans from the 158th Regiment. The report continued, 'They gave us a cap and helmet badge and a box of cigars.' Despite the Christmas spirit, the German soldiers boasted of their impending victory. Wright reported, 'One of them states the war would be over in 3 weeks as they had defeated Russia.'

During the truce, preparations for defence continued with digging and the erection of wire.[32] But staff at brigade headquarters were alarmed by what was taking place. On Christmas Eve, the Divisional General Staff had received instructions from GHQ that an attack was expected and they had passed this to each brigade to filter down to battalions.[33] Half an hour into Christmas Day, the 1st RIRifles received this message from brigade HQ in response to their account: 'No communication of any sort is to be held with the enemy nor is he to be allowed to approach our trenches under penalty of fire being opened.' Yet the order was simply ignored and direct fraternization continued throughout the night. At dawn, the Germans continued to dance and sing in front of their parapet. By this time, the hierarchy had changed its tune, giving the battalion some official sanction for the festivities. On a frosty but misty morning,[34] a message received at 8.40 carried divisional instructions: 'So long as Germans do not snipe, there should be no sniping from our lines today but greatest vigilance must be maintained as Germans are not to be trusted. Our guns will not be firing today unless asked to do so by Infantry or unless German guns fire.' At 11.30 a.m., the battalion reported back to brigade HQ that the 'Situation seems [to be] evolving into a kind of mutual armistice terminating 12 m.n. [midnight] tonight.' It was observed that 'Germans are moving about on their parapets doing odd jobs which seem quite harmless', but that otherwise, trenches on both sides were being strongly guarded. However, the battalion assured their superiors that 'Actual communication with the enemy is forbidden.'

Throughout the truce the battalion officers retained suspicions about the Germans' intentions. Wright noted that 'The German soldiers themselves are probably simple minded enough about the thing but only time will show whether there is not something behind all this.' The officers were also probably conscious that there might come a time when they needed to defend their role in the truce. So Wright also noted in the war diary that 'The truce is sought entirely by the enemy' and that the Germans had asked for a two-day truce, which had been refused by the battalion's officers in the firing-line. Moreover, it was agreed with the Germans that should there be any works 'that the other consider not playing the game' then shots would be fired over heads as a signal.

Yet despite no agreement for a two-day truce, that was effectively what happened. It ended formally at midnight on Christmas Day, with the prearranged signal of Captain Arthur O'Sullivan of the battalion's B Company firing his revolver. Only a few shots were fired by the Germans after the signal. When a small party of Germans tried to approach O'Sullivan's trench, they were not fired upon and were simply told to go back to their own lines. In the morning, the battalion's sentries were above their parapets and the Germans did not fire. A day later, the battalion's Commanding Officer, Lieutenant-Colonel George Brenton Laurie, wrote to his wife, 'Our strange sort of armistice continued throughout yesterday.'[35]

In the early part of 1915, all three battalions were rotated between the front and reserve areas on a regular basis. The 2nd Inniskillings saw out 1914 in billets and did not go to the front again until 6 February, by which time they had been transferred, as battalions often were, to another brigade: 5th, part of the 2nd Division, at Festubert. Three months later, this was to be the site of a bloody battle but, until that point, the 2nd Inniskillings enjoyed relative quiet at the front. They carried out work strengthening breastworks, which were trenches built above wet ground, rather than dug into the ground, using any materials soldiers could find. While doing so, the men were under occasional shell-fire, which could result in one-off casualties at any time. In late March one was Private Joseph Donnelly of Grosvenor Place. He had been a member of the Irish Volunteers who heeded John Redmond's call and enlisted.[36] Otherwise, casualties were light: the battalion was regularly rotated, seldom being in the front line for more than four days.[37]

Better weather from March opened up new opportunities for attack. In early March, the 1st RIRifles were thrown into action at a place which had already cost the 2nd RIRifles dear during the battle of La Bassée: Neuve Chapelle. The March 1915 attack at Neuve Chapelle was a battle in its own right rather than part of a wider operation. The aim was to capture the Aubers Ridge to allow the Allies to threaten German-held Lille. The 1st RIRifles took their position for the second wave of the attack in the early hours of 10 March. At 7.30 a.m. a heavy artillery bombardment of German lines began and continued for 35 minutes. Unlike some such bombardments later in the war, it was highly effective and the first wave of the attack (2nd Lincolnshires and 2nd Royal Berkshires) took the German trenches with ease. The 1st RIRifles had orders to replace the 2nd Lincolnshires on the breastwork of the former front line but so quick had been the advance that the battalion passed through the line and advanced on the second objective: the village of Neuve Chapelle itself, about 400 yards behind the German front line. A Company attacked to the right, with B on the left, supported by C and D companies respectively. B Company secured its goal but as D came up from behind in support, German machine guns opened fire on the continuing advance.

It was now 8.40 a.m., and the battalion could temporarily go no further as the British artillery was not due to stop firing on the land ahead until 9 a.m. But by 9.40 a.m. all the objectives had been gained, with the 1st RIRifles occupying trenches previously taken and briefly held by the 2nd Battalion in the previous October. As the positions were secured, and 'desultory shelling' took place through the night, the battalion counted its losses. These appeared to be 22 men killed, 88 wounded, and 99 missing. Among the officers, two were killed and six wounded. Later, it became clear that 28 of the missing were in fact killed.[38] Over the course of the next two days the battalion lost as many men again. Some of the casualties came from German shelling as the battalion tried simply to hold their gains, but most came from a disastrous attack on the morning of 12 March.

After the attack had already been delayed once, the battalion took up position at 9 a.m. Fog delayed until noon a British bombardment due at 10 a.m., but the Germans shelled the British lines continuously from 9.45 onwards and the battalion took heavy casualties. When they advanced at 12.45, they came under heavy German fire and were hindered by wire in front of trenches, which had not been effectively cut during the bombardment. At 5.15 p.m., the battalion was ordered to advance and take the German line 'at all costs', but it soon became clear that the Germans were so entrenched that there was no question of an advance. The 'at all costs' order was rescinded, and the battalion withdrew at 7.30 p.m.[39] The battle as a whole cost the British over 11,000 casualties.

The battalion remained in the Neuve Chapelle area until the end of March. On one occasion in the front line, the men found the 'Whole place heaped with dead, both British and German'. Casualties were incurred throughout the month from both shelling and sniping. Overall, the battalion's time at Neuve Chapelle was not as costly for the 1st RIRifles as it had been for the 2nd five months before, but it still took its toll with approximately 100 men losing their lives. At least 16 of these were West Belfast men, including Lance-Corporal Rex Ross and Rifleman John Blair who had managed to squeeze in brief visits to Belfast while the battalion had been in England. For some men, death was delayed but it came nonetheless. At the end of April, Rifleman James Wherry of Thames Street died in hospital at Le Havre. He was killed by 'enteric fever' (typhoid) to which he had succumbed after being wounded. A veteran of the Boer War with 16 years' service in the army, he had worked at Queen's Island (part of the shipyards) immediately before the war. His widow, Jane, was left with five children.[40]

The next major action of the 1st RIRifles was to be even more costly than Neuve Chapelle. Close to that village, at what was variously called Rouge Bancs or Fromelles at the time, but was later called the Battle of Aubers Ridge, the battalion made another attempt to take the ridge that had been their target in March. This was all part of the wider Artois offensive, with the French taking action along a front between Arras and Lens. During the battle, having attacked at 5.40 a.m. on 9 May, the battalion secured its objective under heavy fire though with many casualties. But relief from other battalions, necessary to continue the attack, did not arrive, and the battalion was forced to retreat. By 7 a.m., so many officers had been lost that one company placed itself under the command of the officer in charge of the 2nd Rifle Brigade. Fifty of the 1st RIRifles and 150 of that brigade held a line for 12 hours, when they came under attack. The Germans were driven away but at 3 a.m. the next morning, the remains of the two battalions were forced back to the original British line.

Around 600 men from the 1st RIRifles had advanced on 9 May. Around 80 per cent of them (454) were casualties – over 200 at that point simply missing.[41] All officers were killed, wounded or missing, and it fell to the regimental sergeant-major to take the remaining men back to billets. It later transpired that 179 'other ranks' in the battalion had been killed in just one day, including at least 25 West Belfast men. They came from both the Falls and the Shankill. Rifleman Hugh McGrady from Gibson Street had enlisted at the outbreak of the war.[42] Others, such as Rifleman James Owens of Esmond Street, had been reservists. Owens was one of many who had worked at Workman Clark, and he was also a member of the West Belfast UVF.[43] Rifleman Thomas McDonnell of Tralee Street, aged 24, had been a prominent local boxer before the war.[44]

For some families, agony was only just beginning. As late as September 1915, the only news of 32-year-old Rifleman John Adams was that he was missing on 9 May. That would have been trying enough for his parents, David and Elizabeth Adams of 12 Varna Street, but they also had to endure the news only seven days later that his brother, Private Dominick Adams, aged 21, had gone missing with the 2nd Inniskillings.[45] Neither body was ever found, and the brothers who died within a week of each other are commemorated on two separate memorials.

Dominick Adams was killed at Festubert. On the night of 15/16 May, the British launched an offensive there as part of the continued Artois offensive. By this time, the Germans were focused on advancing on the Eastern Front and merely holding ground in the west. At 9 p.m. on 15 May, the 2nd Inniskillings readied themselves for attack, assembled at the front of the British line alongside their 5th Brigade comrades the 2nd Worcestershires to the left and 6th Brigade to the right. These two brigades were also joined by Indian troops of the Meerut Division's Gharwal Brigade. When the attack began at 11.30 p.m., the right half of the 2nd Inniskillings secured their goal in the German lines, but the left half and the rest of the attack failed. Those who had taken German trenches remained

Pte John Adams, 1st Royal Irish Rifles, 12 Varna Street, KIA 9 May 1915
(*Belfast Evening Telegraph* 3 November 1915, p. 6)

Pte Dominick Adams, 2nd Royal Inniskilling Fusiliers, 12 Varna Street,
KIA 16 May 1915 (*Belfast Evening Telegraph* 3 November 1915, p. 6)

there until the evening of 16 May when they were ordered to retreat. Casualties had been heavy. On the day of the battle, the war diary recorded 19 officer casualties, plus 39 other ranks killed, 377 wounded and 239 missing; but it later became apparent that many of the missing were dead and the death-toll for the action eventually reached 245 other ranks,[46] which closely matched the heaviest losses in battalions of the Ulster Division on 1 and 2 July 1916 on the Somme and exceeded many. It was a costly exercise with all gains made surrendered. Over the next few days other battalions made only small advances.

Many of the men killed during 15/16 May were from the Inniskillings' immediate home area around Omagh, but they also came from across Ulster's nine counties, as far south as Dublin and parts of England and Scotland. Of those killed, at least 23 were from West Belfast, and some of their stories illustrate the diverse nature of the battalion. Private Thomas Porter was a West Belfast UVF member, but as a reservist he was among the many who went to the front with regular battalions rather than awaiting the formation of the 9th RIRifles.[47] In the same action, William Montgomery, an Orangeman from Snugville Street,[48] was also killed. So too were Catholics from the Falls, like Dominick Adams and Arthur Connolly. Consequently, the 2nd Inniskillings in the early stages of the war were yet another example of a mixed battalion in which men from both communities served alongside each other. Men from West Belfast continued to serve in this unit throughout the war, but as casualties were replaced by whomsoever was available, it began to lose its Ulster and even its Irish character. After Festubert, relatively few West Belfast men fell in its ranks compared to 1914–15.

The same applies to the 1st RIRifles after their decimation at Neuve Chapelle, but there is one notable exception: Lance-Corporal Peter Sands, who was the first West Belfast man (certainly of three and possibly four) to be shot for 'desertion'.[49] Sands was married to Elizabeth, and lived in Abyssinia Street in the Falls. He had been granted leave from his battalion on 25 February 1915 and this allowed him to return to the UK. The leave was for just four days, but by 1 March he had not returned to his unit and he was struck off the battalion's roll and listed as a deserter a month later. Sands had been due to meet a sergeant from the 1st RIRifles at Victoria Station in London, but did not show. He claimed that he had reported to Victoria Barracks in Belfast on 2 March as he had lost his travel warrant and needed it to get back to France. Sands was told there by a corporal that he was not known at the barracks and he simply went away. He spent the next four months in Belfast until he was apprehended on 7 July after a tip-off and sent back to France. At his trial, Sands argued, 'Had I intended to desert I would have worn plain clothes, but up to the time I was arrested I always wore uniform.' This did nothing to persuade the officers presiding. On 30 August, he was convicted of 'When on active service, deserting His Majesty's Service' and sentenced 'to suffer death by being shot'. Sands' Commanding Officer had described him as a solider of 'very good character both in ordinary situations and as a fighting man'. Brigadier-General R. B. Stephens commanding 25th Brigade argued that 'It is not possible to say that his offence was deliberate to avoid a particular duty', but added that Sands had missed the heavy fighting in early May and had been away for four months. Taking that into account, Stephens believed that Sands had deserted and recommended that the sentence be carried out. At dawn, 5 a.m., on 15 September, Sands was executed at Fleurbaix. Although he was buried in the churchyard there, his grave (and others) could not be located after the war and he is now commemorated along with the others whose graves were lost on a memorial at Cabaret-Rouge British Cemetery, Souchez.[50]

By the time Sands was shot, few West Belfast men were falling in action in his battalion, and although it played a part on the Somme in July 1916, the story of West Belfast at the Western Front for the remainder of 1915 rests with the 2nd RIRifles. The battalion was briefly (in early May 1915) borrowed by the 5th Division for operations at Hill 60. When rotated to the front, the men were regularly on patrol at night, trying to capture Germans if possible, but if not, to locate German listening-posts and digging parties.[51] Men were lost through the daily effects of shell-fire between attacks including, in July, two Woodvale men who had served in the Boer War: Riflemen Robert Johnstone and William Hall. Johnstone was hit in the eye by a bullet and died following an operation to save him. Hall was a skilled footballer before the war. He had played for Cliftonville and was also a member of a representative team consisting of soldiers from Irish regiments. He played in their first match in which they beat their English counterparts.[52]

Losses in the 2nd RIRifles were especially heavy in June and September 1915, when the battalion took part in two attacks at Bellewaarde. In the first of these, on 16 June, 55 of its men were killed, and a further 63 on 25 September. Writing home about the first operation, Rifleman Robert Coates told his mother in Carnan Street:

> The first men out of the trench when the time came were the Liverpool Scottish. We were not supposed to charge at all except they were beaten back, but as soon as our chaps saw them jumping out of the trench the officers could not hold them back. They let out one wild Irish yell and jumped over the parapet and charged over the field like madmen, and of course I went with the rest ... We had to hold the trenches all day and it was something awful. They shelled us for about 18 hours with hundreds of guns, but they could not shift us. We were relieved next morning about one o'clock, and I never was as glad in all my life. Our regiment had about 300 killed and wounded, so thank God I got out safe once more. I think I am the luckiest man in the world.

Coates' luck continued until July 1917, when he was killed in action.[53]

In both June and September, the attacks at Bellewaarde aimed to distract German forces from larger attacks at Givenchy in June and Loos in September. West Belfast men accounted for about 10 per cent of the battalion's losses in the two attacks. One name stands out: Sergeant William Shearer, who had won the Distinguished Conduct Medal the previous November (while a private) for carrying a message under 'most destructive fire' and 'for conspicuous gallantry on all occasions'.[54] Shearer was killed on 25 September. Part of his significance is that he was an Orangeman and a drill sergeant in the UVF prior to the war. As such, alongside Michael McGivern, he illustrates the diversity of the 2nd RIRifles. But Shearer was also presented as a role model by unionist newspapers, which described how, when told of his DCM award, he replied, 'I have only done my duty for my King and country and for the honour of Ulster.' Then, in June 1915, he received a commendation for bravery from Major-General Haldane and was promoted to sergeant. Beyond the stories of heroism, we know of Shearer's last thoughts before going into battle through a letter to his wife. So stirring was this letter that having been read out by the Revd William Corkey at a service in Townsend Street Presbyterian Church it was published in several newspapers. It was Corkey, also a pre-war member of the UVF, who had received formal notification of Shearer's death, because ministers were often asked to break the news to families. Corkey arrived at the Shearer house to find a family party going on, and wrote later that 'It seemed so cruel to bring such news to such a company.' But in fact, Shearer's wife, Sarah, said that she was expecting the news and handed Corkey a letter from her husband. As published in the newspapers, Shearer had written to his wife:

> My regiment is going forward to attack the Hun to-morrow . . . at dawn, and, if possible, give him about turn to Berlin. Now, by the time you receive this I will be lying in a soldier's grave somewhere in France. Keep yourself cool and calm, and when my son William grows a bit older just let him know the part his father took in the great war, 1914–15, and when he is able to look after my D.C. Medal and whatever other ones are given you for me give them to him. I tried hard to get leave home this month, but could not get one, as I knew that sooner or later this trench fighting would have to stop. Well, darling, I am going forward in the fight for freedom with a good heart and putting my trust in God for the Allies to be victorious.[55]

What was left out of this published letter were some personal words to Shearer's wife, and it is difficult to know how these were received by her. After he had referred to his grave in France, he wrote 'and darling, I want you to forget me', adding later, 'forget all about me, we hardly knew each other when war broke out and I am at war one year'.[56] Even if Sarah Shearer had wished to visit her husband's 'soldier's grave', she would not have been able to do so, as it is unmarked. Like Michael McGivern, his body was never identified and they are instead listed on the Menin Gate in Ypres.

Despite Shearer's hopes, the attack at Bellewaarde failed to make any significant impact on German lines despite heavy losses. Some early targets were gained, but nothing was secured, and the battalion was eventually relieved at midnight on 25/26 September. They spent the rest of the year rotating in and out of the trenches. Casualties were light, with only two West Belfast deaths in the remainder of the year.[57] For the nationalists in the battalion, a highlight was the visit of their leader, John Redmond, who inspected them in billets at Le Bizet. Redmond hoped throughout the war that side-by-side service could lead to good relations between Protestant and Catholic, which would translate to Ireland

Sergeant W. SHEARER.

Sgt William Shearer DCM, 2nd Royal Irish Rifles, 29 Seventh Street, KIA
25 September 1915 (*Belfast Weekly Telegraph* 23 October 1915, p. 2)

after the war.[58] Father Gill commented that 'Seeing the regiment is in great part
from the North of Ireland and containing many Protestants the reception of
Mr Redmond was very remarkable.'[59]

Gill's analysis might have glossed over some tensions between the men, although there is no evidence for any, and the fact remains that the 2nd RIRifles
contained men who back home in West Belfast would have been political foes.
The battalion was the clearest example of unionists and nationalists serving
together. However, as the war ground on, and the 2nd RIRifles was refreshed
with drafts of volunteers from across the UK, its Irish character was diluted,
even more so its links with West Belfast. The next stage of the war on the Western
Front would belong to the volunteers of Kitchener's new army, including the 36th
(Ulster) and 16th (Irish) divisions.

4

The Nature of War

The Germans are worse than cannibals, nothing is bad enough for them,
the things they have done.

PRIVATE OLIVER SMITH, ARGYLL AND SUTHERLAND HIGHLANDERS

In the early months of the war, while the regular battalions were retreating from Mons and starting to dig in, the people of Belfast began to form impressions of the war that were to last throughout 1914–18 and to influence the way the war was seen afterwards. They learnt that the war was a world war, in which men were fighting on a range of fronts, and they learnt of the horrors of war in a way that was relatively and perhaps surprisingly uncensored. For example, quite detailed stories of individual battalions were carried in newspapers, which now enable the historian to use newspapers as source of information in a way that would not be possible for the Second World War. At least until mid-1916, any German spy could obtain a significant amount of information about the movements of battalions from daily newspapers. Information such as which battalion was in a particular area was easy to glean from battle reports and only later in the war did this material become a more closely guarded secret.

The clearest signs of the war being a world war came in periodic reports of action well beyond the Western Front. Hugh Roy's parents lived in the Old Lodge Road, and he wrote home to them from South Africa, where he was a trooper in Colonel Enslin's Horse. That unit was engaged in suppressing the Boer revolt, which began in August 1914 as a protest against South African support for the British war effort. Boers had been incorporated into the South African state formed in 1910, and the former Boer commander, Louis Botha, was prime minister of the new state. It was only a minority of Boers who opposed the British war effort, but they posed a threat because of the potential for collaboration with German forces in south-west Africa. The rising was put down by February 1915, and Trooper Roy was unusual in being a non-Boer involved in the conflict. His letter told how he was chased by 20 'rebels' for five miles while carrying despatches on horseback. Roy's 'spirited horse' saved the day.[1] A later example of African service was Private John McConkey of Eton Street, who served in East Africa with the 25th Royal Fusiliers. He was there for over two years and had a difficult time. His discipline was poor and he was punished variously for drunkenness and disorder, at one point spending six months in prison on hard labour. However, his greatest long-term problem was malaria. He spent all of 1916 in hospitals and was eventually sent home in August 1917.[2]

Meanwhile, Quartermaster Sergeant Thomas Booth served for a year in Sierra Leone, although ironically he died suddenly in his house in Sidney Street West in October 1915 while on leave. A veteran of 18 years' previous service, he had been an aide to General Sir Ian Hamilton during the Russo-Japanese war of 1904–5 when Hamilton had been the British army's observer with the Japanese forces.[3]

The sea was also a major part of the 'world' war. In January 1915, Private W. H. Wright of Iverna Street, serving on HMS *Cornwall* with the Royal Marines, sent home a detailed account of the sinking of the *Leipzig* off the Falkland Islands. He described it as 'the finest but yet the saddest sight I have seen', saying that 'I couldn't help thinking of the poor fellows that were struggling in that cold sea, for after all they are only fighting for their country.'[4]

By this time Belfast had already felt naval losses. Naval casualties were mostly killed (or 'lost at sea' in naval terminology) rather than wounded, and were announced to the public in one batch as a ship sunk. Consequently, they had the capacity to shock in an instant those communities with a tradition of naval service. Belfast was one of those, and although naval families seem to have lived more in those parts of North and East Belfast closest to the docks, there were also many sailors from the west of the city. The German submarine U9, lurking in the North Sea, was the harbinger of death on two separate days. It sank the *Aboukir*, the *Hogue* and the *Cressy* in the North Sea on 22 September 1914, with three West

Able Seaman Thomas Doyle, HMS *Hawke*, 18 Warkworth Street, survived sinking
(*Belfast Evening Telegraph* 17 October 1914, p. 6)

Belfast men losing their lives. Then, on 15 October, the cruiser HMS *Hawke* was lost with only about 60 men of a crew of nearly 600 surviving. Of these, around 30 men from Belfast were lost, at least 17 of them from West Belfast. One was David Tully of Bristol Street, who had joined the navy in 1908. By the end of the war, two of his brothers would also be dead.[5]

One West Belfast man on board was Able Seaman Thomas Doyle of Warkworth Street. Doyle's war service was his second spell in the navy, and he served six years from 1903, followed by five years as a reservist while working as a postman. Doyle had been on the mess deck of the *Hawke* at around 10.45 on 15 October when he heard an explosion. He heard three orders. The first was 'Close all watertight doors', but it was impossible to get below decks to do so. The second impossible order was 'Out all boats'. The listing of the ship put paid to that. Soon after came an order that could be carried out: 'Every man for himself', called by the captain through a megaphone. After throwing some wood into the water to use as a buoy, Doyle was fortunate in getting into the only lifeboat that had been launched. He found himself with 48 other men and a brief moment of terror ensued when U9's periscope was seen above water. The survivors feared that they would be rammed, but the submarine went in another direction. Doyle was five hours on the boat, before being picked up at about 16.00 by a Norwegian. They were then transferred to the trawler *Ben Rinnes* at midnight, arriving in Aberdeen on the morning of 16 October. Contact with home was an obvious priority and Doyle's wife received the news of his survival by telegram that day.[6]

Although the largest single loss of West Belfast men at sea was on board the *Hawke*, the greatest naval battle of the war, Jutland, also took its toll on 31 May and 1 June 1916. This battle was the only confrontation of the war between the

Able Seaman John Crothers, HMS *Defence* (left) and Stoker 1st Class Robert Crothers, HMS *Invincible*, 24 Disraeli Street, brothers lost at sea 31 May 1916
(*Belfast Evening Telegraph* 17 June 1916, p. 4)

British Grand Fleet and the German High Seas Fleet: it involved 274 warships, with 14 British and 11 German ships sunk. Dispute over who won continues to this day. The Royal Navy certainly lost more men: over 6,000 compared to just over 2,500 Germans. Among British casualties were at least 13 West Belfast men on the *Black Prince, Defence, Indefatigable, Invincible, Queen Mary* and *Turbulent*. Four were on the *Defence*, including John Crothers of Disraeli Street, whose brother Robert was killed on the *Invincible*. At the time, there were three other Crothers brothers serving in the army.[7]

Aside from appreciating the worldwide nature of the conflict, Belfast people would have been aware of many aspects of life at the front. If news of casualties was slow to reach home, soldiers at the front were sometimes the most ignorant of the fate of members of their families. In December 1914 Private J. McCormick, 2nd RIRifles, of Tyrone Street, was wounded and in hospital in Boulogne. He wrote to his father – and the letter was published in a newspaper for all to see – that 'I have been told by a few wounded men passing through here that my brother Tom was killed. It has greatly upset me, but I hope it is not true. I expect to go back to the firing line very soon, so if it is true I care not what happens to me, I shall have revenge for it.' His father already knew that Tom was not dead but a prisoner.[8]

A surprising amount of detail reached home about life in the kind of camp that was holding Tom McCormick. This was because in the First World War exchanges of prisoners and repatriations of the wounded were routine. So when a prisoner returned home in exchange for a foe, he could tell all. Private J. Pritchard of the 2nd Inniskillings and a resident of Paris Street, was repatriated in November 1915, having been wounded at Mons in August 1914 and taken prisoner. He told of rough handling when he was captured and said that no attention was given to his wounds, while food was minimal.[9] Such stories provided excellent propaganda and were confirmed by later private interviews, which did not reach the newspapers but were told on release. The pattern appears to have been one of dire living conditions, casual violence at the hands of German captors and abuse from German civilians, interspersed with individual acts of kindness, especially from German medical staff.[10]

A celebrated case of a prisoner returning home was that of Corporal John Robinson, captured at Le Cateau. In October 1915 he returned home to Ross Street in the Falls as part of a prisoner exchange. A member of the Royal Army Medical Corps, Robinson injured his shoulder, knee and head, and was blind for ten days after his ambulance was hit. He told the *Belfast Evening Telegraph* how he was treated by two German Red Cross men: 'They were kindly enough to give them their due, and raised my head to help me drink brandy and wine.' When Robinson could speak, he was interrogated by the Germans, who were particularly keen to discuss Ireland's attitude to the war. He was told that he could not be an Irishman if he was in the British army, and several days later, was taken on a train of German and British wounded to Recklinghausen in Germany. There he was interrogated again, bizarrely being shown a photo of an

Orange procession in Belfast on 12 July 1912. The *Telegraph* reported, 'whether the German knew it or not, there was comedy in the situation, for Robinson is of the Falls rather than the Shankill "persuasion" himself'. By October 1914, Robinson was in Sennelager with 4,000 British soldiers and 45,000 French, and was among those whom the Germans tried to recruit for an 'Irish brigade' to fight against the British. He described how one morning all Irish Catholics were ordered to fall in for a parade and 'Seven hundred men filled with curiosity responded, but not all were Irishmen, nor were all Catholics – there were some Shankill Road men.' Over the next weeks, efforts were made to recruit the men into the Irish Brigade, partly through preferential treatment in living conditions. They were then transferred to two more camps, in one of which they believed Roger Casement spoke to them. Casement was a former member of the British consular service, but he was also a committed Irish nationalist and when war

Cpl John Robinson, Royal Army Medical Corps, 45 Ross Street, repatriated in 1915, testified in Casement trial (*Belfast Evening Telegraph* 21 October 1915, p. 6)

broke out he became increasingly radical and sought German support for Irish independence. He tried, with little success, to persuade Irishmen to serve Germany. After being exchanged for German prisoners, Robinson's group came home via neutral Holland. Arriving home, he saw his baby son for the first time. He survived service in the Dardanelles to be the first military witness called in Casement's treason trial.[11]

Other stories concerned luck. Rifleman James Butler, 2nd RIRifles, wrote home to his wife in Scotland Street. The pocket of his trousers was torn clean away by shrapnel, but a purse in the pocket deflected the shrapnel from his leg and saved him from injury.[12] Some stories brought comfort to those who were waiting for news of a missing loved one. Private P. McCarron of Iris Street, serving in the Norfolk Regiment, turned up in a hospital in Norwich in October 1916. When news reached home, he had been missing for two years.[13]

But many more stories focused on the brutality of war. Letters from the front were often reproduced in the newspapers. Many (or at least the reported parts) were always upbeat in tone, but they did not avoid stories of what became known generally as German 'frightfulness' as political leaders and newspapers sought to rally public opinion for the war effort. Letters from men at the front were a way of doing this.

Corporal J. P. O'Farrell was a member of a battalion of the Royal Irish Fusiliers. Before the war he was a well-known Ulster Gaelic sportsman and a member of the Cavan Slashers Gaelic Athletic Club. His mother lived at Chief Street in the Shankill, and received a letter from him in October 1914. He wrote how his battalion had 'chased' the Germans from a town, and was now dug in. He said, 'The Germans are burning all before them as they retire. Last night the sky was lit up with burning houses and hay ricks set on fire. They are behaving very badly to the people in the villages, and there are some terrible stories of their treatment of the inhabitants.'

A more graphic account came from a member of the 2nd Inniskillings' Machine Gun Section, Lance-Corporal William Leeburn, writing to his mother in Beverley Street in Woodvale. He wrote of 'poor people, old women and little children, walking along the roads, homeless and friendless, driven out by the Germans' who 'killed cows and left their carcasses lying in the street'. Private Oliver Smith of the Argyll and Sutherland Highlanders took a similar tone writing to relatives in Eglinton Street in Court ward. He was a Boer War veteran and described by the *Belfast Evening Telegraph* as being 'well-known up Celtic Park ways', which may simply have been a reference to some involvement in Belfast Celtic but may also have been code for being a nationalist. Smith wrote, 'The Germans are worse than cannibals, nothing is bad enough for them, the things they have done.' Such accounts served to reinforce public perceptions of the beastly Hun and justify involvement in the war. But the public were also being prepared for the idea that the war might not be over by Christmas: although O'Farrell said that he was 'pretty sure there will be a day of reckoning soon', he added that 'I expect to get home at the latest early in spring.' Trooper Albert Courtney, a native of the Falls,

Cpl J. P. O'Farrell, Royal Irish Fusiliers, 24 Chief Street, Cavan Slashers player
(*Belfast Evening Telegraph* 28 October 1914, p. 3)

and wounded in the left lung and back by shrapnel, told the *Telegraph* that he
believed the war 'would last a considerable time'.[14]

Although O'Farrell, Leeburn and Smith all stressed the friendliness of locals
and the value of comforts sent from home, others were clear how awful life at the
front was. The most shocking and pessimistic accounts came from wounded men
returning home. Private George Taylor, of the 1st West Yorks, was asked by the
Telegraph, 'What is war like?' He replied, 'It's not hell! . . . it's worse than hell. Hell
could never be anything like so bad.' Taylor was not a native of Belfast, originally
hailing from London, but he settled in the city after marrying a Belfast woman,
and had been commander of J Company of the UVF's West Belfast Regiment. He
had served with the 1st West Yorks on the North-West frontier of India before
the war and rejoined at the outbreak, serving with the transport section, which
meant he was sometimes on horseback. His story told of how his horse had

been shot from under him during fighting on the Aisne in September. Taylor had been trapped under the fallen horse, his knee crushed. He was then stuck in the left shin by a German bayonet but his assailant was simultaneously killed by a bayonet through the body. Taylor added his own story of Hun 'frightfulness', telling how a soldier had surrendered to the Germans having been heavily outnumbered. However, on handing over his bayonet-fixed rifle, the German receiving the weapon had used it on the surrendering soldier.[15]

There were also detailed accounts, couched in the language of heroism and service, of the nature of wounds. One story related to the death of Sapper James Smyth Davison of the Royal Engineers 59th Field Company. Aged 25, from Lake Glen, Andersonstown, he was a pre-war soldier who had rejoined at the outbreak of war. He distinguished himself at the Aisne, rescuing six soldiers from a capsized boat. At Ypres, on 25 April 1915, while carrying dispatches, he was 'seriously injured by a poisoned German shell, which inflicted no fewer than 76 wounds on his body and made 12 holes in his despatch satchel'. Davison managed to shake off the poison in hospital in Boulogne, and was then moved to Stobhill hospital in Glasgow. There he developed tetanus and died. Two hours after his death, a letter arrived at the hospital saying he had been awarded the Distinguished Conduct Medal.[16]

In addition to stories about individuals, there was focus on the contribution of specific families. Especially in the early stages of the war, newspapers focused on families from which many men were serving. These stories were all part of a recruiting effort that encouraged women to push men into the army, the implication of all stories being that 'if this family has given so much, you can do the same'. One of the earliest from West Belfast was the Magee family of Braemar Street, Broadway, on the southern edge of the Falls. By January 1915, Mrs Magee had six sons serving: Robert in the 4th Hussars, George and Edward in the 6th RIRifles, William in the 8th Inniskillings, Joseph in the 2nd RIRifles, and Jack on HMS *Lance*. The *Belfast Evening Telegraph* hailed them as a 'FINE ENCOURAGEMENT FOR LADS TO ENLIST'.[17] In March 1915 all five Boyd sons from 17 Bromley Street were a similar case: James in the Royal Marines, David in the 8th RIRifles, John in the Army Service Corps, Joseph in the 9th RIRifles and Hugh in the Royal Engineers attached to the Ulster Division.[18]

But the risks of many members of the same family serving were steadily brought home by the story of the Quinn brothers. Robert Quinn lived at 15 North Boundary Street with his widowed sister, Eliza Jane McAteer. Quinn's wife, Ruth, died when his three boys were young and his sister had acted as mother to them. All three served in the Inniskillings and all three were killed, William with the 2nd Battalion in November 1914, James with the 1st in May 1915 and Robert with the 2nd in April 1917.[19] The McDowells of Malvern Place, about whom there is less information, lost four sons.[20]

Aside from hearing about casualties in their own immediate circle and from newspapers, the public actually saw wounded soldiers in Belfast from November 1914. They came for transportation to other parts of Ireland, and some stayed in

Pte William Quinn, 2nd Royal Inniskilling Fusiliers (left), KIA 4 November 1914; Pte James Quinn, 1st Royal Inniskilling Fusiliers, KIA 22 May 1915, brothers from 15 North Boundary Street (*Belfast Evening Telegraph* 1 July 1915, p. 6). A third brother, Robert, was also killed with the 2nd Inniskillings in April 1917.

Belfast hospitals, including the UVF Hospital, which opened in Belfast in January 1915 and treated soldiers from all backgrounds. Such soldiers were embraced by members of the public who organized events to entertain them and assist their recovery.[21] Further charitable contributions to the war effort came through fundraising activities. From the earliest days of the war, volunteers raised funds for comforts for soldiers. The girls at St Aidan's School in West Belfast sold badges to buy tobacco for the 2nd RIRifles.[22]

For Christmas 1914, the Shankill Road Mission congregation sent their members at the front parcels made up of clothing (such as mittens and socks), plus matches, cigarettes, boracic ointment, Vaseline, chocolate, liquorice, and a New Testament.[23] The Falls and Smithfield branch of the Queen Mary Guild (which originated in a group providing clothes for the poor from the 1880s) sent tobacco and other items to the 16th Division. In 1915 these were presented to the division in person by Joseph Devlin at training camps in Ireland and England.[24] Throughout the war, one-off activities included a Belfast Rotary Club sale of Allied flags to raise money for the wounded, a 'Horse Show and Gymkhana' at Celtic Park in aid of the Red and Blue Cross societies and the Lady Mayoress's

Chrysanthemum Day. There was also and a football match (friendlier than in 1912) between Linfield and Belfast Celtic to raise funds for prisoners of war.[25] There was also fundraising for projects such as the provision of recreation huts at the front by both the Belfast Boy Scouts and the Soldiers' Christian Association, and the Revd William Corkey of the Townsend Street presbytery went to the front in 1918 to work in a YMCA hut.[26] Longer-term plans were made to help former members of the UVF through the UVF Patriotic Fund launched in May 1916. Funds were raised by subscriptions, but also through events such as gold and silver collections.[27]

Such charitable work grew as the war went on. The launch of the Patriotic Fund was a sign that the political establishment had understood the challenge of looking after the wounded and the families of the dead, and knew that charity must be about more than sending cigarettes to soldiers at the front. Such a realization by early 1916 was informed not only by the experiences of the men on the Western Front, but by the Allies' first disaster: Gallipoli.

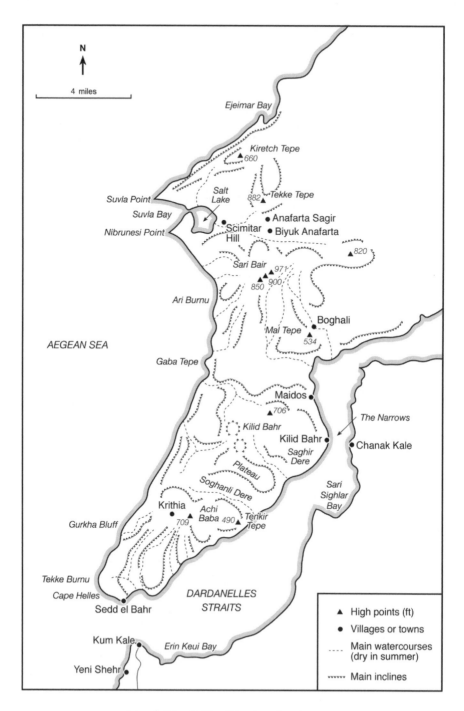

N

4 miles

Ejeimar Bay

Kiretch Tepe
▲ *660*

Tekke Tepe
882 ▲

Salt Lake

Suvla Point

Suvla Bay

Nibrunesi Point

● Anafarta Sagir

Scimitar Hill

● Biyuk Anafarta

▲ *820*

Sari Bair ▲ *971*
850 ▲ ▲ *900*

Ari Burnu

Boghali ●

Mal Tepe
▲ *534*

AEGEAN SEA

Gaba Tepe

Maidos ●

▲ *706*

The Narrows

Kilid Bahr

Kilid Bahr ●

● Chanak Kale

Saghir Dere

Sari Sighlar Bay

Plateau

Soghanli Dere

Krithia ●
Achi Baba
▲ *709* *490* ▲ *Tenkir Tepe*

Gurkha Bluff

Tekke Burnu

Cape Helles

Sedd el Bahr ●

DARDANELLES STRAITS

Kum Kale ●

Erin Keui Bay

Yeni Shehr ●

▲ High points (ft)
● Villages or towns
- - - Main watercourses (dry in summer)
 vvvvv Main inclines

Map 3 The Gallipoli Peninsula, 1915–16

5

Gallipoli and the Eastern Front

*There was not a falter, they followed like one man, soon catching me up
and we tore forward like driven birds.*

CAPTAIN F. E. EASTWOOD, 6TH ROYAL IRISH RIFLES

While the 1st RIRifles were decimated at Neuve Chapelle, the men of West Belfast faced equal challenges fighting the Turks at Gallipoli. Handfuls of West Belfast men served in a wide range of infantry units at Gallipoli.[1] Others were lost in the naval aspect of the campaign.[2] But along with the 6th RIRifles, the 1st Royal Inniskilling Fusiliers carried the flag for West Belfast at Gallipoli.

Turkey entered the war in October 1914, initially fighting Russia on the Caucasian Front. Hostilities with Britain began on 5 November. The Russians desperately wanted a new front opened against Turkey to relieve pressure. The Dardanelles Straits were chosen because they controlled access to the Sea of Marmara and consequently the Turkish capital, Constantinople. Moreover, entry to that sea would open up the Black Sea through the narrow Bosporus Channel, offering a new supply route between the Mediterranean and Russia.

The initial attack on the straits on 19 February 1915 was naval. After an un-successful month, the British Cabinet decided to launch an amphibious landing at Gallipoli, in which the British would cooperate with Australian, New Zealand and French troops. However, liaison between the British commanders on the spot, Admiral de Robeck and General Hamilton, was exceptionally poor and is one reason why Gallipoli has become a byword for failed planning. Delays gave General Otto Liman von Sanders, the German officer commanding the Turkish Fifth Army, time to strengthen the Gallipoli defences, making the 25 April land-ings far more difficult than they might have been a month earlier.[3]

The British element of the initial landings was the 29th Division. The 1st Royal Inniskilling Fusiliers were members of 87th Brigade, alongside other battalions formerly in India: the 2nd South Wales Borderers, 1st King's Own Scottish Borderers and the 1st Border Regiment. Thus comprising English, Scottish, Welsh and Irish battalions, the brigade was known as the 'Union Brigade'. The battalion had been in India when war broke out, and had not left until 7 December, arriving at Avonmouth in England on 10 January 1915. From there, the battalion went to Rugby where the brigade was formed.[4] The battalion trained for two months before making the seven-day sea voyage to Malta, arriving on 24 March. After a two-day rest, the battalion embarked on the short trip to Alexandria, and assembled with the rest of 29th Division at the Greek island of Lemnos on 12 April.

The 29th Division was due to head for Gallipoli on 23 April, but bad weather struck. The men were on ships in Lemnos harbour for two days, during which time the 1st Inniskillings practised ladder-climbing in full equipment, along with rowing and landing boats.[5] At 17.00 on 24 April, a convoy of troops for the landing departed Lemnos. They reached their destinations at dawn the next day. The 29th Division (later joined by French reserve troops) headed for Helles, the southern tip of the peninsula, while the ANZAC force went for Gaba Tepe, and the French were to land at Besika Bay, on the Asian side of the Dardanelles. The attacks on these three points were joined by a fake landing at Bulair at the far north of the peninsula carried out by the Royal Naval Division, which had some success in confusing the Turks.

The ANZACs encountered problems first: they landed further north than intended and faced steep cliffs, suffering heavy casualties despite relatively light initial resistance. Indeed, one West Belfast man, Private William Calderwood, whose parents lived in Beverley Street, was killed while serving with the 11th Australian Infantry.[6] But 87th Brigade's landing was remarkably easy. The guns of HMS *Implacable* made a great impact on the Turkish defences, and the brigade landed without any casualties. By mid-afternoon, the 1st Inniskillings had landed and were digging in. The differing fortunes of other parts of the landing force meant that rapid advance was difficult. However, by the time further advances were planned on 28 April, the Turkish forces were clear exactly where the Allies had landed, and had been able to reinforce their defences. As a result, the conditions of the Western Front were soon transported to Gallipoli. By the time of the advance on 28 April, the 1st Inniskillings had lost six men from Turkish counter-attacks, including the first West Belfast loss in the battalion, Lance-Corporal James McCalmont of Woodvale Street. Much heavier losses were to occur when the attack began and continued throughout May.

The attack at 8 a.m. on 28 April was the first of three battles for Krithia. On the first day, progress was halting, and after three hours of fighting they could advance no further.[7] That evening 29th Division consolidated its position in new trenches, holding the line until a new attack on 6 May. During this time the 1st Inniskillings had to deal with a heavy Turkish attack on the night of 1 May, after which about 150 Turks were found to have dug in just 250 yards or so in front of the British line. A successful raid on the Turkish line brought back 132 prisoners. The next day, Lance-Corporal Herman Henderson of Warkworth Street was one who lost his life not in a large battle but through shellfire or snipers. Henderson had seven years' service, having been in India with the battalion before the war; his was a military family with his father also serving, as a sergeant, with the 13th RIRifles.[8]

At 11 a.m. on 6 May, the second battle for Krithia was launched. It lasted for three days. By dusk on 6 May, 600–700 yards had been gained, with new trenches dug. On 7 May, following naval bombardment of the Turkish position, the advance was 'entirely held up by cross fire from enemy machine guns which cannot be located'. Even by the evening of 8 May only limited gains of a few hundred yards had been made. A day later, the 1st Inniskillings were relieved at the front by the 89th Punjabis. For the remainder of May the battalion was periodically at the front, often facing heavy counter-attacks. The regimental history records how there was an especially fierce and unexpected attack on 22 May at Gurkha Bluff, with the Turks breaking British lines. While the Inniskillings were at dinner, 'The enemy bombers came forward shouting "Allah, Allah", careless of death. Fierce hand-to-hand fighting followed in the trenches.'[9] This representation of the Turkish soldiers as fanatics was typical of the Allies' impression of their enemy. The surprise Turkish attack on 22 May was costly for the battalion, with 49 men falling on that day alone. Among them was Private James Quinn of 15 North Boundary Street, one of three brothers to be killed in the war.[10]

Although another attempt on Krithia took place on 4 June, the 1st Inniskillings were in reserve throughout and did not leave their trenches. It was not until the middle of June that the battalion was again in action.[11] It came under fire from high-explosive shells on the night of 18/19 June, and men went forward in bombing parties to hold back an enemy breakthrough. However, June and July passed with relatively light casualties, although on the night of 1 and 2 July, in response to a Turkish attack, two Victoria Crosses were earned by the battalion, the first ever awarded to soldiers of the regiment. One award was made to an Ulsterman, Sergeant James Somers, a native of Belturbet, County Cavan, who held a 'sap'[12] all night long on his own, and then led a charge taking a Turkish trench the next morning. The other award was made to Captain Gerald O'Sullivan, of County Cork, who led a bombing party to take a trench. Neither man survived the war. O'Sullivan was dead just a month later, while Somers was later gassed in France and died of the effects at home in May 1918.[13]

As on the Western Front, units at Gallipoli were not constantly in the firing-line. The 1st Inniskillings were even withdrawn from the Gallipoli peninsula for rest at Mudros between 11 and 21 July. When they were at the front, their task was mainly holding hard-won ground rather than making further advances. Many casualties came from Turkish shell-fire. One soldier, Lance-Corporal Samuel Fallon, died after being mortally wounded by a shell on 2 July. The report of his death came from his brother who was in the trench alongside him, and who sent news back to their aunt in Hutchinson Street in the Falls.[14]

Soldiers were not only in danger from the Turks. Illnesses such as enteric fever and dysentery flourished as the terrain made it impossible to bury many of the dead, which is one reason why so many of the British dead at Gallipoli are on one memorial at Helles instead of having marked graves. In the 1st Inniskillings, fatalities continued even when they were not advancing. Private Hugh Thompson died of wounds on 11 July. He was a reservist before the war and his loss was not the only one from Gallipoli for his parents in Carnan Street: on 25 April his brother, Private John Thompson, a regular in the 1st Royal Dublin Fusiliers, was killed on the first day of the landings.[15]

In the face of these losses, a desperate bid to regain the initiative was launched on 6 August. This offensive took place mainly at Suvla Bay, north of the ANZAC landing. Although the 1st Inniskillings were to be involved in this operation later in the month, another battalion containing West Belfast men was at the forefront of the attack: the 6th RIRifles. This battalion had not seen action and was part of the new army, in 29th Brigade of the 10th (Irish) Division. Although consisting of battalions raised in Ireland at the start of the war, the 10th Division was self-consciously non-political, in contrast to the highly politicized 16th and 36th divisions. The 6th RIRifles drew on men from across Ireland, although the majority were from Ulster counties.

The 6th RIRifles landed slightly to the south of Suvla Bay, at Sari Bair, aiming to take the ridge that dominated the terrain. The ANZACs had made such sacrifices there that it was already known to the Allies as Anzac Cove. The landing was complete by 4.30 a.m. on 6 August and they waited, dug in, for orders to attack.[16] Captain F. E. Eastwood, a company commander on that day, wrote in 1931 about the operation: 'After landing at night . . . we wandered where we liked as long as we got away from the sea-shore.' The next day, after dawn, although under fire, all Turkish shells fell short. Orders had come for an attack on the afternoon of 6 August but were subsequently cancelled. It was not until the early afternoon of 8 August that the 6th RIRifles advanced with the 10th Hampshires. The men moved up in half-company blocks, but those at the front had not actually received clear orders and succeeded in blocking the trenches. Eastwood, commanding D company, only got his men to safety 'by a sort of Rugby scrimmage under cover'. They entrenched on 9 August and on the morning of 10 August as 'the sun rose higher and higher' the battalion was ordered to attack the Turks. Eastwood led the first attack himself because his platoon commander had been missing since shell-fire the previous afternoon. He described the advance:

> There was not a falter, they followed like one man, soon catching me up and we tore forward like driven birds. A mine did not explode at our feet, but shrapnel, machine guns, rifle fire poured into us, a sort of enfilade fire as the man on my left seemed to take my lot. I only got a bit of shrapnel in the neck, enough to bring me down. I did not see a man rise again.

A second platoon followed, and was also cut down. Eastwood tried to lead those who could still walk in another attack, but that turned out to be only seven men. He was hit in the wrist, and then by a bullet through his helmet which scraped his head and ear. Unable to continue, Eastwood retired, and the attack was suspended. The Turks had been thoroughly dug in and Eastwood later concluded 'even with to-day's knowledge of the ground . . . the task, owing to the nature of the ground, was impossible'.[17]

A later Turkish counter-attack inflicted further heavy casualties on the 6th RIRifles on 10 August, as did shelling on the next day. By 14 August, the battalion was in relative safety behind the front line and was eventually withdrawn from the peninsula on 30 September, moving to Salonica days later. On 10 and 11 August alone, the 6th RIRifles lost 65 men, with at least another 250 wounded. All of its officers at the front had been killed, and command passed temporarily to a captain who had been in reserve. Another 23 men would lose their lives before the withdrawal at the end of September, mainly through wounds or illness. Among the 65 killed in the attack and counter-attack at Sari Bair were at least 19 West Belfast men. Rifleman Robert Cooley of Bow Street was at 49 one of the oldest in action at the front.[18] But for many relatives, formal confirmation of death was not immediate. Rifleman Patrick Canavan, aged 28, of Servia Street was declared missing in September. But his wife, Mary Teresa, and three little sons waited 14 months after his death before receiving official notice that he was presumed killed.[19] The family of Private Owen Conlon, living in Omar Street in the Falls, waited until January 1917 to be given official news. His mother, Margaret Conlon, had tried without success to find information from the Red Cross in Dublin.[20] Other families received news of a wound or illness, only for death to follow later. Rifleman John McLaughlin of Leeson Street in the Falls, aged 19, died of wounds on the hospital ship *Dunluce*.[21] Rifleman Harry McClune of Denmark Street in the Shankill, and formerly of the North Belfast UVF, succumbed to dysentery in St Andrew's hospital, Malta.[22] In December, rifleman John Kirkpatrick of Burnaby Street died closer to home in Stobhill hospital, Glasgow.[23]

West Belfast men had also been in action at Sari Bair in the 31st Brigade of the 10th (Irish) Division. Two Boer War veterans lost their lives in the 6th Royal Irish Fusiliers: Lance-Sergeant Patrick Hamill of Grosvenor Road and Private John McPherson of Alton Street.[24] In the same brigade, in the 5th Royal Irish Fusiliers,[25] was Daniel McKeown, one of those volunteers with a previous record in soldiering who enlisted early in the war. He only served at Gallipoli from 7 to 16 August, before being wounded and returning home.[26] Another West Belfast soldier of the 5th Royal Irish Fusiliers, Thomas Donnelly of Inkerman Street, fell as the battalion went into the attack on 7 August. His body was never identified. He had enlisted with his brother, Patrick, who was serving elsewhere. Before going overseas, Thomas had been photographed with his sweetheart, Elizabeth Adams of Varna Street. She lost not only Thomas in the spring and summer of 1915 but also her two brothers, Johnny and Dominick, who died within a week of each other in May 1915 on the Western Front. After the war, she married Thomas's brother, Patrick, who had survived his service.[27]

Soon after the 6th RIRifles were engaged at Sari Bair, the 1st Inniskillings took part in another operation at Helles, which aimed to draw Turkish troops away from the wider Suvla Bay offensive. On 6 August, the Inniskillings were not involved in a direct assault. But they did take part in an effort to confuse the Turks, cheering and moving about in their trench, while showing the tips of their bayonets above the parapets to indicate preparation for an attack. On 17 August the battalion was moved from Helles to Suvla Bay itself. Four days later they took part in an assault on Hill 70 or 'Scimitar Hill' during which 123 men and seven officers (including Captain O'Sullivan who had won the VC in July) were killed in action, not counting those who later died of wounds.

The attack began at 3.30 p.m., preceded first by a half-hour bombardment and

L/Sgt Patrick Hamill, 6th Royal Irish Fusiliers, Boer War veteran, 24 Alton Street,
KIA 9 August 1915 (*Belfast Evening Telegraph* 5 October 1915, p. 4)

then half an hour of machine-gun fire. It was hoped that an afternoon attack
would mean that the Turks had the sun facing directly towards them, which
might help to obscure the advance. However, the day was dull and the attackers
were robbed of that advantage. The 1st Inniskillings led a 400-yard front with
the 1st Borders in support. Although the first trench towards the crest of the hill
was reached and taken in ten minutes, casualties were heavy, with officers and
men 'swept down as by an invisible scythe'.[28] Moreover, the trench provided no
shelter from Turkish machine guns and a field battery on higher ground. Those
who could still move retreated to organize a new attack. Captain William Pike led
an attack in which nobody survived, and Captain O'Sullivan led another charge
calling out, 'One more charge for the honour of the Old Regiment.' From that
charge of 50, only one man returned.[29] This was the end of the operation for the
battalion. It had begun the afternoon with 19 officers and 758 men. Before the
end of the day, only four officers and 230 men answered a roll-call. So in addition
to the 123 who would eventually be confirmed killed that day, around 400 were

wounded and out of action. At least 17 of the dead were from West Belfast, among them Private Thomas Seeds of 13 Crosby Street, who was just 17. He was in the West Belfast UVF and worked in the shipyards at Queen's Island when he enlisted.[30] In honour of this action the battalion was, in 1922, given sanction to wear the badge of the 29th Division (an ace of diamonds halved) in perpetuity to mark the sacrifice at Scimitar Hill.[31]

Having marched 2½ miles behind the lines on 22 August, the remnants of the battalion spent a week digging and clearing communication trenches. That was the pattern until the battalion was withdrawn by sea to rest at Imbros, arriving there on 23 September. The rough weather made a landing impossible, but the men eventually went ashore a day later and spent a week in the rest camp before heading back to Helles on 1 October. There was no question of further efforts to advance by this point, and the British government was now seriously considering evacuation. That was foreshadowed in mid-October with the replacement of General Hamilton as commander at Gallipoli with General Monro who soon recommended full withdrawal. Kitchener visited the Dardanelles in mid-November and agreed.

By this time, there was little activity on the front, and the 1st Inniskillings were even able to take part in a football tournament, dubbed the Dardanelles Cup, in which they beat the 1st King's Own Scottish Borderers 1–0 on 4 November. However, from mid-November, the weather put paid to further football.

Pte Thomas Seeds, 1st Royal Inniskilling Fusiliers, ex-UVF, 13 Crosby Street, KIA 21 August 1915 (*Belfast Evening Telegraph* 11 November 1915, p. 4)

Conditions matched those associated with the Western Front. On 17 November the battalion war diary noted just how desperate the situation was:

> Very heavy tropical downpour, the whole of the dug-outs being nearly wash[ed] out. The lines being 6 inches to 2 feet deep in water and mud. An extra issue of rum. But nothing could be done except to turn men out to redig the washed away drains, and to make new ones. Kept the battalion occupied in digging to keep them warm.

Despite the rum and digging, some men died of the cold. For others, a wound was the best thing that could happen to them in Gallipoli during this time because it meant a ticket home. A Boer War veteran, Corporal John Harper of the Military Mounted Police, was wounded late in the campaign on 10 December having already received a Military Medal. An Orangeman and a member of the North Belfast UVF, he was shipped off to hospital in Malta. For his seven children, the eldest of whom was serving in the Royal Navy by 1915, it was especially fortunate that he survived, for they had already lost one parent during the war: their mother had died while their father was at the front, leaving their uncle to care for the youngest of them.[32]

By this time, even though the Turks were dug in and showing no intention of fighting, the tough winter conditions made withdrawal ever more urgent. The evacuation of Suvla Bay and Anzac Bay was completed without casualties on the night of 19/20 December. That left only Helles, and from 3 January the 1st Inniskillings prepared for 'retirement', much of which involved making the Turks believe that a withdrawal was not actually happening. This involved such tricks as dummy figures, and attaching clockwork mechanisms to rifle triggers so that shots could be fired periodically after all troops had departed. Moreover, for some weeks in advance of the withdrawal no shots were fired between 11.30 p.m. and 5 a.m. to acclimatize the Turks to silent nights.

The officers of the 1st Inniskillings feared casualties from three sources during a withdrawal: a general Turkish attack along the whole front, a 'local' attack at specific points, or shelling of the beaches. The last was considered 'probable and to many minds unavoidable'. Incredibly, none of these threats materialized: although the Turks seemed to be aware that something was happening, they did not know if it was a retreat or an attack and opted to stay in their lines.[33] When the retreat began just before dusk on 8 January, all trenches not needed for the evacuation were blocked to slow up the Turks should they advance. Moving back, the men's footsteps were muffled by strips of sandbags or blankets tied to their boots. By 4 a.m. on 9 January the battalion was sailing away on several different vessels, without casualties.

Unlike most other operations at Gallipoli the withdrawal on 8 January 1916 was a 'success' in that as few as three Allied casualties were registered – all accidental. At one point, when asked to estimate casualties in a withdrawal, Hamilton had reckoned 50 per cent. However, the ease of withdrawal could not hide the scope of the complete and utter failure of the operation at Gallipoli, at a cost of at least 37,000 British Empire soldiers dead, along with 5,000 French fatalities and perhaps 65,000 Turkish dead.[34] For the 1st Inniskillings, there would be no further danger until May, by which time they had been deployed in France, where they were soon to play a part on the Somme on 1 July. At Gallipoli, 441 men of the 1st Inniskillings had lost their lives, including at least 50 from West Belfast. Twenty-five of the 6th RIRifles' 109 dead were from the same area.

The withdrawal from Gallipoli did not signal the end of West Belfast's involvement in the war against Turkey. The 6th RIRifles were in Salonica soon after leaving Gallipoli.[35] Greece entered the war in the middle of 1915 and in October, the British and French landed troops at Salonica as it was strategically important for supplying Serbia to aid its fight on the Balkan Front, which meant that the Bulgarians threatened it. By January 1916, 160,000 Entente troops faced Bulgarian and German forces in defensive positions similar to those in France and Belgium.

At Salonica, malaria was a particular hazard and casualties from illness were high. However, the fighting was nowhere near as intense as at Gallipoli. The 6th RIRifles' first engagement in the region came in Serbia, alongside at least one other 10th Division battalion containing West Belfast men: the 6th Inniskillings. Having landed at Salonica the division was sent to Serbia to aid its fight against Bulgaria. In difficult mountainous conditions, they took part in the battle of Kosturino on 7/8 December, successfully delaying the Bulgarian advance, although by 12 December all British troops in Serbia had been forced back to Salonica where they dug in. The Salonica posting was a relatively safe one, and in the whole of 1916, the 6th RIRifles lost only 24 men. One of these was Private Robert Fitzgerald of Dover Street, on 24 February 1916. He was reported in newspapers as having been killed in action, and that was probably all anyone at home was told. The truth was that he had been killed in an accident during machine-gun training. The battalion war diary recorded on 24 February, '1 man accidentally shot during M.G. instructions . . . This man died at about 1800.'[36]

The 10th (Irish) Division remained at Salonica until September 1917, when it moved to Egypt taking part in the Palestine campaign. The 6th RIRifles were involved in the defence of Jerusalem, which had been taken from the Turks in December 1917. The battalion lost only 15 men from their arrival in Egypt in mid-September 1917, to June 1918, when the final fatalities of the battalion died of wounds. A month before, the battalion had been disbanded, with most of the units of the 10th Division replaced by Indian battalions as part of a process of 'Indianization' of British units in the area.[37]

Almost all of the fighting on the British 'eastern' front was against the Turks. The action in Salonica against the Bulgarians (supported by Germans) represented a relatively small part of the British war effort. Even more unusual was the engagement of a discreet part of the Royal Naval Air Service: the Royal Naval Armoured Car Division. This fought in a number of theatres including Mesopotamia, East Africa and France. On the Eastern Front it verged on being a private army, led by Oliver Locker-Lampson, who had been a Conservative MP since 1910, and was a Commander in the Royal Naval Volunteer Reserve.

Although his elder brother, Godfrey, later became a government minister, Oliver was always on the right-wing margins of his party, and was later an especially zealous anti-Bolshevik. Soon after the outbreak of war, he and some friends in Ulster provided £27,600 to equip an armoured car unit, initially of 15 cars, and was given command of the unit which was designated 15 Squadron. The money was a combination of personal funds and (secretly) UVF resources. Consequently, three of the cars were called *Ulster*, *Londonderry* and *Mountjoy*. The men were recruited through Locker-Lampson's connections in East Anglia and London, plus Ulster.[38] By June 1915, there were 150 men and a dozen officers, who had been, in Locker-Lampson's words, 'specially recruited in the North of Ireland'.

The funders initially wanted the unit to be part of the Ulster Division, but this idea was not pursued. The unit served briefly in Belgium, but the army disliked Admiralty involvement in land operations, and for a time it looked as if the squadrons would be disbanded. However, the Belgian military had sent armoured cars to Russia as they had little military value in the trench conditions of the Western Front, and Lampson successfully argued that the same should be done with his squadron. By October 1915, the cars prepared for the sea voyage to Russia.[39]

Arriving in January 1916, 33 armoured cars, 455 men and 44 officers, were first used to guard prisoners of war at Alexandrovsk.[40] There then occurred an incident which is still shrouded in mystery. As news of the Easter Rising reached Russia, many of the men were concerned about the safety of families back home in Ireland. They seem to have demanded to be repatriated and then, when this was refused, a mini-mutiny took place. Royal Marines from nearby British warships were sent to control the situation, but the storm seems to have passed before they arrived. There are suggestions that alcohol had fuelled tempers, but veterans were later reluctant to discuss what happened.[41] It remains unclear whether the incident was at all influenced by sympathy for the Easter Rising, but it does reveal the unease that some officers felt about the potential for trouble in Irish units.

During the summer of 1916, the unit was moved to the Caucasus and supported Cossack cavalry against Turkish troops in Kurdish territory. In October it moved to Odessa on the way to Romania, which had entered the war on the Allied side in August. However, Romania soon collapsed and the unit did not spend long there, although its role led to the award of many Russian decorations to its men.[42] Working closely with Russian soldiers throughout the early part of 1917, often in trenches, the men of the unit were eyewitnesses to the unfolding Russian Revolution while based at Tiraspol, but by the middle of 1917 they were again on the move to Galicia, where their opponents were Austrians. On the morning of 1 July 1917 the armoured cars were due to lead an advance on heavily fortified positions at Brzezany. They did so at 9.55 a.m. and forced the Austrians back from the first line of trenches. However, on moving down the road to Brzezany their path was blocked by barbed wire. Volunteers went forward to clear the road, but one man was killed and several were wounded. The dead man was Chief Petty Officer John McFarland.[43] Locker-Lampson sent a letter to McFarland's wife Mary, in Langford Street. It was typical of the kind of letter that commanding officers sent home in its praise for McFarland's bravery, but was somewhat unusual in the amount of detail it contained:

> Your husband was a splendid soldier. He joined me early in the war, and it was my special wish that he was promoted to be chief petty officer. Coming out to Russia in the great storm which nearly wrecked the ship, he was on duty at the gun which we mounted against submarines, and he then lashed himself to the gun throughout the time he was on duty sooner than leave it. Later on he did excellent work in Roumania, constantly exposing himself, and winning more than one Russian medal. It was his pluck with the 'Ulster' car that led to his recommendation for an English decoration, which I hope he will get. Finally, we reached the Galician front, when the attack began. One of the roads was blocked, and our cars could not go down it. Lieutenant-Commander Smiles asked for volunteers to clear it under heavy shell-fire. Your husband volunteered, and was instantaneously killed after clearing the road. He was one of the finest fighters in the force, a most splendid soldier, and had the heart of a lion. I sincerely hope this record of courage and manful service, and the sympathy of all his comrades, will indeed comfort you and help you bear your loss.[44]

Chief Petty Officer John McFarland DSM, Royal Naval Air Service,
19 Langford Street, KIA 1 July 1917 (*Belfast Evening Telegraph* 23 August 1917, p. 6)

McFarland did indeed receive another decoration after his death, the Distinguished Service Medal, and is commemorated in a cemetery in Poland, which contains mainly Allied prisoners of war from the Second World War.

McFarland's case demonstrates how far the stories throughout the war continued to come from well beyond the Western Front. However, after the withdrawal from Gallipoli, the vast majority of casualties were from France or Belgium. News of those losses came in bulk and without much personal information attached. After Gallipoli, the story of West Belfast at the front turned to a new breed of soldier: the volunteer who joined for political reasons, following the call of Carson or Redmond, and whose service would in the years after the war be used to advance a claim to special treatment by the British government. These volunteers, in the 16th and 36th divisions, arrived in France at the end of 1915.

6

Arrivals and Executions

*I was feeling very ill; with pains all over me. I do not remember
what I did.*

PRIVATE JAMES CROZIER, 9TH ROYAL IRISH RIFLES

*I wasn't going to look at the poor fellow lying there without doing
something ... His hand was swinging by the skin from his arm ... well, I
just brought him in. That's all.*

SERGEANT JOHN TIERNEY DCM, 7TH LEINSTERS

Not until the autumn of 1915, when the war had been raging for well over a year, did Belfast's volunteer battalions arrive on the Western Front. The 9th RIRifles left their base in Hampshire on 3 October 1915, making the short trip to France by sea from Folkestone to Boulogne.[1] They were commanded by Lieutenant-Colonel G. S. Ormerod, who succumbed to pneumonia soon after the battalion first entered the trenches. He was replaced by F. P. 'Percy' Crozier, whose memoirs, including *The Men I Killed*, and style of command, have made him a controversial figure. He had resigned a previous commission in the 3rd Loyal North Lancashire Regiment in 1909 over dishonoured cheques but was one of the UVF officers (in this case, from West Belfast) who was commissioned in the Ulster Division.[2]

During the battalion's first week in France, it faced routine training and inspections, and was moved inland first by train and then on foot, marching up to 10 km each day. At night, the soldiers were in billets in houses or farm buildings, or more often under canvas. On 10 October, the battalion arrived at Hédauville, a tiny settlement two miles north-west of Albert, in the area that is now described as the Somme. It was now only a few miles due west of Thiepval where many would meet their deaths on 1 July 1916, and where the memorial to the 36th (Ulster) Division stands today.

When volunteer units arrived in France, there were at least two different approaches to easing them into fighting. In the Ulster Division, men were sent to the front attached to experienced units as soon as possible, whereas the officers of the 16th Division hoped to spend time acclimatizing the men to France by placing them in billets with French civilians.[3] For the 9th RIRifles, the first approach meant attachment to the 1st Hampshires and the Rifle Brigade. Soon before daybreak on 12 October, C Company of the 9th RIRifles incurred its first casualties, none fatal. During a heavy bombardment lasting three-quarters of an hour, 62 shells, 50 trench mortars, and '50 other projectiles (mostly whiz-bangs)' fell.[4] Most damage was done in one dugout, which was packed with men. Five from the 9th RIRifles were wounded. They escaped relatively lightly: two from the 1st Hampshires were killed outright.

C Company faced enemy soldiers for the first time the next day, being surprised by a German patrol while themselves patrolling. One man from the 9th was killed, his body retrieved by the Germans, and one wounded. The dead soldier was Rifleman John Hanna. Born in Carnmoney in County Antrim, he had enlisted in Belfast. He was buried by the Germans at Miraumont, but his grave was later destroyed by shell-fire and he is now recorded on a memorial at the Queen's Cemetery in Bucquoy.

Over the next four days, the four companies of the 9th were rotated between the trenches and Hédauville. All except D Company incurred casualties. Then, on 18 October, after nearly a week in and out of the trenches, the entire battalion moved away from the front to be billeted in Vignacourt. There they faced the unpleasant but potentially life-saving experience of passing through a barn filled with gas to check their gas helmets. Over two weeks of training, parades and inspections followed, both as a battalion and as part of the wider division. This was punctuated, on 26 October, with a drive past in an open car by King George V and the French President, Poincaré.

During the Ulster Division's initiation at the front, a number of concerns became apparent about its discipline and training, and order appears to have been particularly poor in 107th Brigade, which contained the 9th RIRifles and the other three Belfast battalions. Captain Montgomery in command of the 9th RIRifles' A Company believed that facing the enemy improved morale. He wrote home, 'It is very extraordinary to note the effect of fire on different people. Almost all my previous real bad eggs, especially drunks, have turned out well.'[5] Yet indiscipline persisted. The replacement of Major-General Powell with Major-General Nugent as divisional commander before departure for France, was possibly a result of this, and Nugent subsequently put new officers in key positions.[6] More drastic action was taken with 107th Brigade as a whole by temporarily transferring it to the 4th Division, in exchange for 12th Brigade, which joined the Ulster Division.[7]

Although discipline did not seem to have improved by the time 107th Brigade returned in early February 1916, the transfer did have some practical benefits. George McBride, a Shankill man in the 15th RIRifles recalled:

> We learned a great deal from these regulars, they taught us all we needed to know about trench life. How to dig a proper trench, how to fill sandbags, and how to bring up supplies safely. We learned just about all we would need to know when we eventually took over our own line of trenches.[8]

Throughout this time, the trenches were in a 'very bad state' according to the battalion war diary, and the brigade war diary noted that on 4–7 December, they were 'in [a] very wet state and communication Trenches mostly flooded and impassable'.[9]

Sniper fire was also a hazard. In late November the 15th RIRifles lost its first man with West Belfast connections, Rifleman William Kearney. He and his wife lived in County Monaghan, but his parents lived in North Boundary Street. He was hit by a sniper and died in hospital that evening.[10] A sniper accounted for the second loss in the 9th RIRifles on 8 December: Rifleman Daniel Crilly of B Company. Aged 37, he left a widow, Martha, in Francis Street. News of his death came through just before Christmas. It was reported that the day after his death his children, ignorant of events, had 'sent him Christmas cards in a parcel of comforts from their mother, not knowing that he would never receive them'. Lieutenant W. J. Shanks wrote to Martha Crilly, 'Your husband was standing on the fire step in the trench and looked over the parapet, when a bullet hit him in the head, death being instantaneous.' Shanks added words that were common in letters from officers, and may or may not have been true, but had a clear purpose: 'I am sure it will be a great relief to you to know that he suffered no pain.' Captain Gaffikin also sent a letter of sympathy, in which he said, 'Your husband was a splendid soldier in the trenches, and had just got a first-class certificate as a bomber.' He was perhaps more realistic about how much he could ease Martha Crilly's pain adding, 'I am afraid that nothing I can say will be much consolation to you in your sorrow, but I am sure it will be a help for your children to know that their father died doing his duty for his country like a good soldier.'[11]

From late December, the 9th RIRifles took part in regular patrols to collect information or prisoners and inflict damage. Sometimes, more was left behind than was intended. On 23 and 24 December, two West Belfast men were wounded and captured by the enemy. They died soon after. One was Rifleman James Gallagher, aged just 19. He was a Congregationalist from Cambrai Street and had

Rfn Daniel Crilly, 9th Royal Irish Rifles, 7 Francis Street, KIA 8 December 1915
(*Belfast Evening Telegraph* 12 February 1916, p. 6)

Daniel Crilly's grave at Sucrerie

been working as a shipping apprentice clerk in 1911, but had moved to the New Northern Spinning and Weaving Company by 1914. One of four children, with two older brothers and one younger sister, he had been a member of the North Belfast UVF and the Edenderry Brass and Reed Band. Thirty-three members of the band had enlisted by the end of 1915 and Gallagher was the first to fall. Second-Lieutenant Berry, one of few officers from West Belfast, wrote, 'He was one of the grenadiers attached to the company patrol and was shot while bombing the enemy at a distance of about 20 yards.'[12] Berry also wrote to the wife of Rifleman John Pritchard, in Little Sackville Street. Margaret Pritchard, who had six children, was told, 'Your husband was always a keen and courageous soldier on patrol, and was one of the first party to go out when we first occupied our present line of trenches. On that occasion I noticed the fearlessness which he showed every time he went out on patrol.'[13]

For some of the Ulster Division, Christmas 1915 was a peaceful one. The 14th RIRifles were in billets at Ergnies, which may partly explain the origins of bitterness elsewhere in the Division among those who saw the battalion as being given easier tasks than others.[14] The battalion war diary noted on 25 December, 'A most enjoyable holiday was spent by all ranks.' Turkey, geese, chicken and plum pudding were followed by impromptu concerts. A prize of £2 was awarded to A Company for having the best decorated billet. Boxing Day was a holiday, and the day after, the battalion's officers beat the sergeants 1–0 in a 'strenuous' morning football match, before the battalion team drew 1–1 with the 11th Inniskillings.[15] Local people took part in celebrations, some having provided food for the soldiers.[16] This was despite the later recollection of George McBride of the 15th RIRifles that there were some strained relations with local people in France. He said, 'I did get the impression that we were actually in the way and that we were a bit of a nuisance to them, trampling over the land. They did not seem to appreciate the fact that we were there to help them fight the Germans, and that many of us would die doing this.'[17]

Christmas was altogether different for the 9th and 15th RIRifles at the front with the 4th Division. There was rain all night and early in the morning on Christmas Day itself. The 9th's war diary simply records, 'Xmas Day. At stand to in the morning great activity was shown on both sides. In the evening we were relieved by the 2nd Dublin Fusiliers and returned to billets.' Four days later, the 9th returned the favour to the Fusiliers and welcomed 1916 from the trenches. In three months in France, six men had been lost by the 9th.

They lost more than that in the first two weeks of January 1916. By this time, the weather meant that patrols were few and far between. But each side was exploding mines and exchanging shell and trench mortar fire, which meant that increasingly men died of wounds caused by shelling rather than being killed outright. It is striking that whereas previously the battalion war diary had noted the cause of death, it stopped doing so around this time, perhaps because fatalities were becoming more usual. So in the case of Rifleman James McCormick of Hutchinson Street, the diary just notes, 'One man killed', but it was reported at home that he had been struck by a rifle grenade.[18] McCormick's grave in the Sucrerie Military Cemetery at Colincamps is unusual for carrying a slogan that illustrates his or his family's politics: it reads, 'Died For Ulster and Freedom'. Such losses indicated that the battalion was tried and tested at the front. By late January 1916, they were taking on platoons of Royal Inniskilling Fusiliers for instruction, as they had been nursed by the Hampshires.

News of life at the front was brought back home by the Revd James Quinn, of St Michael's Parish Church in the Shankill. He was serving as a chaplain with 107th Brigade and was in Belfast on leave in early January 1916. Preaching to his own congregation, he gave a vivid account of life in France divided into two parts: 'in the trenches' and 'out of the trenches'. As regards the former, he described the layout and conditions. Quinn told how on one day when he visited the 9th RIRifles at the front, 'the mud on the floors of their dugouts was inches deep. It was impossible to lie down'. Yet he also stressed that life was more comfortable when in billets, and added that 'whether in trench or in billets, our men are wonderfully cheerful'. Later, there would be periodic visits to the front by clerics making goodwill visits. One such trip, in April 1917, involved the Revd Dr Henry Montgomery of the Shankill Road Mission who took part in a Presbyterian delegation visiting troops in billets and hospitals, and also paid tribute to the dead in cemeteries.[19]

Despite the cheerfulness that Quinn reported, there were tensions in the battalion around the trial of Second Lieutenant A. J. Annandale on 1 February, and the execution of Private James Crozier at the end of the month. Annandale was one of the battalion's many non-Ulster officers, originating from Midlothian. He was charged with leaving a dugout during a discussion with his Commanding Officer (CO) and not returning. Unlike many such records, the file on his General Court Martial is thin on details of the trial.[20] There are no statements and it was simply recorded that the accused should be dismissed from the army on the grounds of health. His CO, Percy Crozier, took a dim view of the case. In one later account Crozier thinly disguised Annandale as 'Rochdale' and described how when the Germans began to mortar the trench, 'He rises, rushes past me, and bolts down the trench in front of his men as fast as he can go. After daylight he is discovered in a disued French dugout behind the lines, asleep.'[21] In a later account Crozier claimed that Annandale 'got off . . . because of a legal quibble raised by influential friends'.[22] Whether there was such a 'quibble' is unclear, as is the identity of the 'friends', although he was given a character reference by Lieutenant-Colonel A. S. Blair of the 9th Royal Scots. But regardless of quibbles, the surviving records suggest that Annandale had serious medical problems. When he appeared before a medical board in August 1916 he was described as suffering from neurasthenia (a diagnosis covering fatigue, headaches and depression), speaking 'with hesitation and jerking' and experiencing muscle tremors. Moreover, he had 'a considerable degree of myopia in both eyes, and with his present lenses can only read large type'. These conditions were not, the board believed, caused by military service, but had been worsened by shell-shock. As a result, Annandale was declared permanently unfit for duty and discharged.

Percy Crozier remarked later that 'had justice been done according to our code' in the case of Annandale, there would have been fewer regrets in the battalion than there were for a Rifleman who was shot for desertion. This was James Crozier,[23] no relation to his CO, but who had been personally recruited by the elder Crozier. In two accounts, the latter told the story of the young soldier, giving him pseudonyms on both occasions (Crockett and Crocker). Crozier's mother, Elizabeth, lived in Battenberg Street. She had not wanted him to join up, for obvious reasons, but also because he was slightly underage. Percy Crozier witnessed the mother's pleas to her son and promised 'Don't worry . . . I'll look after him. I'll see no harm comes to him.' Percy Crozier later remembered the young man as a good soldier in the winter of 1915–16. When James Crozier first disappeared from sentry duty it was presumed that he had drowned. Two weeks later according to Percy Crozier (the actual absence was 31 January–4 February), James appeared again under arrest. Percy Crozier argued that there was no alternative but to shoot him and was a hostile witness at the trial. His signed statement said, 'From a fighting point of view, this soldier is of no value.' He added, 'His behaviour has been that of a "shirker" for the past three months.' Meanwhile, a medical examination suggested that he was fit.

That medical verdict wrecked James Crozier's case, which was based on being ill. He said, 'I was feeling very ill; with pains all over me. I do not remember what I did. I was dazed: I do not remember being warned for any duty. I cannot remember leaving the trenches even.' Nothing is known about what then happened until a Corporal Taylor from another unit found Crozier walking about 25 miles behind the front line, without any form of identification and no rifle or equipment. Taylor said that Crozier told him his name and regiment and described himself as a deserter. This evidence was damning and Crozier had nothing to say in response. Given all the established procedures of the time, it was therefore no surprise that Crozier was found guilty and sentenced to death. Whether Percy Crozier reflected at this point on his words to James's mother is not clear, but he did write later that he had arranged 'that enough spirituous liquor is left beside him to sink a ship'. As a result, when the time came for his execution on 27 February he was 'far too drunk to walk' and 'practically lifeless and quite unconscious'. Percy Crozier knew this because he was waiting close to the walled garden at the back of a villa in Mailly-Maillet where the firing squad was lined up. With him were the 9th RIRifles who were there to learn at first-hand what happened to deserters, although only their CO, standing on a mound, could see over the wall. There he could see the soldier put up against a post and 'hooked on like dead meat in a butcher's shop'. At 7.05 a.m., the firing squad took aim, but their volley did not kill Crozier, and the officer in charge of the party had to fire a shot from his revolver. Following this, the battalion marched back to breakfast.[24]

Crozier's death remains controversial to this day, and many campaigners have pointed to the different treatment he would now receive.[25] Such attitudes have informed the pardon of all those who were 'shot at dawn', which was given by the British government in 2006.[26] Yet by the standards of the day, it was widely believed by officers that execution for desertion was necessary to maintain discipline, and it has been argued that such a strategy, combined with the replacement of inefficient officers, actually worked.[27]

Crozier was not the only West Belfast volunteer who fell to tough discipline. Rifleman James Templeton of Enfield Street was a member of the 15th RIRifles. At 5 p.m. on 20 February 1916 he had been with his battalion in the trenches, but four hours later he was absent.[28] He was not seen again until the evening of the next day when he gave himself up to a lance-corporal of the battalion about six miles behind the front line. Templeton's defence was short and simple,

This document records that

Rfn J Templeton of the 15th Battalion,
Royal Irish Rifles

who was executed for desertion on
19 March 1916 is pardoned under Section 359
of the Armed Forces Act 2006.

The pardon stands as recognition that he was
one of many victims of the First World War
and that execution was not a fate he deserved.

Secretary of State for Defence

This document records that

Rfn James Crozier of the
9th Battalion, The Royal Irish Rifles

who was executed for desertion on
27 February 1916 is pardoned under
Section 359 of the Armed Forces Act 2006.

The pardon stands as recognition that he was
one of many victims of the First World War
and that execution was not a fate he deserved.

Secretary of State for Defence

This document records that

Rfn P Sands of the 1st Battalion,
Royal Irish Rifles

who was executed for desertion on
15 September 1915 is pardoned under
Section 359 of the Armed Forces Act 2006.

The pardon stands as recognition that he was
one of many victims of the First World War
and that execution was not a fate he deserved.

Secretary of State for Defence

Pardons (pictures courtesy of the National Archives, Kew). Files on soldiers shot at dawn held at the National Archives in Kew now contain copies of the pardons granted in 2006.

'I am sorry for what I have done.' But the prosecution had gathered evidence of previous absences or disobedience. His Commanding Officer, Major William B. Ewart, stated, 'This man's character is poor, indeed, and his general conduct is always open to complaint.' However, Ewart did speculate that Templeton may not have realized the serious nature of his offence as there had been nothing similar in the battalion. This became a decisive argument in favour of a severe penalty. Major-General Nugent, commanding the 36th Division, argued that because the 'extreme penalty' had not been awarded for three previous cases of desertion in the battalion, it should be carried out for Templeton 'as a deterrent to other men in this Unit'. At 7.06 a.m. on 19 March 1916, Templeton was executed. Alongside Templeton that morning was another of his battalion, Rifleman John Ferguson McCracken, who is believed to have been from Belfast but cannot be linked to a particular area. He was convicted of desertion and of feigning injury to avoid service.[29] Like Templeton, McCracken was offered as an example to the battalion. The two men lie next to each other at Mailly-Maillet Communal Cemetery extension.

By the time of these executions, 107th Brigade had been living with heavy snow for about three weeks; they soon suffered the consequences of the thaw. Meanwhile, there was a steady growth in enemy aircraft activity, both in reconnaissance and in bombing of trenches.[30] Snipers continued to take their toll. Corporal William J. Bell of the 9th RIRifles was killed by a head shot on 8 March; he was a member of Revd Quinn's congregation back in Belfast, and Quinn himself officiated at the graveside. April came as a much-needed break as the battalion was away from the front for the entire month, partly occupied in working parties on a railway. Later in April, and in the first week of May, the battalion was practising attack in dummy trenches. Then on 9 May they moved to an area that would be forever associated with not only the 9th RIRifles but the 36th Division more widely: Thiepval Wood, which the battalion found 'still unspoilt, save on the fringe. Birds sing and squirrels jump from tree to tree.'[31]

While the 9th RIRifles prepared to move to Thiepval, West Belfast men fell in many other places. In the 2nd RIRifles, one was Private Herbert Smith of Heather Street. He had clearly enlisted underage because it was reported that he had reached his 17th birthday the day before his death on 26 April.[32] Earlier in the month, Private William Rosbotham of the Royal Army Medical Corps was among the oldest West Belfast deaths in service during the war years, but he was not lost in action. Aged 57, Rosbotham died in England on 8 April at Tidworth Military Hospital, although the cause of death is not clear.[33]

Closer to home was the death of Lance-Corporal Nathaniel Morton of Woodvale Street in the Shankill. As a member of the 18th RIRifles, one of the reserve battalions based in Ireland, Morton might have expected to have been out of harm's way. However, his battalion was sent to Dublin at the end of April 1916 to put down the Easter Rising. That began on Easter Monday, 24 April, when the Irish Republican Brotherhood, Irish Volunteers and Irish Citizen Army collaborated in declaring a republic and seizing key buildings by force. For five days, a bloody battle raged in the city centre, with the leadership ensconced in the General Post Office, until battered and surrounded, they surrendered on 29 April. It was on this last day that Morton died of wounds sustained in the fighting, one of 108 British soldiers killed during the Rising. He was only 19, and his mother had to cope with the news of his death knowing that her husband James also faced daily danger while serving in France.[34]

Also in Dublin during the Rising was another West Belfast soldier. Michael Brennan, a staunch nationalist, had joined the 6th Connaughts after Redmond had called on nationalists to enlist. Having been gassed and frostbitten in France, he was lying in a Dublin hospital when the rebels took over the hospital. He remained in bed the whole time.[35] Brennan was one of many nationalists who took the view that they could advance their cause by fighting for the British rather than against them, and it was this that enabled them to serve in the same army, against the same enemy, as unionists. Such men in the 6th Connaughts and 7th Leinsters formed the core of 47th Brigade within the 16th (Irish) Division. That division was more 'mixed' in terms of religion than the 36th: the 7th Leinsters held both Catholic and Anglican church parades on their first Christmas Day in France. Meanwhile, a former Orangeman, who had resigned from the Order due to his left-wing political views, claimed that he was one of a hundred Protestants serving in the 6th Connaughts.[36] Nevertheless, these men were largely nationalist in their politics, and it is 47th Brigade that best represents West Belfast nationalism at the front, which is why it paraded in front of Joseph Devlin even in England in early December.[37]

The 47th arrived in France from training a few months after the 9th RIRifles.[38] Having arrived at Le Havre early on 18 December 1915, 36 officers and 952 other ranks of the 6th Connaughts arrived by train at Hesdigneul near Béthune. There were similar numbers in the 7th Leinsters and with them, in the 47th Brigade, were the 6th Royal Irish Regiment and 8th Royal Munster Fusiliers. As the 6th Connaughts disembarked from the train at Hesdigneul, the men heard for the first time the sound of guns on the front line. Unaware of the privations to come, the battalion's war diary noted that the journey was uneventful 'except that hot water was not available along the railway route'. Meanwhile, the 7th Leinsters were at Gosnay, a village neighbouring the Connaughts. Although the aim in the 16th Division was for men to stay in billets as long as possible without being placed at the front, there was a rapid introduction to fighting for some. The 7th Leinsters were first into the trenches, with six officers and 18 NCOs attached to the 6th London Regiment for instruction on 23 December. One of the officers was John Staniforth, a native of Yorkshire, and the son of a country doctor.[39] On the basis of his mother being Irish, he had enlisted as a private in the 6th Connaughts but had risen to second lieutenant and been transferred to the 7th Leinsters prior to arrival in France. He wrote home about how he and his men had been sent on a five-mile journey to the front in a London bus, which still carried 'Camberwell Green' as its destination. He then described the trenches vividly:

Imagine a garbage-heap covered with all the refuse of six months: rags, tins, bottles, bits of papers, all sifted over with the indescribable greyish ashen squalor of filthy humanity. It is peopled with gaunt, hollow-eyed tattered creatures who crawl and swarm about upon it, and eye you suspiciously as you pass; men whose nerves are absolutely gone; unshaven, half-human things moving about in a stench of corruption . . .

And the keynote of the whole thing is boredom and weariness, utter and absolute. You sit in a dug-out and read or play cards from morning till night, and your nerves get worn out with watching against Hun attacks which never come, and with shoring up parapets that crumble-in even as you dig, and pumping out water that fills up again as fast as you get it out.[40]

On Christmas Eve, the 6th Connaughts entered the same part of the line, with 25 men moving to the trenches for two days' instruction. For those still behind the front line, Christmas Day was marked in the 7th Leinsters with plum pudding but celebrations were subdued with 'very little drunkenness' noted in the war diary.

When the second draft of 6th Connaughts went on Boxing Day, they were in a trench one mile north-east of Merville when the Germans exploded a mine under the British front line. There were no casualties, but the men gained an early taste of the noise and mud of the front. These sensations were especially vivid for an unnamed machine-gun sergeant who was buried for half an hour before being removed alive. Men also faced problems with the most basic clothing: boots. The brigade war diary recorded on 5 January that the boots issued to all units of the brigade 'have been very badly reported on, many showing signs of wear after only being in use a fortnight'.[41]

Throughout January and early February, both the 7th Leinsters and 6th Connaughts formed working parties, trained and spent time at the front attached to more experienced battalions, sometimes on the Loos Salient. The first casualties in the Leinsters came at Les Brebis, when two companies were shelled while assembling in the church square. Ten were wounded.

The Connaughts were the first at the front as an entire battalion. On 26 January, they moved to the 'Puits no. 14 bis' sector, near to Loos, temporarily attached to 46th Brigade, with companies parcelled out to different battalions. At about 5 p.m. on 27 January, after an artillery bombardment, they faced their first enemy advance. The Connaughts' machine guns held the Germans off, but the battalion lost its first man, Private John Lavery, born in Warrenpoint, County Down, but living and having enlisted in Belfast. The next day, B Company 'had to undergo severe handling by the enemy's artillery', with two killed and 13 wounded. By the end of the month, the total losses were seven killed and 29 wounded.

Early in February, the battalion lost its first West Belfast INV recruit, James Patrick Canavan of Varna Street, who died of wounds at a base hospital. News of his death was conveyed to his parents in a letter from the French priest who had administered the last rites.[42] Around this time, the 6th Connaughts faced regular shelling and took part in occasional patrols. A point of curiosity for the men was that the Germans were digging small round trenches, which they feared would be used to hold either gas cylinders or *Flammenwerfer* which would spurt flames at British troops. Much of the Connaughts' activity was focused on destroying these trenches.

One of the battalion's casualties during shelling on 7 February was Private Patrick McCormack of Carlisle Street. The *Belfast News Letter* reported that he was killed 'during a heavy bombardment of our position. He and two comrades most gallantly went out to repair a broken telephone wire when a shell exploded in the middle of them killing Signaller McCormack on the spot.' In early April, his mother Margaret received a standard text card from General Hickie, Commander of the 16th Division: 'I have read with much pride the reports of his regimental commander and brigade commander regarding his gallant conduct and devotion to duty in the field on his day of death, and have ordered his name and deed to be entered in the record of the Irish Division.'[43]

When the 6th Connaughts left the trenches on 8 February, their training period over, they returned to the Béthune area. The battalion war diary noted a number of problems. Shells that did not explode were branded as 'duds' and 'were too many to inspire confidence in the care exercised in their manufacture'. Meanwhile, the water supply was a serious problem, and men were forced to drink from wells in the trenches, many succumbing to diarrhoea as a result.

The 7th Leinsters went into the trenches for the first time as a whole battalion three days after the 6th Connaughts left. They spent 11 and 12 February in trenches at Annequin and La Bassée with the 98th and 19th brigades. Two days later the battalion relieved the 18th Royal Fusiliers at Cambrun and lost its first men on 17 February. These included one native of Belfast, Private John Comiskey, the other men being from Dublin and Limerick. Meanwhile, on the morning of 16 February, Sergeant John Tierney, a McDonnell Street resident and member of the 7th Leinsters' H Company, became the first member of the Belfast INV to win the DCM. He rescued a Corporal Murphy, who was trying to bring barbed wire back to the lines and had a hand blown off. When asked by a journalist why he had saved the man, Tierney said, 'I wasn't going to look at the poor fellow lying there without doing something. No man with a heart could do that.' Tierney added, 'His hand was swinging by the skin from his arm', and, 'well, I just brought him in. That's all.' As for Murphy, there was some excited newspaper speculation that he had been recommended for the Victoria Cross for the initial expedition but he did not receive it.[44]

Following the 7th Leinsters' withdrawal from the front on 18 February they, like the 6th Connaughts, spent the remainder of February marching, drilling and training. The 6th Connaughts were joined by drafts of soldiers, many of whom had served with other battalions of the Connaughts either on the Western Front or in the Dardanelles. On 2 March the Connaughts moved into trenches in the Hulluch sector, a few miles east of Béthune. They fought the Germans for craters created by the British exploding mines close to the German position. In some places German lines were only 15 yards away from the craters, so fighting was at close quarters, with the Connaughts used principally as grenadiers, carrying buckets of grenades to the craters and then throwing them. The Germans were using mines, and on the morning of 5 March, nine men of A Company were buried when a mine went off, though all were saved.

Between arriving in the Hulluch sector on 2 March and leaving on 10 March, ten men were killed in action with a further 31 wounded. Four of these later died of their wounds. Meanwhile, other men suffered from the sheer exhaustion of being 'knee deep in mud and the long nights standing in that mud during cold wet and almost arctic weather'. About 50 were sent to hospital suffering from exposure. When the battalion left the trenches, it welcomed not only the relief of simply drilling and training, but also the holiday given to mark St Patrick's Day. Brigade sports and a battalion concert provided special entertainment for both the 6th Connaughts and 7th Leinsters. The shamrock that was presented in the traditional way had been sent by the man whom many regarded as their political leader and who had urged them to join up: John Redmond.

During late March to mid-May, both the 6th Connaughts and 7th Leinsters were regularly at the front. On 28 March, at 'Puits no. 14 bis' sector, the 7th Leinsters came under heavy shell-fire losing four men together, including the battalion's first West Belfast fatality: Private James Johnston of Alexander Street West.[45] When 47th Brigade was later at the front in the Hulluch trenches, it spent five weeks in a simple routine: repair trenches, survive German bombardment and repair trenches again, periodically relieved by other battalions to allow for a few days' rest behind the front. The wire was in a particularly poor state and because it was a crucial part of trench defence, repair was a priority. Yet the brightness of the moon, and the close proximity of the German trenches could make that difficult. Each time there was a bombardment, the men prepared for German attacks but this did not happen in April or May. The 6th Connaughts' war diary noted on 14 May that this was 'much to the disappointment of our men whose fighting spirit is now of the highest degree'. But there were periodic gas attacks, with four of the Connaughts' machine-gunners killed by gas on 29 April.

It was difficult to take the war to the German lines because of a shortage of shells. The Connaughts' war diary noted the Germans' 'very decided readiness to use more shells than our artillery who were on short rations'. The effect on the morale of the men was marked, and any attack they made with the weapons at their disposal (trench mortars and rifle grenades) 'was not as enthusiastic as it might have been' because the Germans were always likely to reply with greater firepower. However, the Allies were about to attempt a fightback on a scale never before seen.

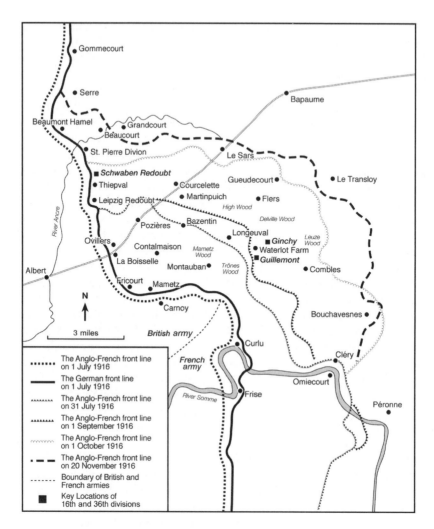

Map 4 The Battle of the Somme, July–November 1916

7

The Ulster Division on the Somme

*The Brigade moved off as if on parade . . . but alas . . . the slow tat tat of
the Hun machine guns . . . caught the advance under a deadly cross fire,
but nothing could stop this advance and on they went.*

14TH ROYAL IRISH RIFLES WAR DIARY

Planning for an offensive in the Somme area began in late 1915 with the aim of
making a decisive impact on overall German numbers. However, the aim of the
offensive changed from February 1916 in light of the German onslaught against
the French at Verdun. The Somme offensive, in which French troops would play
a relatively minor role, now became a diversionary attack to ease pressure on the
French who were being bled dry by wave on wave of German attacks at Verdun.
For the Ulster Division, preparations for the 'great advance' on the Somme began
in May 1916. The 14th RIRifles had seen far less action in their first six months in
France than battalions of 107th Brigade, but was among the earliest of the Ulster
Division to be moved to Thiepval. They came under heavy fire in the early hours
of 6 May losing nine men during a bombardment described by one officer as a
'perfect inferno'.[1]

The 9th RIRifles arrived at Thiepval three days later, but it was a month before
they were under heavy attack. Then, on the night of 5/6 June, came the battalion's
first losses on the Somme. In one shell attack seven men were killed, four of
whom lived no more than a few hundred yards off the Shankill Road: Lance-
Corporals Edward Mooney and Samuel Gorman, and Riflemen Samuel Todd
and Thomas McKee. Two more, Riflemen William Quinn and James Fowler were
also from West Belfast. The seventh dead soldier, Rifleman James McIlwraith, had
been born in the Shankill. Mooney, once of the West Belfast UVF, left his widow
with six children. Six of the seven (all except McKee) were buried in a cemetery
at Authuile, in one row alongside Rifleman George Barnes who died suddenly
on 15 June.[2] It is relatively unusual to find so many men from one unit buried
in such a row. Rupert Brooke wrote of a corner of foreign field being forever
England; if there is any corner of a foreign field that is forever West Belfast, and
particularly the Shankill, Authuile has a claim to that.

The preparations for the battle were far from gloomy for some. One veteran,
Jack Christie, recalled:

There's all this emphasis on the Somme, and while it was unique because of the slaughter,
I still had some happy times there. I was in Thiepval Wood for maybe a couple of months

L/Cpl Samuel Gorman,
1 Tennent Street,
(*Belfast Evening Telegraph*
3 June 1916, p. 4)

Rfn Samuel Todd,
26 Heather Street,
(*Belfast Evening Telegraph*
24 June 1916, p. 4)

Rfn William Quinn,
27 Little Sackville Street,
(*Belfast Evening Telegraph*
17 June 1916, p. 4)

L/Cpl Edward Mooney,
11 Third Street,
(*Belfast Evening Telegraph*
21 June 1916, p. 4)

9th Royal Irish Rifles from Shankill killed on night of 5/6 June 1916

Authuile Cemetery

Row of six of seven Shankill men killed on 5 and 6 June 1916,
plus one killed on 15 June 1916

preparing for the 1st July, and although they were throwing shells over at us, and the work was hard, somehow it still didn't detract from the enjoyment of the night being with your mates in the dug-outs.[3]

The preparations in which Christie was involved ended on 24 June when a heavy bombardment of German lines commenced. It was due to last until 28 June, but poor weather meant the advance was delayed by two days, so the bombardment continued.[4] The objective of this bombardment was to lay waste to the German lines so that infantry could advance easily.[5]

The delay of the attack to 1 July provided a coincidence of history. The anniversary of the Battle of the Boyne in 1690, when King William III defeated King James II consolidating a Protestant rather than Catholic monarchy, is today marked on 12 July. But this is only due to the adoption of the Gregorian calendar throughout the British Empire in 1752, which added 11 days to the dates marked by the Julian calendar. Thus in 1690, the date of the Battle of the Boyne was 1 July. Consequently, the 36th Division's war diary, commented that 'No date could have been more auspiciously chosen for the day on which the Ulster Division was to prove its value as a fighting force.' It added, 'The cries of "No surrender, boys" . . . showed how well the men appreciated the historical associations of the day and the example they were called on to follow.' This may be overstating the precise historical awareness of the men, for 'No Surrender' is a phrase that is uttered in Ulster on more occasions than the anniversary of the Battle of the Boyne and is more accurately associated with the siege of Derry. Moreover, one veteran wrote on the 50th anniversary of the battle: 'Nothing was further from my mind than the Boyne on the Somme.'[6] But we can at least be sure that those who wrote the records were aware of the coincidence.[7]

The specific goal of the Ulster Division was to advance around 3,000 yards from their position at the north-east of Thiepval Wood. That meant taking the Schwaben Redoubt and moving to the German position marked on trench maps as the 'D Line', just short of the village of Grandcourt (see map 5). The division's front was just under two miles long, with 109th Brigade, half of 108th Brigade and part of the 15th RIRifles in the right and right-centre sectors. Behind this line was 107th Brigade, which, after the initial attack, was to take part of the D Line, described as D8 to D9, and then extend its front north-west along the D line. To its left (north) was the other half of 108th Brigade and 29th Division, operating north of the River Ancre. To the right (south) of 107th Brigade was the 32nd Division, whose target was the village of Thiepval.

On the 'fine but misty' morning of 1 July 1916, the 8th, 9th and 10th RIRifles gathered in assembly trenches in Aveluy Wood at 4 a.m. By 6.15 a.m., they had reached a position where they lay down for the duration of the intense final bombardment of German lines beginning ten minutes later.[8] Each man carried a heavy load: a waterproof sheet, a woollen waistcoat, two Mills grenades, 170 rounds of ammunition, two sandbags in their belts, two smoke helmets, goggles and rations, in addition to their rifle. They wore their battalion's distinguishing badge at the top of a sleeve. In 107th Brigade, badges were triangular, worn with one point downwards, yellow/orange for the 9th and red for the 15th.[9] In 109th Brigade, rectangles were worn, pale blue in the case of the 14th.

The advance began at zero hour: 7.30 a.m. From the outset it was clear that much of the German forward line had survived the bombardment. Even the barbed wire was undamaged in many places. So advancing men walked into a storm of bullets when they had expected to stroll into empty German trenches. The 14th RIRifles' war diary described the scene:

> The Brigade moved off as if on parade, nothing finer in the way of an advance was ever seen but alas no sooner were they clear of our own wire, when the slow tat tat of the Hun machine guns from THIEPVAL VILLAGE and BEAUMONT-HAMEL caught the advance under a deadly cross fire, but nothing could stop this advance and on they went.[10]

On the other side, a German describing the advance later wrote in similar terms: 'The waves hastened their steps, disappeared for minutes on end in dead ground, then rushed forward again in agile bounds.'[11]

The 14th was taking prisoners as early as 7.45 a.m. Meanwhile, by 9 a.m., parts of the 15th RIRifles took the C Line, which included one edge of the Schwaben Redoubt.[12] Yet although the 14th and 15th had gained ground, it was clear by 8 a.m. that the 'advance' was floundering. The 32nd Division, including the 15th Lancashire Fusiliers (1st Salford Pals) and the 16th Northumberland Fusiliers (Tyneside Commercials), failed to take Thiepval. They could not overcome the entrenched and determined machine-gunners who had survived the British bombardment. Meanwhile, the half of 108th Brigade operating north of the Ancre was unable to advance. This made 107th Brigade vulnerable to attack from both sides as it advanced.[13]

Knowing this, General Nugent, commanding the 36th Division, tried to stop 107th Brigade's attack. Seeking authority, he sent two messages to his superiors at Corps HQ, at 8.32 a.m. and 8.54 a.m. The first response was that a new attack was to be made by 32nd Division on Thiepval village and that 107th Brigade must support that by continuing the advance. However, at 9.16 a.m., permission came for Nugent to hold back the brigade. It was too late. No telephone wires were intact, and no runners could get through.[14]

Yet from 7.30 a.m., 107th Brigade had been moving steadily forwards through Thiepval Wood. By 8 a.m., they were in position for advance, lying down as a precaution against enemy fire. Five minutes later, when the 9th advanced, they were fired on by machine guns from Thiepval village. An hour later, the 9th were still facing machine-gun fire from Thiepval, but communications had also become a major problem. Communication between companies was to be carried out by cable, but the lines had been broken, and when linesmen attempted repairs at 9.15 a.m., they were killed or wounded. In the place of cable, a system of runners was introduced. As they moved forward through empty German trenches, the 9th gained control of areas given Ulster names for ease of memory. By 10 a.m., both Lisburn on B Line and Lurgan on C Line were taken. D Line (Coleraine,

Portadown, Enniskillen, Strabane and Omagh) were still occupied by Germans. But right along the advance of 107th Brigade the earlier bombardment had been much more effective at breaking the wire than in other parts of the British front.[15] At 10 a.m., about 35 men of D Company, on the right of the battalion's advance, got into the D Line trench, but finding parts 'strongly held and a great number of them became casualties through hand grenades'.

Men led by Corporal Short, who was later killed, continued to fight in the D Line for 40 minutes. Over the next two hours the 9th came to a halt. Captain Berry led men on the left of the battalion's advance, but was so pinned down by machine-gun fire that his men had to dig in between C and D lines. There were also shortages of ammunition, with Major Gaffikin close to running out of Lewis gun magazines by 11 a.m. In a desperate search for ammunition the soldiers became scavengers: Lieutenant Garner took a small party to search the area for discarded magazines. The battle for D Line continued to rage, but with little support from elsewhere some of those already there had to fall back and consolidate in C Line by 12.30 p.m. In the chaos, Crozier as battalion CO began to lose track of what was happening. His efforts to find out more by sending two intelligence scouts to the furthest point forward did not solve the problem. Neither man returned.

This was part of a general loss of direction along the front, partly due to the loss of so many officers. George McBride, serving in the 15th RIRifles recalled, 'to me it seemed more like a riot than a battle. Disorder set in, my group reached the German third line, when we got there we discovered that we didn't have any officers with us, they must all have been killed or wounded.'[16] Only by 1 p.m. had it become clear to Crozier, having received a message from his superiors, that the failure to take Thiepval village 'was the crux of the problem'. Poor communication continued to hamper the 9th in their defence of C Line. At the front, both Major Gaffikin and Captain Montgomery, the only two company commanders who remained uninjured, decided that holding on to their gains so far was the most they could achieve. Meanwhile, the men were beginning to tire, which Crozier attributed to them throwing rather than bowling grenades, which also reduced the range of the grenades. From early in the afternoon the Germans had been bombing the D Line, which had been taken by the 9th. This was a prelude to a German counter-attack by the 180th Regiment and the 8th Bavarian Reserve Regiment.

One of the key factors that had allowed the 9th to move forward was the effectiveness of the brigade's machine-gun company. But at around 4 p.m., Crozier discovered that they had been 'wiped out'. Meanwhile, Second Lieutenant Harding, the battalion intelligence officer, had gone forward to try to find out how Gaffikin and Montgomery were faring. He returned with the message that they could hold on if there was a steady supply of grenades, and he then took his report back to brigade headquarters. Crozier 'collected odd men together' and sent Sergeant Cully, whom Crozier described as 'the most dependable NCO. I could put my hand on at the time', to the front with supplies.

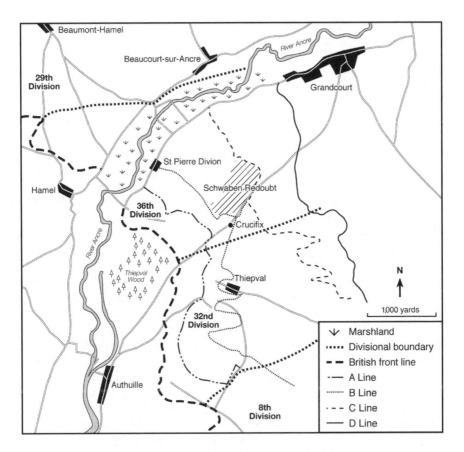

Map 5 The Somme: Thiepval area, 1 and 2 July 1916

Although the 9th and the rest of 107th Brigade were hanging on to the Schwaben Redoubt, they had been surrounded on three sides by early evening. The arrival of two companies of the 4th West Yorkshires boosted numbers but did not alter the basic problem faced by the 9th: they were almost surrounded, nearing exhaustion and had dwindling supplies of ammunition. Some British soldiers had decided to retreat of their own volition. George McBride recalled of his officer-less men of the 15th RIRifles, 'someone decided we could make no further progress as we were running out of ammunition and water. So we made our way back into the shell-holes for cover when we could, we eventually ended up back in our own reserve line trenches.'[17] At 6 p.m., Crozier reported to 107th Brigade 'that 70 men 108th Bde who were retreating had been sent back and that Lt Finlay had to fire on them', although doubts were cast on this account later in the evening and on the next day.[18] What was clear was that Gaffikin's position was becoming desperate. He reported to Brigade soon after 6 p.m. that 'We advanced too soon for our artillery, and in some places the barrage came back, and nearly all our casualties were from that. There was no fight in the Bosch. We are in considerable difficulty . . . I do not think we shall be able to hold out tonight.' It was the German reply to the British barrage that had done for so many men of the 9th. Gaffikin said: 'If it had not been for barrage we could have taken D line sitting. The wire was sufficiently cut.'[19]

Between 7 p.m. and 9 p.m., Harding again surveyed the front. He found 'heavy grenade fighting in progress', but believed that the line could be held. He recommended that water and ammunition should be taken to them, but this was slowed up by enemy fire. Then, at 9.40 p.m., reports came through that Major Gaffikin had been injured and that Captain Montgomery was taking over. Around this time, German bombing increased and 'the men were very much fatigued, so much in fact that in many instances they were unable to do anything'. Attempts to bolster the leadership at the front were weakened as officers sent to the front were killed or wounded. Those at the Schwaben Redoubt faced Germans on three sides and the 9th were forced to retreat when the Germans attacked in force at 10 p.m., soon finding themselves back at the A Line, the position of the German front earlier in the day. A German who was there described how the bodies of 'courageous members of the Ulster Division littered the Redoubt, every foot of which was soaked in blood'.[20] Crozier noted that at 10.30 p.m. Montgomery reported to him 'in a state of collapse' with a head wound, 'his life being undoubtedly saved by his steel helmet'. Officers returned to the 15th RIRifles HQ with only a few men. That battalion began 1 July with 583 men of all ranks, but by the next morning only about 120 were left standing. Of the 460 or so of all casualties, 74 other ranks were killed on 1 July, along with four officers.

The next morning, as the war diary of the 14th RIRifles noted, 'a few bare poles of trees . . . that were once a wood, bore eloquent testimony to the severity of the fire' from the day before. But the surviving men were soon back in action. Early on 2 July, brigade observers spotted men remaining in the A Line and ordered Crozier to collect all the able-bodied soldiers that he could find among the remnants of the 8th, 9th 10th and 15th battalions as reinforcements. Crozier pulled together 360 men: about 100 each from the 9th, 8th and 15th RIRifles and 60 from the 10th. He planned to lead the hybrid Belfast battalion himself, but was stopped by the 9th's Adjutant, Lieutenant E. E. Hine. Major Woods went in Crozier's place. At 2 p.m., Woods led his men forward and over the next four to five hours consolidated the British position in the A Line, facing heavy German bombardment throughout. What he and his men found in places must have horrified them. One message said 'Have found nothing but dead in these trenches.' Another reported that, in one trench, wounded men from various battalions said the Germans had recently visited them and taken prisoner all the wounded who could still walk. By the early evening, Woods' work was done: A Line was secured. Of the 360 men he had taken forward, about 80 were casualties, almost all of these wounded rather than killed. The 9th battalion lost five men that day. A day later, the entire division was withdrawn from the front and, after various movements over the next week, they were sent to the area around Bayenghem-les-Eperlecques, inland from Calais.[21] In the 9th RIRifles, five officers and up to 107 other ranks were dead on 1 and 2 July, at least 61 of these being from West Belfast. On 1 July alone, across the division, there were around 5,550 casualties (with as many as 2,000 dead) and 58,000 in the British army as a whole, around one-third of them dead.[22]

It was not until a few days later that news of the true nature of the Somme offensive would reach Belfast. On the evening of Saturday 1 July, the *Belfast Evening Telegraph* carried news of the start of the attack, and boasted of British artillery superiority. On Monday 3 July its headline read 'GOOD DAY FOR ALLIES'. The *News Letter* hailed 'A BRILLIANT OPENING'. But on Wednesday 5 July, the *Telegraph* referred to heavy casualties in the Ulster Division. The next day, it reported that the next of kin of many officer casualties had been contacted by the War Office, but there were as yet no official lists to give the public an idea of the scope of casualties. Despite this, the Orange Order decided to suspend 12 July celebrations. This was partly to do with a UK-wide request that workers should continue to work their hardest to support men at the front, and from 1915 12 July celebrations had been muted.[23] But the Somme casualties made public celebration of 12 July even less appealing, and on 7 July detailed lists began to appear, first for officers and then, from 10 July, the longest lists of rank-and-file casualties that the Belfast newspapers would print in the entire war.[24] The casualties of 1 July continued to dominate the news during the rest of July and into August, and although reports were dwindling by the end of that month, they were steadily supplemented by casualties from later days of the battle.

For most of the bereaved, news came by telegram. In some cases this was not the first bad news of the war. Sergeant Henry Foster of Canmore Street, a former UVF member in the 9th RIRifles was killed on 1 July. His brother, Rifleman John Foster had been lost in December 1914 in the 2nd RIRifles.[25] Two other brothers, the Mabins, both lost their lives on 1 July: Jeremiah known as 'Jerry', in the 9th RIRifles, and George in the 1st Inniskillings. Confirmation of their deaths seems not to have come until May 1917, but the family story has it that when the initial news that they were missing was received, the postman arrived at their parents' home in Crosby Street to find that he was carrying two letters and held one back.[26] Certainly, for many families, confirmation of death was delayed in just the way it had been in the early stages of the war during the retreat from Mons. It was not for another year that John and Jane McRoberts of Leopold Street would receive confirmation that their son James, serving with the 9th RIRifles, had been killed on 1 July.[27] Alexander Gray's wife Jeannie, in Broadbent Street, waited until November 1917.[28] The bodies of such men were never found, or at least if they were, they were never identified, and their names are among those on the Thiepval memorial to the 73,357 lost who have no known grave.

So long were the casualty lists that, unlike in earlier stages of the war, individual stories of how men had died or survived were few and far between. But they did appear gradually. Although surviving officers had little time for long

Sgt Henry Foster, 12 Canmore Street

Rfn Jeremiah Mabin, 16 Crosby Street
(RUR Museum)

Rfn Thomas Lewis, and Agnes,
24 Fourth Street

L/Cpl Bertie Holohan,
129 Glenwood Street
(Somme Heritage Centre)

9th Royal Rifles KIA on 1 July 1916

letters home to the families of those killed, they did send them whenever possible. Second Lieutenant McGranahan wrote to Sarah Stevenson, living in Tennent Street with her four children. He told her that her husband, Lance-Corporal Joseph Stevenson, 'was, without exception, the finest man in my platoon. He was a good soldier, a splendid shot, and a thorough gentleman in every way.'[29] Percy Crozier wrote to Eliza Jane Martin, wife of 35-year-old Company Sergeant-Major Joseph Martin of Woodvale Road and a former member of the North Belfast UVF, saying: 'Your husband was killed just as the battalion was about to deploy from the wood for the attack . . . He has persevered to remain with the battalion all this winter, in spite of being ill, and when he came back from hospital it only was because he knew it was his duty to be in the firing line, come what may.'[30]

One of the reasons that Crozier had written to Eliza Martin was that the Captain in Joseph Martin's company, J. H. Berry, had been taken prisoner. Berry was one of only a handful of officers from the West Belfast area. His father, Robert, lived at 304 Springfield Road and received a letter from his son in mid-August saying that he had been wounded in his abdomen and right groin on 1 July. Berry's right leg was paralysed and he could only crawl slowly. He appears to have become lost in No Man's Land on the night of 2/3 July. When he fell into the B Line on 4 July, he did not realize that it was in German possession but, fortunately, his captors carried him to a dressing station. At that point he was interned in Germany, before being transferred to Mürren in Switzerland in December. He was operated on and received both electric treatment and massage for his paralysed leg which steadily regained movement. In September 1917 he was repatriated. Having been an accountant before the war, Berry was ideally suited to the administrative work he then carried out for the Ministry of Munitions in Belfast.[31]

Some distressing news was wrong, as in the case of Company Sergeant-Major Arthur Hill of the 9th RIRifles. His wife Alice, of Enfield Street, received a letter from Captain Montgomery in mid-July. She was told that her husband had been killed between the B and C lines on 1 July 'when most gallantly leading his company'. Montgomery told a story of Hill's heroism:

> Within the first minute and a half after we deployed all his company officers, myself included, were hit. To his undying honour be it said that after I called to him (being half-stunned with a bullet through my helmet) to 'carry on' . . . I shall never forget the sight of him, as cool as if he were on a church parade at home.

It would have been strange for Montgomery to have made a mistake in the case of Hill for he told the soldier's 'widow': 'I feel that I have lost not only an invaluable company sergeant-major and born leader, but an esteemed friend. I ask you to permit me to share your great grief.' This news came through to Alice Hill relatively soon after 1 July and she placed a death notice in the *Belfast Evening Telegraph* on 18 July, which published Montgomery's letter a day later.

When Montgomery received a copy of the newspaper soon after, his reaction is an insight into the reasons why officers wrote such letters to bereaved wives and families. He told his father:

Captain John H. Berry (back row, second from left) with fellow officers of the 9th Royal Irish Rifles, 304 Springfield Road, wounded on 1 July 1916, PoW repatriated in 1917 (RUR Museum)

I have written some awful balls to poor women who have lost husbands etc. One of the worst was to Company Sergeant Major Hill's wife. To my horror I saw the most of it in the *Newsletter* . . . I wish you would tell the newspaper from me that the 9th Battalion people object to seeing that kind of waffle published. It is sent only to try and give these poor people something – some very little thing out of the wreck . . . It simply comes to this, that we will write nothing to these people for the future. I certainly won't. The unfortunate women of course take a ghastly delight in putting the beastly letters in the papers . . . but if the papers are told that these people won't get the letters unless they (the papers) refrain from publishing them when asked to do so by the unfortunate recipients, perhaps they will quit. My blood ran cold when I saw the balls I had written Mrs Hill in print.[32]

Perhaps Mongtomery was sounding off his anger, rather than making a statement that nothing he said about Hill was true. But it is a disturbing letter and raises questions about other accounts of valour on the battlefield, although where medals were awarded there must have been little doubt about what had taken place. But in any event, Mrs Hill was soon to get some greater relief: her husband was not dead. On 24 August news came to the battalion that several officers and men who had been presumed killed were actually wounded and held prisoner. Among them was Arthur Hill, and he even made it home to Belfast after the war. During his time in prison, Hill corresponded with Montgomery's father, and his wife was visited by Montgomery's mother.[33] The officer–soldier relationship, and the duty of care that many officers felt, clearly even influenced his family at home. It was a paternalism that was common in many Irish regiments.[34] However, when Hill returned home, he did not survive long, succumbing to wounds on 24 August 1919 and being buried in Belfast City Cemetery.[35]

Another survivor was Rifleman Isaac Burns of the 15th RIRifles. A Brownlow Street member of the North Belfast UVF, he made it through 1 July due 'to a Testament and hymn book he had in his tunic pocket. They were the means of saving his life by stopping a bullet which permeated both books.' His fortune did not see out the war as he was later killed in November 1917, a death that was not confirmed for nearly a year, during which time he was declared missing.[36]

While such individual stories were gradually reaching home, key aspects of the way the Somme was seen by the public were put in place through newspapers. The *Telegraph* in particular reported how the men had continued to press forwards despite heavy casualties, resisting successive counter-attacks. The ineffectiveness of the artillery bombardment was mentioned as early as 7 July, emphasizing the extent to which the division had advanced against a largely intact German line. Two strong and enduring images were also put forward. The first was of the men advancing 'as if on parade'. The second was of the division advancing to Orange battle cries: 'No Surrender' and 'Remember the Boyne'.[37] A section of a poem by the *News Letter*'s regular poet, Samuel Cowan, offers a good example of such sentiment:

Flinging his fun in the face of Death –
Above the roar of the cannon's breath

Singing his sacred shibboleth
Of 'The Boyne!' and 'No Surrender!'
Wherever a man of Ulster is
Honour and Glory shall aye be his!
Was ever a fight in the world like this
Or a charge of sublimer splendour?

FROM 'THE CHARGE OF THE ULSTER DIVISION AT THIEPVAL,
1 JULY 1916', BY SAMUEL K. COWAN[38]

The reality may have been different. Some contemporary accounts stress that there were men who wore Orange sashes as they went into battle, while Gaffikin was said to have waved an orange handkerchief.[39] Others like Malcolm McKee said that the Boyne anniversary had no impact on them.[40] Whatever the historical events, the fact remains that linking the two remains the dominant unionist narrative in Belfast today. The link must remain central to any understanding of the battle because its impact on the way the battle was described at the time was significant. However, there is another aspect of the Somme that has been told far less often. It concerns West Belfast men outside the Ulster Division who laid down their lives on 1 July, and the men of the 16th (Irish) Division who fought as the battle continued in the months after.

8

The Other Somme

Not a tree stands. Not a square foot of surface has escaped mutilation.
There is nothing but the mud and the gaping shell-holes . . . and, in the
bottom of many, the bodies of the dead.

CAPTAIN ROWLAND FEILDING, 6TH CONNAUGHT RANGERS

Although the vast majority of West Belfast casualties on 1 July 1916 came in the Ulster Division, there were also men serving on other parts of the line on that day. The battle-hardened 1st Inniskillings arrived in the Thiepval area in June from Gallipoli via Egypt and Marseilles. Immediately to the left of the Ulster Division on 1 July, their task was to advance in the area between the River Ancre and the village of Beaumont-Hamel. But machine-gun fire was so heavy that they could make no headway and their casualties were some of the heaviest of the battle. At the end of the day, 50 from 916 other ranks were confirmed killed, but over 200 were missing, and the battalion's death-toll for the day eventually rose to 228. Another 265 were wounded. The vast majority of these were from the Inniskillings' own recruiting area but a handful, at least 15, came from West Belfast, principally from the Shankill area. Among them was George Mabin whose brother Jeremiah had been lost in the 9th RIRifles. As the regimental history said, 'In that field of fire nothing could live.'[1]

Meanwhile, there were West Belfast men in the 1st RIRifles, a few miles south of Thiepval, at Ovillers. In their part of the line, in addition to machine guns, German shelling was a particular problem. By the middle of the day they had been forced back to their starting-point and made no further advance. Their casualties had been only a little lighter than many of the Ulster Division battalions. Having started the day with 600 other ranks, 348 men were wounded, and the final figure of dead on the day was 56. Among these were at least 10 West Belfast men, including Lance-Corporal Joseph McShane from Servia Street in the Falls and Rifleman John Clarke of Derry Street in the Shankill.[2]

Like the Ulster Division, the 1st RIRifles and the 1st Inniskillings were withdrawn from the front line soon after 1 July. The Battle of the Somme entered a new phase as fresh units were sent to hold the small areas of ground gained, and to make incremental gains instead of pursuing a further great advance. One of the first battalions to take part in the new phase was the 2nd RIRifles. On 7 July they assembled for an attack at La Boisselle, close to the area in which the 1st RIRifles had been on 1 July. Conditions were difficult. The battalion's Jesuit chaplain, Father Gill, wrote that rain fell as the attack opened, and because the soil was chalky 'soon the hollows of the trenches began to fill up with a white liquid mud like thick whitewash'.[3] Before being withdrawn in the early hours of 10 July, the battalion held lines gained by other units, advanced further forwards, and because of their success in gaining ground came under friendly fire from the British artillery which did not expect them to be so far ahead. By the time of their withdrawal, they had been forced by a heavy German counter-attack to surrender some but not all of the ground gained, and had lost 83 men, 11 of whom came from West Belfast, among them Rifleman John Duffy of Conway Street in the Falls.[4] Such numbers meant that the battalion had nothing like the connection with the Falls and the Shankill that it had earlier in the war, but it also shows that after 1 July, the losses from these areas continued even though the remnants of the Ulster Division were behind the lines.[5] That continued to be the case throughout the rest of July and August, as the 2nd RIRifles was periodically at the front taking part in efforts to advance the line. Even when they were attacking, hazards remained, as Private William Burns of Derby Street discovered on 28 September when a sniper shot him while he was on sentry duty.[6]

By this point the 2nd Inniskillings had also taken part in tough fighting. They were part of the 32nd Division held in reserve on 1 July. They eventually supported 49th Division when it plugged the gap between the 32nd and Ulster

'Death Penny', commemoration of Rfn John Duffy, 2nd Royal Irish Rifles, 134 Conway Street, KIA 7 July 1916

divisions which had emerged due to the disastrous attack on Thiepval village. However, the heaviest losses for the 2nd Inniskillings came on 10 and 11 July at La Boisselle when the battalion lost 41 men, compared to their relatively light losses of only 16 on 1 July. Their aim had been to extend the British lines at Ovillers, and that was achieved over two days, with German counter-attacks repelled by Lewis guns. Among five West Belfast losses in the 2nd Inniskillings on 10/11 July was another of the small number of officers from the Shankill district: Lieutenant Claude Walker, son of the Revd Robert Walker of Shankill Rectory in the Ballygomartin Road.[7]

The front line remained virtually unaltered in August, with the next great push coming in early September. In this, both the 6th Connaughts and 7th Leinsters played a significant role. Neither battalion had been inactive while the Ulster Division was preparing for 1 July, although they had not been on the Somme, fighting principally in the Loos sector. Their time was notionally 'rest', but one officer, Blake O'Sullivan, noted how 'This term "rest" became a standard joke.' He described how due to the 'back-breaking work parties' in which men fetched and carried material from the front line, 'many a tired man welcomed the return to the death-dealing "line"'.[8]

Around this time, men at the front would have received news that dealt a blow to former INV members. On 5 June 1916 HMS *Hampshire* had hit a German mine off the Orkneys. The incident attracted worldwide attention because one passenger lost was Lord Kitchener. But for Belfast nationalists a more personal loss was that of Surgeon Hugh McNally, who had been Commander of the Belfast INV and was serving as the ship's doctor. McNally had attended Raglan Street Boys' School in West Belfast, before working as a chemist's apprentice prior to studying medicine at Queen's University. Having graduated in 1915, he applied to be a naval doctor, leaving his command position in the INV, which he had gained due to his experience in the University Officers' Training Corps.[9]

Such news was received while men of 47th Brigade were facing heavy shellfire whenever they were at the front. But an opportunity to hit back against the Germans came through raids. On the night of 26/27 June, the 6th Connaughts and 7th Leinsters collaborated on a raid. Two units of the Connaughts provided smoke cover, while another two held craters and dug communication trenches back to British lines.[10] The men placed wire around the edge and constructed bombing posts, to make it difficult for the Germans to counter-attack and to provide a base for further attacks on German lines. Considering that around 200 men went out into the thick of the battle, the fatalities, two in number, were light indeed, but they were heavier in the 7th Leinsters who carried out the actual raids.

The raid began at 12.15 a.m. on 27 June when two mines were exploded close to German positions.[11] Three minutes later, the 7th Leinsters entered German lines in six parties, each led by an officer and consisting of between 20 and 25 men. Each party was accompanied by a piper playing 'Ballyhooly', who subsequently acted as a stretcher-bearer. The sound of the pipes and the mud thrown into the trenches by the exploding mines must have caused great confusion among the Germans. However, parties 1 and 2, led by Second Lieutenant Hickman and Lieutenant Johnstone, met with 'formidable opposition', not from the trenches themselves, but from a machine gun at a strong-point on slightly higher ground. The main fighting fell to parties 3 and 4 led by Captain Lynch and Second Lieutenant Hodgson. Lynch himself was wounded, but NCOs continued the attack. Extensive use was made of bombs thrown into dugouts with their effectiveness 'proved by the shrieks and groans of the occupants'. Heavy casualties were inflicted on the enemy in a bitter fight. There was desperate handto-hand fighting and 'our raiders had to use their fists' when there was too little room for bayonets. A report in the brigade war diary stated that few prisoners were taken because although some Germans surrendered when cornered, 'there were three gross acts of treachery'. This probably means that the Germans turned on their captors and were killed in the process. Among the 14 dead in the 7th Leinsters was Private Samuel Irvine of California Street, but for the information gained and the damage done (at least 140 Germans killed or wounded), it was seen by staff officers to have been a highly effective operation.[12] Meanwhile, it began to build a reputation for this volunteer battalion as skilled raiders.

Aside from raids, simply being in the trenches was costly as the Germans responded wherever they could to the Allied advance on the Somme. The 6th Connaughts lost 26 men in July and August, mainly through daily bombardments, while the 7th Leinsters lost 16. During this time a great act of individual heroism was performed by Private Patrick McKillen, an enlistee in the 6th Connaughts from the INV and a resident of Oranmore Street. On 27 July, McKillen 'continued to work his machine gun, single handed, under a heavy fire, after all the remainder of the section had been put out of action. Private McKillen stuck to his gun and held the position for 24 hours.'[13]

In September, 47th Brigade moved to the Somme area, close to the small village of Guillemont, around five miles south-west of Thiepval. On arriving in the area, the Connaughts faced the familiar routine of improving badly damaged trenches, and the Germans continued to inflict heavy casualties through shelling. On 2 September alone, the 6th Connaughts' B Company lost ten men, with a further 30 wounded.[14] The next day, they did what they had come to the Somme to do.

At 5 a.m. on 3 September, the battalion drew up for the attack. The whole of 47th Brigade was temporarily attached to the 20th Division. The plan was for three successive waves of troops to take the village. C and D companies of the 6th Connaughts were to attack in the first wave. In the second and third waves, platoons of B Company would plug the gaps in C Company's lines, and platoons from A Company would do the same for D. At 8 a.m., the Germans received the familiar warning of an imminent attack: a heavy bombardment from British lines. Yet some of the heavy trench mortars being used in the attack fell short with tragic results. Waiting in 'Rim Trench' the Connaughts' C Company endured not only retaliatory fire from the Germans but 'friendly fire' from the British lines.

By 12 noon, as the bombardment continued, casualties numbered nearly 200. W. A. Lyon, an officer with the 7th Leinsters, later described their ordeal as 'a six hour plastering' and wondered how the men had carried on.[15]

Some had not done so. With C Company in no fit state for the first attack, troops intended for the second wave replaced them. Then, for three minutes, the Royal Field Artillery let go 'an intense barrage' of the German front. Unlike the bombardment in late June, this was successful. Advancing on the enemy, the Connaughts found 'Very little opposition . . . as the enemy surrendered at once' on the left of their advance – the area that was originally to have been attacked by C Company. They were joined by the 7th Leinsters who had not endured the problems of friendly fire, and both battalions found it comparatively easy to take their first objective. Casualties might have been higher from a dug-in machine gun, which fired 'a hurricane of . . . bullets sounding like hosts of bees, whistling swooshing and shrieking past our heads with blood-curdling intensity'. Yet many were saved because the gunner had fired a few feet too high.[16]

On the right, there was heavier resistance, but 47th Brigade soon overcame that, before cleaning up pockets of resistance holed up in various areas. Private Thomas Hughes of the 6th Connaughts (and a native of County Monaghan) was wounded in the initial attack, but had wounds dressed and returned to the firing-line. Having done so, he located a German machine gun that was causing great damage. Hughes ran out ahead of his company, shot the gunner and captured the gun. He was wounded doing this but went on to bring back three or four prisoners. For these acts of 'most conspicuous bravery and determination' Hughes was awarded the battalion's only Victoria Cross of the war.[17] Another VC went to Lieutenant John Holland of the 7th Leinsters, once an Irish Volunteer, and from County Kildare. He led the battalion's bombers into Guillemont, not stopping even for British artillery fire.[18] As a result of such bravery, the first three objectives had been reached before 1 p.m., and around 140 men of the 6th Connaughts joined an attack by other parts of the 16th Division on the final objective, the 'Sunken Road'. Meanwhile, the remainder of the battalion dug in with the 7th Leinsters to hold the territory gained until they were relieved the next day. Inevitably, Guillemont village, which they had taken, 'had been reduced to matchwood'.[19] Among the dead and wounded, one soldier took grim pleasure in what he found: Blake O'Sullivan noted how a soldier 'came running out of a corpse-strewn trench. His hands were holding something cupped in one of those round German fatigue caps, and grinning like a maniac, [he] apparently wanted to share the joke. He came up and showed me the cap – filled and quivering with its owner's brains.' O'Sullivan, who was wounded by this time, 'retched convulsively' and turned away.[20]

In total during 2–4 September, the 7th Leinsters sustained 219 casualties among the other ranks, of whom 38 men were killed. Ten officers were wounded but none killed. Another four men died of wounds in the three days after. Those killed included at least six West Belfast men all from Falls or Smithfield wards: Privates John Sharkey, John Breen, Charles Doherty and Patrick Duffin, plus

Corporals Frederick Campfield and Edward Sharkey.[21] During the same period
the 6th Connaughts had lost 55 men, along with two officers. At least three of the
men were from West Belfast: Privates James Conway, William Ferris and Patrick
McGinney.[22]

   One of the dead officers was the 6th Connaughts' Commanding Officer,
Lieutenant-Colonel J. S. M. Lenox-Conyngham. He was replaced on 6 September
by Major Rowland Charles Feilding, whose letters home to his wife, published
in 1929, provide an invaluable insight into details of the Connaughts that would
never find their way into the battalion war diary. Feilding was Shrewsbury-born

Delville Wood Grave of Pte Patrick McGinney, 6th Connaught Rangers,
34 Balkan Street, KIA 3 September 1916

and the son of a Church of England cleric with English and Austrian aristocratic connections. A civil engineer by training, he was in South Africa during the Matabele rebellion of 1896 and joined 'Gifford's Horse', which protected white settlers. He later served in the Lancashire Fusiliers, and married Edith Stapleton-Bretherton, converting to her Catholic faith. At the outbreak of war in 1914, Feilding was serving in a territorial unit, but he transferred to the Coldstream Guards, with whom he served in France until joining the 6th Connaughts. His conversion to Catholicism had marked him out for this battalion as efforts were made to attach Catholic officers to Irish (as distinct from Ulster) regiments.[23] Feilding had few connections with Ireland, and none with Belfast, but is a crucial figure in describing the lives of the Belfast men in his battalion. Even though one officer who wanted command of the battalion tried to undermine him, Feilding was hugely popular with his men.[24]

When Feilding took over, the 6th Connaughts had taken part in one of the few gains of the Somme campaign in the late summer months of 1916. However, they had sustained heavy losses, as had 47th Brigade as a whole. Of the 2,400 soldiers from the brigade who took part, nearly half were injured.[25] When Feilding joined the battalion as its CO he found 365 other ranks bivouacking at Carnoy 'amid a plague of flies'. Of these, on 7 September, some 250 men and officers of the 6th Connaughts, and nearly 300 of the 7th Leinsters, marched from Carnoy towards the front. Before departing, the 6th Connaughts (and probably other Catholic soldiers in 47th Brigade), 'kneeling down in the ranks, all received general absolution' from the division's senior chaplain.[26] They now had a fresh objective: to take German trenches close to the village of Ginchy, as part of a wider attack on the village itself, with the rest of the 16th Division. A British attack there on 6 September had failed as the Germans were well dug in.

On the way to the front, Feilding led his men back to Guillemont where so many had been lost days before. He recorded the scene in a letter to his wife:

> ... not a brick or stone is to be seen, except where it has been churned up by a bursting shell. Not a tree stands. Not a square foot of surface has escaped mutilation. There is nothing but the mud and the gaping shell-holes; – a chaotic wilderness of shell-holes, rim overlapping rim; and, in the bottom of many, the bodies of the dead.

The Connaughts' passage to the front was dangerous. German flares lit the land-scape, with the Connaughts' helmets flickering in the light. Without recognizable landmarks the battalion's guide lost his way. For some of the men, it was their first taste of battle as 91 of those going forward were new drafts who had only just joined the battalion. Seven men were lost through shell-fire on the way, but the battalion reached their destination at 10.30 p.m. They found themselves in trenches that had been German only a few days before.[27]

At 4.45 p.m. on 9 September, there was an intensive bombardment of the German lines for two minutes. As at Guillemont, some shells fell short. Fortunately, many were duds, and casualties were lighter than on 3 September. However, with duds also falling on German lines, the impact of the bombardment was not nearly as great as planned. When British troops moved forward at 4.47 p.m., they found the Germans 'very little disturbed'. So in the first wave of the attack, the 6th Royal Irish Regiment and the 8th Munster Fusiliers were 'mown down by a devastating fire from machine guns'. The original plan had been for the 6th Connaughts, plus one company of the 7th Leinsters and two from the 11th Hampshires, to follow behind the first attack, but with the Munsters so badly hit, their men had stopped advancing. A and B companies of the Connaughts realized what had happened and stayed in their trenches, but C and D companies plus the Leinsters and Hampshires did not. When there was a pause in the fighting, they judged that it was their turn to attack. Under Captains Steuart and Bain they advanced, but moved only a few yards before they came under heavy fire. Both officers were hit and the men could make no impact on the German lines. At 5.43 p.m. a runner was sent back with a message for divisional HQ saying, 'It appears that the trench opposite is full of Germans and that they were well prepared.'

Elsewhere, 48th Brigade was more successful. By 7.30 p.m. they had taken control of the village. But the attack on Ginchy was disastrous for the Connaughts. The bombardment had done too little damage to the German lines. The war diary noted that the German line 'had escaped our preliminary bombardment almost entirely and that it was thickly manned'. Feilding later revealed that this trench had been overlooked in the British bombardment. It was 'hidden and believed innocuous' and was expected to be the easy part of the attack. For that reason it 'had been allocated to the tired and battered 47th Brigade'. Instead, it was 'a veritable hornets' nest'.[28] By the evening of 9 September, the Connaughts had lost ten men, with more than 70 others wounded. The Leinsters had lost 11 men. Captain Steuart died of his wounds six days later. The battalion was withdrawn from the front the day after the attack, and spent the next ten days in billets before going by train north to the Bailleul area. For the 16th Division as a whole, their operations on the Somme had not been as futile as those in July. However, across the division, between 1 and 10 September, there were 4,090 killed, wounded or missing from 10,410 other ranks, and 240 from 435 officers. Of the 4,090 other ranks, 586 were confirmed killed and 846 were missing at the end of the month.[29] At least 1,079 of those were later confirmed killed.[30] For the nationalists and others of the division, these losses at both villages made the September stage of the Somme their incarnation of Thiepval, and it is appropriate that a divisional memorial now stands in Guillemont.

One effect of an advance was that the dead could be identified and buried. They were not left on land held by the enemy or in No Man's Land. Almost all the men who died as a result of 47th Brigade's attack on the Somme were buried close to where they fell. It was unusual for bodies to be returned home for burial when killed in action, although that did happen to a Falls Road sailor, John Trainor, lost on HMS *Fauvette* earlier in the year.[31] When men were wounded and later died in hospital, even in England, their bodies were sometimes returned to their families in Belfast. In early November, the *Irish News* reported on the burial in Milltown Cemetery, with full military honours, of two members of the 7th

Leinsters: Privates John Quirk of Milan Street and E. Cunningham of Millfield. Quirk had been commended by General Hickie for distinguished conduct on the Somme and had died of wounds at Woburn Cottage Hospital. Cunningham, a member of the Ancient Order of Hibernians, had been wounded at Guillemont and died in Tunbridge Wells.

In future years, Belfast's Troubles would see many members of the IRA buried in Milltown. In those times, despite its Cross of Sacrifice erected after the war in memory of the dead of 1914–18, it offered no welcome to British soldiers. Instead, the military tone to funerals was provided by masked men. However, in 1916 it was different. For the funeral of Quirk and Cunningham, the band of the RIRifles attended and shots were fired by men of the same regiment.[32] A few months earlier, Milltown had also seen the military funeral of Sergeant John McManus of the 18th RIRifles, a 64-year-old soldier with extensive service between 1868 and 1901, who had been brought back to train men after 1914. He had died of natural causes and was the oldest West Belfast man to die in service in 1914–18.[33]

Guillemont and Ginchy ended major West Belfast involvement on the Somme in 1916. The battle continued until November when snows came, by which time the British had made several further advances. The challenge now became a different one: how to survive the winter.

9

On and On

How long, O God! till Right shall conquer Wrong
Shall Hatred rage, and in her red right hand
Brandish her bloody falchion, thro' a land
Where Death is lord. How long, O God! how long?

FROM 'HOW LONG' BY SAMUEL K. COWAN[1]

In the aftermath of the Somme, the prospect of defeating Germany with a decisive 'big push' seemed remote. The broken volunteer battalions had to be rebuilt before they could again be an effective fighting force. As this happened, the winter of 1916–17 was bleak and tough. Men in the ranks did not know how far lessons had been learned from the early days of the Battle of the Somme, although some had seen them already acted on in the later stages of the battle.[2] Men in the 36th and 16th divisions did not know that they were part of a machine slowly but surely being built for an advance at Messines the next summer, which would be one of the most effective British operations of the war. So from the perspective of the trenches, and the people at home, the war in late 1916 and early 1917 ground on and on, with no end in sight.

While it was still summer, efforts were made to replenish the Ulster Division with Ulster men. As part of the drive, Captain Montgomery, Sergeant McAllister and Sergeant Murdoch of the 9th RIRifles arrived in Belfast on 11 August 1916. They took part in several meetings, including one at Brown Square in West Belfast on the evening of 23 August. Montgomery said that 'if the recruits necessary to fill up the gaps in the Irish regiments were not forthcoming under the voluntary system the Government would eventually decide on applying the Compulsion Act to this country'. He called on women to encourage men to enlist. In an earlier speech before a performance at the Royal Hippodrome, Montgomery had spoken how the men of his battalion from the Shankill Road were 'the right sort'. At that meeting he put pressure on 'the shop-boy class' saying that he had noticed too many of them on the streets of Belfast. He said that if they joined the army, 'he would give them a job that was more manly than selling ribbons'.[3] The *News Letter* printed a poem which included the lines, 'Then pity the man who hears the call yet/Dares to disobey, fearing to venture.'[4]

However, the campaign appears to have had little impact, and Irish recruitment generally was stalling. At the outbreak of war, 21,000 Irishmen were serving in the British army, joined by 30,000 mobilized reservists. Between August 1915 and December 1915, 90,500 more enlisted, but only 43,700 joined up in the rest of the war. That later figure was just 3.8 per cent of unenlisted men aged 15–49, compared to 22.1 per cent in England and Wales (aided by conscription) over the same period. Even prior to January 1916, when Irish recruitment ran at 7.8 per cent of men aged 15–49, it was 24.2 per cent in England and Wales, and 26.9 per cent in Scotland.[5] In Ulster, recruitment among both Catholics and Protestants was higher than in other parts of Ireland throughout the war. However, it still fell away from 1916.[6] In West Belfast specifically, figures mirrored that.[7]

A range of factors affected recruitment. For example, farmers' sons were historically unwilling to join up, and many agricultural workers could not in any case be spared from the land.[8] The radicalization of nationalist opinion after the Easter Rising of course played a part. In London, political leaders debated how to respond. They considered, and rejected, merging the 16th and 36th divisions.[9] Instead, drafts were sent from elsewhere in the UK, in the case of the 9th RIRifles, particularly from London and the Norfolk Regiment. Meanwhile, where there were new Irish recruits, these were drafted into regular battalions such as the 1st and 2nd RIRifles, which led to the eventual merger or disbandment of many service battalions.[10] The effect of these changes on the nationality of notionally 'Irish' and/or 'Ulster' units was marked. Soldiers who were Irish-born comprised 86 per cent of these units in 1914, but only 56 per cent in 1918. Despite this, the geographic titles of divisions were kept, even though there was a proposal to drop 'Ulster' from the name of the 36th. This was never done and it should be noted that although the local links of the Irish units were being undermined, they were no more affected by this than other part of the British army, which also struggled to maintain links to their recruiting areas.[11]

However, before new recruits flooded into the 16th Division, Rowland Feilding was able to reflect on the nature of the Irish soldiers who still dominated his battalion immediately after Ginchy. Many English officers saw Irish soldiers as having distinct characteristics. F. W. S. Jourdain, also an officer with the 6th Connaughts, said when interviewed in 1990: 'Irish troops are a bit different to English troops. They've got, in a way, less individuality, I suppose. But I never found I had any difficulty with them at all.'[12] Feilding, writing to his wife, described them as 'difficult to drive, but easy to lead', reflecting one dominant stereotype of Irish soldiers as enthusiastic fighters if pointed in the right direction. He also saw them as 'intensely religious' and 'loyal to their officers', many of whom were Irish themselves. While the men would 'report sick pretty readily' when they were behind the lines, there were only one or two men ill per day in the whole battalion while at the front. This, Feilding believed, was 'a matter of honour with them', adding that 'where Mass is concerned, they are never too tired to attend. Their devotion is quite amazing.'[13] Consequently, Feilding took the spiritual well-being of his men seriously. In April 1917 his wife sent miniature crucifixes to be distributed throughout the battalion. They had been blessed by the Pope and brought from Rome by Cardinal Bourne, the Archbishop of Westminster.[14]

As new recruits arrived in the Ulster Division, the 9th RIRifles had been moved to the Franco-Belgian border at Kortepijp, a few miles east of the French town of

Bailleul. Meanwhile, 47th Brigade was sent a few miles south-west of Ypres, the 6th Connaughts to Locre (now Loker) and the 7th Leinsters to Scherpenberg. This meant the 16th and 36th divisions were no more than a few miles apart, due to post-Somme reorganizations, which put both divisions in IX Corps. Their stories were now intertwined. Units from the two divisions regularly relieved each other at the front, and they had the chance for much contact.

It is difficult to know how the men of the 16th and 36th divisions got on as there are so few accounts from the ranks. Accounts from officers differ. Feilding cited a joke about 'fraternizing with the enemy' when the 6th Connaughts played the 9th Royal Irish Fusiliers at football in April 1917, and there were certainly some tensions.[15] Walter Collins served in the 9th RIRifles but, as a Londoner, was an outsider. He later remembered 'an air of restraint' between the two divisions.[16] But other sources suggest good relations. Private Jack Christie of the Ulster Division recalled, 'We should never let politics blind us to the truth about things – bravery and loyalty wasn't all on one side. The 16th Division played a vital part alongside us.' He told the story of how he was one of four men at an advance post dealing with the wounded: 'just over the brow of the hill some of the 16th had their wee dug out, and we went across, a couple of us at a time, to have a yarn with them, and they came across too, a couple at a time, always leaving a couple at the first aid post – and we became great friends.'[17]

From these limited accounts it is difficult to draw firm conclusions, but it seems likely that the relationship was mixed. The men collaborated in the shared tasks of fighting and survival, and enjoyed good relations on an individual level. Yet the joke about fraternization with the enemy hinted at an underlying sense of difference that was not extinguished by being away from Ireland.

The political slant of the two divisions certainly still existed for anyone who cared to look. A symbol of this was the return to the 6th Connaughts in October 1916 of a former officer: the Nationalist MP Captain Stephen Gwynn. He was one of several Nationalist MPs who had made a strong political statement by joining up. Others included Daniel Sheehan and Willie Redmond, plus the former MP Tom Kettle, the latter two later killed in action.[18] Gwynn had trained in the cadet corps of the 7th Leinsters and previously served with the 6th Connaughts from December 1915 to May 1916, at which point he had gone back to London for parliamentary debates on the Easter Rising. Feilding noted that Gwynn was 'adored by his Company'. He found Gwynn 'a refined, polished, brave gentleman', the antithesis of Feilding's 'preconceived ideas' formed in England of the nature of an Irish Nationalist MP.[19]

In general, the 6th Connaughts found this sector of the front much easier to cope with than the Somme area. Feilding described is as 'like coming from Hell to the Thames Valley in summer-time'.[20] When in the actual firing-line, battalions of both divisions carried out patrols of No Man's Land, but raids on German lines were the main offensive action. Crozier, in command of the 9th RIRifles, was especially fond of raids which other officers felt had no purpose except bravado.[21] The weather had to be right for raids to take place. On 31 August, the 9th RIRifles' war diary noted: 'set out for the trenches intending to visit Fritz under cover of gas', but the wind 'declined to blow so our raiding party returned thankfully to bed to dream of glorious raids'. However, a successful raid took place on the night of 15/16 September. A month later, on 12 October, three officers, 30 other ranks and four sappers attacked the enemy lines. They had been given seven tasks: to assess the damage caused by British trench mortars; capture prisoners; bring back personal effects of Germans (to help identify units); 'to kill Germans'; destroy machine-gun emplacements; 'destroy everything too heavy or impossible to remove'; and to obtain telephone and signal equipment. Heavy damage was inflicted and a prisoner was taken, but few papers were found.

During the raid, Sergeant Robert Moore played a crucial role. A resident of Springfield Road, he had been in the West Belfast UVF before the war, and worked at Mackie's Foundry as an apprentice fitter before enlisting as a private in 1914 aged 18. He had been promoted to sergeant in September 1915 and, as we shall see later, in 1917 he rose through the ranks to become an officer, only to be killed in action in March 1918. Just a month after the raid, the *Telegraph* reported how Moore volunteered to form a raiding party and to establish a telephone communication line:

Under heavy fire, he remained at his post in the German trenches, and sent his messages clearly, showing great coolness. He would not take his instrument away until he was assured by his officer that all the party was clear of the German trenches. He then with

Sgt Robert Moore MM, 9th Royal Irish Rifles, 227 Springfield Road
(*Belfast Evening Telegraph*, 21 November 1916, p. 4)

great coolness brought his instrument, rolled up his wire and the guiding tape, under heavy fire in our trenches.[22]

Moore was awarded the Military Medal.

That was the last raid of the year as the men dug in for the winter. When they arrived in the Bailleul area they had found that the trenches were relatively shallow, with few deep dugouts due to the spongy nature of the soil. However, during the final months of 1916 the trenches were strengthened with frames and duckboards, while bullet-proof parapets were reinforced.[23] Meanwhile, they faced a different problem due to a range of illnesses then described by the general name of 'venereal disease'. Percy Crozier, who was soon to relinquish command of the 9th RIRifles due to promotion, had been persistently concerned about the men's sexual health since they left Belfast for England. He put a number of measures in place to treat the men because he regarded promiscuity as unavoidable in time of war. However, during this time around Bailleul, such casualties gave him greater concern than losses at the front. Eventually, the source was tracked down to 'an infected girl who hops from camp to camp and ditch to dyke like the true butterfly that she is'.[24]

Throughout the winter months, most fighting ceased because the weather was so bad, with heavy snow and severe frosts. From the start of October to the end of January 1917, there were only 23 fatalities in the 6th Connaughts (15 of those in January), 12 in the 7th Leinsters and just seven 9th RIRifles. Such relatively light casualties illustrate how unusual fighting was as the winter began to bite. The greatest danger from the Germans was shell-fire, not only at the front. On the night of 8/9 February 1917, the 6th Connaughts were behind the lines and lost four men when the Germans managed to strike their huts. (Usually shells hit the trenches.) In the 9th RIRifles, Lance-Corporal Alexander 'Sandy' Johnston, a resident of Bristol Street and member of the North Belfast UVF, had been a keen sportsman before the war, training the junior team of Distillery FC and being a member of the Northern Cycling Club. He won the Military Medal in October 1916 for digging out several comrades who had been buried by a German shell, despite the shelling continuing while he rescued them.[25] Unlike in 1914, shelling continued even on Christmas Day that year: Riflemen Robert Bleakley of Argyle Street and William Matthews of Springfield village were both killed on 25 December 1916.[26]

The cold also had a severe impact. Walter Collins, a Londoner who transferred into the 9th RIRifles after the Somme recalled a method of overcoming the cold in late 1916: 'at morning stand-down all troops rubbed vigorously into their legs and feet a glutinous thick whale oil concoction that was intended to retain inward heat but stank to high heaven'. The operation was inspected by an officer and an NCO, and only when they were satisfied did the men get their rum issue and went to the cookhouse for breakfast of bread and bacon. That was supplemented by hard tack biscuits, and a main meal around midday, usually of corned beef immersed in baked beans and tinned vegetables.[27]

Meanwhile, the war ground some men down. Some popular opinion takes the view that many of those who were shot at dawn would not have been executed had 'modern medical and psychiatric experience' informed the opinions of courts.[28] Yet there were clear cases where the plight of men with mental health problems was treated seriously. As early as 17 January 1916, the 9th RIRifles war diary noted a case of shell-shock.[29] In late 1916 Private Joseph Fleming of Broadbent Street and the 14th RIRifles was buried after an explosion and became hypersensitive, suffering from headaches and trembling hands. He was discharged with shell-shock in October 1916.[30] James Kelly of Wilson Street had suffered from epilepsy from the age of 9, but served for a year at the front before being discharged in December 1916, when it was found that his condition was aggravated by service. During his time in the 9th he had won the Military Medal.[31] Private Bernard Donnelly of Cupar Street had served with the 1st Royal Irish Fusiliers in France in February and March 1916. He was discharged for 'mental deficiency' in December 1916. His record states that 'If left to himself [he] sinks into oblivion and remains completely uninterested in anything but repose of mind and body.' This was attributed to the stress of service.

During this time, some men took desperate steps to get out of the trenches, including self-wounding, often by shooting their hand or foot. Suspicions of such behaviour in the 6th Connaughts led to the trial of Sergeant James Conlon of Omar Street, but he was found not guilty, the victim of a genuine accident. Eventually, he was discharged in May 1918, having succumbed to tuberculosis, but he died the next month. His brother, Owen, had already been killed earlier in the war, at Gallipoli, in the 6th RIRifles.[32] Despite the weather and other problems, officers reported good morale. In late 1916, the 6th Connaughts spent much time repairing trenches, 'practically without rest' and 'wet through much of the time'. Feilding wrote on 16 December: 'They work all night and every night, and a good part of each day ... The temperature is icy. They have not even a blanket. The last two days it has been snowing.' Yet, he added, morale remained good: 'you may ask any one of them, any moment of the day or night, "Are you cold", or "Are you wet?" – and, you will get but one answer. The Irishman will reply – always with a smile – "Not too cold, sir", or "Not too wet, sir".'

If the 16th and 36th divisions dug in for most of the winter in relative safety, the same could not be said for the 1st Inniskillings in 29th Division. They were in the Somme area in January 1917, and were ordered to attack trenches near Carnoy on 27 January. They achieved their goal, gaining two lines, and then repelled a fierce German counter-attack the next day. However, it was a costly operation with about 140 casualties, of whom 44 were killed on 27 and 28 January, and more died of wounds in days after. This battalion had a sizeable West Belfast contingent in it, some of whom would have been regulars. Among the dead were Private Matthew Coates of Sidney Street West and Lance-Corporal James McKenna of Maria Place in the Shankill, plus Privates Patrick Birney of Oranmore Street and Alexander Houston of Abyssinia Street in the Falls.[33]

Fighting resumed more generally in mid-February as the weather improved.

On 19 February, the 6th Connaughts raided German lines. Uniforms were stripped of insignia so that the Germans could not identify which battalions were in the area, but many advanced with 'green miniature Irish flags' tucked into their caps or buttonholes.[34] Dense fog provided cover, but made it difficult to find precise points in the destination. Two hours after the raid began, the Germans offered an armistice, and the Connaughts were able to retrieve their casualties. It was an unusual offer in Feilding's eyes, begun simply by the Germans calling out in English, 'Send out your stretcher men', followed by the Connaughts doing exactly that. When Feilding saw what was happening, he found it hard to believe. The German and British lines were as close as 40 yards apart in this part of the front and Feilding 'found numerous Germans – almost shoulder to shoulder – leaning over their parapet, exposed from the waist up: on our side it was the same. All were watching the stretcher-bearers at work in No Man's Land.' Feilding concluded, 'These people cannot always be so bad as they are painted.'

Yet there was a price to be paid. The terms of the armistice were that arms should be left in the trenches, but one officer, Second Lieutenant Gordon-Ralph, violated this and was taken prisoner. A subsequent inquiry from above examined whether there had been 'fraternization'. This would have breached an order that had arrived while Feilding was on leave and which he had not seen. A court of inquiry led to more stringent orders, in which any assistance from the enemy in collecting the wounded was forbidden. Feilding was dismayed, saying that it marked the scrapping of 'English' qualities of 'Sportsmanship, chivalry, pity'. Instead, 'our methods henceforth are to be strictly Prussian; those very methods which we claim to be fighting in this war to abolish.'[35]

The failed raid cost the 6th Connaughts three officers and eight men. A further 24 were missing, with another five believed to be prisoners. Reflecting on the failure, the Commander of the 16th Division, Brigadier-General Pereira pointed to the bombardments of previous days, other raids on two previous nights and preliminary wire-cutting as having made the Germans suspect an attack. If this was stating the obvious it was still a valid explanation. However, Pereira's report also revealed a difference of opinion among senior officers. Feilding had suggested a one-minute bombardment with Stokes mortars of the frontline immediately before the attack. Pereira had vetoed it as 'I considered at the time that surprise was everything'. He conceded that as it was now clear that the front line was especially strongly held, a short bombardment might have helped to clear it.[36] Pereira was quite open with General Plumer (in command of the Second Army) about having rejected Feilding's recommendation and taking full responsibility for that. Feilding said that this was 'why every officer and soldier of his Brigade swears by him'.[37] But it also pointed to a recurring dilemma: time and time again, the Germans were alert to a likely attack after a bombardment had tried to soften them up, and they were right to be.

Just over a fortnight later both the 6th Connaughts and 7th Leinsters were forced into a defensive posture when German soldiers penetrated British lines close to the Connaughts' position, at around 4.40 p.m. on 8 March. This was not something that the Connaughts had faced before, being used either to digging in or being on the attack, and both they and the Leinsters had been hard hit by a preliminary bombardment. Nearly two hours of close fighting took place, with the Connaughts' bombers trying to drive the Germans back beyond their lines. They managed to do so, but lost seven men in that action and the bombardment before it, among them Private William Hutton of Linview Street on the southern edge of the Falls.[38] The next day, events were repeated, with a raid on trenches held by the Connaughts. Over the two days, 11 men of the 7th Leinsters were killed by German artillery, including Sergeant William Morgan of Abyssinia Street in the Falls.[39] Nine men of the 6th Connaughts died, with 42 wounded.

The 9th RIRifles had an easier time in February. They spent much of the month in 'recreational training'. This included football matches, a bayonet-fighting contest and boxing. Although the weather was cold throughout February, it was also 'clear and bracing'. When the men returned to the front in the Spanbroek sector north-east of Bailleul on 25 February they were much rested. On their first day back, the 9th was hit by the death due to wounds of Sergeant Andrew McAllister. A letter from the battalion CO to his mother, Isabella, in Westmoreland Street, said that he had been encouraged to apply for a commission but had refused to do so. The CO added that, 'I'm sure you will feel pride in the knowledge that your boy was always known to be one of the finest and bravest soldiers who ever left Ulster to fight for his country.'[40] These were not merely words meant to console a parent as the battalion war diary, unusually, described McAllister as 'a most efficient NCO and fearless of all danger'.

The 47th Brigade got away from the front in mid-March. A series of football matches were organized as part of a varied training programme. The 6th Connaughts won several matches within the division, though they lost a game of hurling to the 1st Royal Munster Fusiliers. Catholic soldiers of 47th Brigade attended Mass at Mont des Cats Trappist Monastery, a change from the usual hut or makeshift open-air service. Anglicans in the battalion were served by a chaplain attached to the 6th Royal Irish Regiment.[41] The religious mix of the battalion (at least post-Somme) is indicated by an October 1916 service for Jewish officers and soldiers.

From April onwards, both 47th and 107th brigades focused on training. This sometimes brought the two divisions together. Most notably, the 6th Connaughts played two football matches against the 9th Royal Irish Fusiliers of what Feilding described as 'the Carson (36th) Division'. The Connaughts lost the first match 2–0. The rematch was quite an occasion. Feilding wrote to his wife of 2,000–3,000 soldiers watching 'the two great opposing factions of Ireland, in a spirit of friendliness which, so far as I am aware, seems unattainable on Ireland's native soil'. Again, the 9th Fusiliers won 2–0.[42] Meanwhile, battalions were approaching the full strength of numbers that they would need for an attack. Everything now pointed to Messines, which would become firmly etched into the shared story of the Ulster and Irish divisions.

10

Messines

We should never let politics blind us to the truth about things – bravery and loyalty wasn't all on one side. The 16th Division played a vital part alongside us.

JACK CHRISTIE, ULSTER DIVISION VETERAN

The Rout of the Hun was very complete . . .

MAJOR H. F. N. JOURDAIN, 6TH CONNAUGHTS, DIARY 8 JUNE 1917

By mid-1917, the British army was very different from that which had arrived in France in the summer of 1914. In some cases, men had risen through the ranks to be officers. One such was Second Lieutenant William Rainey who was married with three children in Bristol Street in the Shankill. He had first enlisted as a rifleman with the 2nd RIRifles in 1906. At the outbreak of war he had risen to sergeant, but was severely wounded in September 1914. He spent the next year in hospital and then in a reserve battalion before returning to the front with the 2nd RIRifles in October 1915. A year later, he was in hospital with neurasthenia, but stayed there less than a month. Discharged into his old battalion at the end of October 1916, he was promoted from sergeant for service in the field in February of the next year. But Rainey survived only ten months as an officer, being killed in action at Moevres as part of the battle of Cambrai.[1]

Another man who rose from private was Robert Moore, a former UVF member who had volunteered for the 9th RIRifles. As we saw earlier, he had received the Military Medal. At the end of 1916 he was picked out for officer training, and was away from the front for over six months, four of which were spent training. That began when he reported to No. 5 Officer Cadet Battalion in February 1917 at Trinity College, Cambridge. His promotion to second lieutenant was despite a somewhat poor disciplinary record. In March 1916 he was severely reprimanded for not greeting a sentry properly (which was risky behaviour in case the sentry fired) while leading a working party and also for insolent conduct. In April he was again reprimanded, this time for unspecified 'neglect' of duty. However, such a record may well have indicated the confidence and spirit required of officers. It was no barrier to promotion in Moore's case and he was back in the 17th (Reserve) battalion of his regiment by June 1917.[2]

Meanwhile, the post-Somme drafts and reorganizations had undermined the local links of battalions throughout the army. Consequently, as men from outside Ireland served in Irish regiments, West Belfast men were spread far and wide.

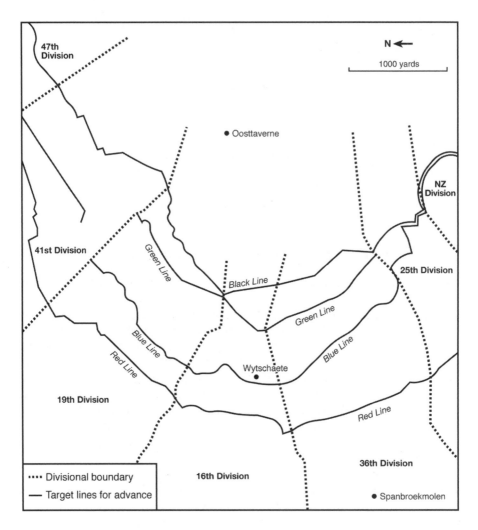

Map 6 Messines, 7 June 1917

Consequently, news of casualties was even more likely to come from a variety of operations than it had done earlier in the war. One case was that of R. J. 'Bertie' Johnston and Ernest Barnett, both Shankill men of the 8th Black Watch. Johnston was from Fortingale Street, Barnett from Lyle Street. Both were killed on 9 April in the first Battle of the Scarpe at Arras, and were described in the *Telegraph* as 'chums' who had enlisted together.[3]

There was to be one further major offensive, which, with the Somme, is particularly closely linked to Belfast men. Messines Ridge is one of the few First World War battles, which evokes thoughts of unqualified success. It was also the site of joint action by the 16th and 36th divisions, and for this reason today's

Messines – now called Mesen – has been the site of joint British–Irish commemorations of those from the entire island of Ireland who served in the war. It is core to the story of Belfast's unionists and nationalists serving together.

Messines was a prelude to the third Battle of Ypres, which was planned for late July. Possession of the ridge gave the Germans an excellent vantage point over the Ypres area, making unobserved troop movements difficult. Holding the ridge would theoretically give the Allies a great advantage in a future attack. The preparation for the action at Messines was markedly different from that for the Somme. The officers of 47th Brigade had seen the model of the area at the end of April, and other ranks had begun practice attacks late that month. From mid-May, 47th Brigade used observation posts on Kemmel Hill to gain a clear view of their target. Such preparation was not limited to broad strategy. There were also trips to the front line so that the battalion could familiarize itself with the precise nature of the trenches to be used both for assembling and 'jumping off'. On the last day of May the entire battalion carried out a mock attack. Such preparations are a clear sign of how lessons from the Somme had been learned.

During this time, some officers worried about the 'loyalty' of soldiers in Irish regiments due to the growth of support for Sinn Féin back home following the Easter Rising. There were certainly some republicans in British ranks during the war, even before the Rising radicalized so many nationalists. One Belfast man, Seán Cusack of Corporation Street close to the city's docks, was stationed at Carrickfergus with a reserve battalion when the Rising erupted, and tried (unsuccessfully) to join the rebels. He was already a member of the Irish Republican Brotherhood.[4] Yet the only major study of discipline in Irish regiments shows that in the aftermath of the Rising, some Irish units actively asserted their opposition to it. It might expected that Stephen Gwynn, as a Nationalist MP, would describe men in the 6th Connaughts as feeling 'stabbed in the back' by the Rising,[5] but there was certainly evidence of that. The 7th Leinsters, when the Germans taunted their lines, responded by playing 'Rule Britannia' and Irish tunes on a melodeon. As time moved on, there appears to have been no growth of support for Sinn Féin in the ranks, despite fears that there might be. In November 1917 this would influence the decision to move reserve units from Ireland to England.[6] Meanwhile, in the 2nd RIRifles, which was also preparing at Neuve Eglise for the attack at Messines as part of the 25th Division, Father Gill noted:

> One morning the Brigadier sent for the CO and myself and asked if we thought it likely that any of the Irish would think of deserting and if it would be advisable to talk to the men . . . I said that nothing could do greater harm than to suggest that any of the men were thought capable of treachery. As a matter of fact no further step was taken.[7]

In the 6th Connaughts, one company carried 'an enormous green flag with a yellow Irish harp on it' when they marched. Feilding said, 'It has not got the Crown, and therefore would be ranked by some people as "Sinn Fein", I feel sure. But it does not seem to make any difference to their loyalty and devotion.'[8] If disloyalty was not a concern, Feilding believed that a handful of men – described by him as 'perhaps half a dozen' – fell into the 'scrimshanker' category. He believed that 'scenting danger ahead' they were committing minor crimes so that they would be imprisoned when the attack took place. However, by this time, field punishment was the usual result of minor crime.[9]

The men of the 9th RIRifles were in working parties for much of May, but their officers prepared for the attack. From their base near Méteren, between 8 and 12 May, the battalion Commanding Officer, now Lieutenant-Colonel P. G. Woods, along with company commanders, carried out reconnaissance missions, familiarizing themselves with the landscape. The officers also took part in various courses, mainly focused on schemes of attack. The 107th Brigade war diary notes that these courses had 'the object of informing the imagination and initiative of the officers', showing how more leeway was given to officers than on the Somme.[10]

On 3 June, the 9th RIRifles moved to the front, marching to the assembly trenches at 9 p.m. on 6 June. The battalion war diary noted 'a fine summer's night'. Aside from their usual equipment, all ranks carried a knobkerry (a club-headed stick) for close combat, six mills grenades, and wire-cutters. Several men in each company carried coloured flags on their rifles to mark the position of the battalion, enabling brigade HQ to keep sight of each battalion's position. Each battalion in 107th Brigade had a flag divided in two, diagonally from bottom left to top right, with yellow in the bottom half, and, in the case of the 9th, blue in the top section.

Overnight, to cover the assembly of the massed ranks, patrols went out to engage any Germans who might be watching from No Man's Land.[11] By 2 a.m. on the morning of 7 June, the battalion was in position, with 107th Brigade on the right of the 36th Division's line and 109th Brigade on the left. Within 107th Brigade's formation, the 9th RIRifles (to the left) and the 8th RIRifles (to the right) were the front line. They were to be followed by the rest of the brigade (10th and 15th RIRifles) with one battalion, the 12th RIRifles, borrowed from 108th Brigade joining them to 'mop-up'. The division had four objectives of different German lines, named simply red, blue, green and black lines, with the 9th focused on the red and blue lines. With these secured, the battalions behind them would move forward and take the green and black lines. To the right of 107th Brigade was the 25th Division, part of II Anzac Corps. This included the 2nd RIRifles. On the immediate left of the 9th RIRifles, as part of 109th Brigade, was the 14th RIRifles. The 8th and 9th were to work closely together in reaching the division's first objective of the red line, joined by the 14th in taking the blue line. They also found themselves shoulder-to-shoulder with the 16th Division, lined up as part of IX Corps (with the 36th and 19th divisions) to the left of 109th Brigade.

In the 14th RIRifles trenches, nerves were evident from early on 7 June. At 1.30 a.m., the battalion war diary noted, 'We can hear a plane flying very low overhead and are in doubt as to whether it is ours or theirs.' Had it been an Allied fighter, the pilot would have been alarmed as 'we are firing on it to make certain'.[12] Zero hour was set for 3.10 a.m. From 2.45 a.m., the officers of the 14th kept 'looking at our watches and counting the time still to go'. At 3.05 a.m., only a few guns were firing. A minute later, there was 'perfect stillness'. The 9th's war diary noted, 'All was now tense with expectancy only awaiting the hour of zero ... to give full rent to that eagerness for the fray which was so marked in this battalion ... A heavy mist enveloped the whole front.' The Germans clearly had no expectation of an attack as their unit in front of the 9th was being relieved, which would never happen if an attack was expected.

Silence was broken at 3.10 a.m. when 'a blinding flash of yellow-green light leapt from the enemy front-line'. This was the Spanbroekmolen mine. Nearly five miles away, Major H. F. N. Jourdain, who had commanded the 6th Connaughts when Feilding was on leave, was working as an observer and recorded that 'The whole earth trembled in a most remarkable way.'[13] Earth and debris were hurled high into the sky[14] and a large crater replaced the previously 'dominating defence of the enemy'. A captured prisoner later reported that almost his entire company had been blown into the air.[15] In the 14th RIRifles trench, the noise was 'too terrible to describe. Even in this deep dugout we cannot hear each other speaking.' Some of the men of that battalion moved over the top as soon as the mine had gone off and when there was a second explosion some were thrown off their feet.

The contrast with 1 July 1916 was marked. Although there had been an artillery bombardment of German lines from 31 May (often followed by raids), it did not end and give the tell-tale sign of an imminent attack.[16] Instead, 'The first flash of the exploding mine revealed the 9th R.I.R. going over the top line after line unheeding of the falling debris.' At that point, the men advanced behind a creeping artillery barrage (supported by targeted machine-gun fire), which moved forwards with the men, a tactic that had been perfected towards the end of the Battle of the Somme. Each move forward in the barrage was of about 100 yards. So unlike the battalion's experience of 11 months before, the Germans did not have the warning period immediately after a barrage had stopped in which to regroup to defend. Indeed, the men were perilously close behind the barrage – just 40 yards – but they were not hit by friendly fire as the calculations were spot on. The level of precision in preparing for this had been considerable. From 1 June, all watches had been synchronized daily at 12 noon. The orders for battle had even warned men 'to prevent bayonets flashing in the moonlight'.[17]

The 47th Brigade had moved to the front on 2 June, with the 6th Connaughts raiding German lines two nights later. On 7 June they also saw mines explode in front of them, in the areas known as Maedelstede, Petit Bois and Peckham. Feilding described the mines exploding 'with a roar to wake the dead'.[18] The 16th Division lined up, to the left of the Ulster Division, with 47th Brigade on the right and 49th Brigade on the left, with 48th Brigade in reserve. In 47th Brigade, the first wave was provided by the 6th Royal Irish Regiment on the right and the 7th Leinsters on the left. The 6th Connaughts were designated as 'moppers-up' to go in behind their comrades from 47th Brigade, the 1st Royal Munster Fusiliers.

Their target, as for the rest of the 16th (Irish) Division, was the capture of Wytschaete village.

As the 9th RIRifles advanced, the huge crater caused them some problems. Faced with a devastated landscape still shrouded in mist some men briefly lost their direction. Speaking in 1994, Walter Collins, who was a lance-corporal in the battalion at Messines, remembered how, 'It got a bit of a shambles in the end . . . all mixed up regiments . . . going up the ridge together.'[19] But it was not until close to the red line, at Bone Point, that serious opposition was encountered from a machine-gun position which had somehow survived the barrage. However, this was soon dealt with by Sergeant Reid and a party from C Company, which moved to the side of the post and shot the gunner. With the red line now taken and the Germans fleeing in shock and chaos, the 9th had lost very few men and had taken many prisoners. Although all had gone to plan in terms of reaching the red line, there was some disorder on the British front line, with men from the 16th and 25th divisions mixed up with the 9th RIRifles.

By this time, nearly an hour into the battle, part of the 107th Brigade's machine-gun company had moved to the lip of the Spanbroekmolen crater. It was too dark for them to fire without risking hitting British troops. But they were in position for daybreak when they could bring further destruction to German lines. This was fortunate for the 9th as the battalion was about to encounter stronger resistance, behind the line of the Spanbroekmolen mine. Although this area had been subjected to the artillery barrage, the Germans were solidly dug in. It turned out to be a stiff fight. Captain Kane led D Company and a platoon from the 14th Rifles to rush a machine-gun post and took the position by bayoneting the gunners. Encountering a nest of dugouts, the battalion then had to bomb the Germans out. They took over 200 prisoners. By 4.50 a.m., as dawn broke, the blue line was in British hands. The 9th RIRifles consolidated their position with wire and stakes found in the German trenches as not enough could be brought forward during the attack.[20] The battalion also saw tanks for the first time. Four were used to support the Ulster Division at Messines, although they did not enter the battle until the blue line had been secured, having the black line as their main target.[21] Meanwhile, the war diary recorded, 'The Royal Flying Corps had complete mastery of the air.'

As the 9th and the 14th consolidated, the 10th and 15th RIRifles moved forward around 5 a.m. to take first the green then the black lines. They faced an enemy barrage, but it was not accurate and their casualties were relatively light. When they moved into the green line at 6.50 a.m. after a British barrage they found little opposition. The black line was a harder fight, but even that was secure by 8 a.m. Meanwhile, Lieutenant O'Brien of the 14th reported back to battalion HQ: 'Everything A1. We are merry and bright. If you could send up shovels I should be obliged. "God save the King".' At 11.55 a.m., A Company of the 9th was sent to help consolidate.

As the 36th Division had found, the German front line offered little resistance to the 16th Division or to the 25th. The war diary of the 2nd RIRifles recorded problems consolidating lines due to destruction wrought by the barrage, but that the advance itself was relatively trouble-free.[22] By the end of the day the 2nd RIRifles had captured 200 prisoners, five machine guns and two trench mortars.

The red line was captured by the 7th Leinsters in little over half an hour. The blue line was all but taken by 5 a.m., although the battalion faced some stubborn machine-gun fire. By 7.30 a.m., the Munsters, in front of the Connaughts, and moving through the Leinsters, had taken the green line, with the final black line secured 30 minutes later. The Leinsters took around 60 prisoners and killed between 80 and 100 Germans. Unfortunately, and unusually for the 6th Connaughts, the war diaries covering 47th Brigade and its division are not nearly as detailed as those for the 9th Rifles at Messines. Even a special narrative prepared by the division after the operation focused mainly on the plans for the attack.[23] However, key points can be deduced. Divisional papers commented on the 'extra-ordinary enthusiasm' of those involved in the attack, and say that 'The energy and determination shown by all ranks were remarkable.' However, as the 36th Division had found, the explosion of the mines had unintended consequences. Some of the assaulting troops were wounded, buried or gassed as the mines went off. Confusion was caused by the glare of the explosions, the smoke and the falling debris, although those who had lost direction soon recovered. In the 7th Leinsters, debris which hung in the air made some men 'visibly ill'. Meanwhile, the preliminary bombardment and mines had such an effect on the Germans that the resistance they offered 'was nowhere very formidable'.

As regards the 6th Connaughts, just before reaching Wytschaete village, the men encountered a German strong-point which they rapidly overcame, captur-ing 98 prisoners in the village itself. The division concluded that the operation had been such a success that there were few areas of the plan that could have been improved, other than not including smoke shells in barrages to reduce confusion.[24]

With the lines secured, 107th Brigade and the 14th RIRifles were relieved on the front line by 108th Brigade the next day.[25] The operation had been a complete success with all targets gained in good time. In the early hours of 8 June, Captain J. A. Mulholland of the 14th noted,

> It is strange to think that last night we sat in our front line in fear and trembling that the Boche would spot us assembling in our trenches, and tonight we are three miles behind his lines and some of his big guns are in our possession and we now see the dugouts and roads, woods and railway lines we have watched so carefully on the map.[26]

Lieutenant-Colonel G. R. H. Cheape, commanding the 14th RIRifles, argued that in future, mopping-up should be carried out by men from the battalion that was attacking, rather than by other units, to avoid confusion over lines of command. However, nothing could detract from the gains made on the day. As Major H. F. N. Jourdain noted on 8 June, 'The Rout of the Hun was very complete.'[27]

As regards casualties, the 7th Leinsters lost only 13 men at Messines, only one of whom appears to have come from West Belfast, Private P. McLoughlin of McDonnell Street.[28] Another 92 men and ten officers were wounded. The 6th Connaughts lost just five men (with just one of these, Private John McKenna, hailing from Belfast), with a further 32 wounded and two missing. There were clear advantages to mopping up, although even the 1st Royal Munster Fusiliers out in front of the Connaughts had also lost only five men that day. In the 14th RIRifles, 41 men and two officers were killed, among them Rifleman Johnston Simpson of Battenberg Street, who had already been wounded three times.[29] For the moppers-up of the 15th RIRifles, fatalities were ten men and no officers.[30]

The 9th RIRifles' casualties for the day were five officers wounded, with 21 other ranks killed, 93 wounded and one missing (later found dead). Compared to the Somme, these casualties were light. The records of the dead men show how far the character of the 9th Rifles in terms of its Belfast connections had changed by this point. Of the 22 dead, ten had transferred into the battalion from other regiments: six from the Norfolk Regiment, three from the London Regiment and one from the King's Royal Rifle Corps. These men had enlisted in places like Norwich, King's Lynn, Battersea, Hackney and Bethnal Green and had no apparent Ulster connection of any kind, although one was from Limerick. Their role had been to fill the boots left by earlier casualties. Of the other 12 men who died at Messines, six were definitely from West Belfast: Lance-Sergeant John Brown (Bellevue Street), and Riflemen Robert Best, J. Lyness (both Ghent Street), Samuel Matier (Ainsworth Avenue), William Frazer (Northumberland Street) and William McCracken (Matchett Street).[31] The mother of Matier received a standard letter from a chaplain, E. J. McKee, which said, 'His sacrifice has not been in vain as our victory was substantial and complete.'[32]

Indeed, more from West Belfast were killed in the 8th RIRifles, which was notionally linked with East Belfast. There were seven of these, including 38-year-old Rifleman Thomas Kyle, who had been commander of half a company in the West Belfast UVF prior to the war, while working as chief pay clerk in the weaving department of the New Northern Spinning and Weaving Company. His wife, Eveleen, was left with three children in Mountcashel Street in Woodvale.[33] That Kyle was in the 8th RIRifles shows how far the local divisions even within the Ulster Division had been broken down by Messines. Meanwhile, the casualty figures for the 2nd RIRifles illustrate its continued link to West Belfast. It lost 23 men and two officers on 7 June. Four were from West Belfast: Bugler David Ayre and Riflemen William John Finn, Samuel Gibson, and Patrick O'Donohoe, of Coates, Paris, Beresford and Waterford Streets respectively.[34] The relatively light casualties meant that the days after 7 June were not nearly as bleak for West Belfast as in July 1916, but there would still have been an air of mourning in that part of the city after the success at Messines.

Some mourning elsewhere in Ireland focused on a figure who has become symbolic of the collaboration between the 16th and 36th divisions: Major Willie Redmond. He was brother of John Redmond, and also a Nationalist MP, and

Officer's letter to Mrs Matier, mother of Samuel Matier, 9th RIRifles,
KIA at Messines (Somme Heritage Centre)

was serving in 16th Division in the 6th Royal Irish Regiment. Aged 56, he had previously been discouraged from leading his men into battle, but he did so on 7 June and was wounded in the leg and wrist. Stretcher-bearers of the 36th Division took him to an aid post, where he died after being given the last rites by a chaplain, also of the 36th, which by this time contained many Catholics. In the months to come, officers and men of both divisions took part in tributes to Redmond, but in Ireland his memory was soon eclipsed by that of the leaders of the Easter Rising.[35]

11

Mud

*There's all this emphasis on the Somme, and while it was unique because
of the slaughter, I still had some happy times there . . . But a place like
Ypres was never like that. Ypres was hell from beginning to end.*

JACK CHRISTIE, STRETCHER-BEARER IN THE 36TH (ULSTER) DIVISION

Messines was a triumph for the 36th and 16th divisions, yet over the next year
reorganizations took place that saw the end of the 9th RIRifles, 7th Leinsters
and 6th Connaughts. Consequently, during 1917 and 1918, West Belfast men
were scattered across different army units more than ever before. Some served
well away from the Western Front. Private Henry Hesketh of Malcolmson Street
was with the 1st Connaught Rangers in Mesopotamia when he succumbed to
heat-stroke in August 1917. He lies in a grave in Baghdad.[1] Closer to home, Stoker
1st Class Albert Brewer of Bellevue Street was lost at sea when HMS *Penshurst*
was torpedoed by a U-boat off the Bristol Channel on Christmas Eve 1917.[2]
Losses from the U-boat war escalated, and there were several other West Belfast
naval deaths in early 1918. George Ross of Woodvale Avenue was First Mate on
the Mercantile Marine ship SS *Teelin Head* when it was attacked by a submarine
on 21 January 1918.[3] Two days later, Private William Campbell of Fingal Street
was serving with the Royal Marine Light Infantry on the SS *Baykerran* when it
went down off Nova Scotia.[4] On 31 January, Isaac Gibson of Tennent Street was
serving in the engine room of HM Submarine K.17 when it collided with HMS
Fearless in the North Sea off the Firth of Forth. All hands were lost, and the site
of the wreck is now protected against pilfering by the Protection of Military
Remains Act (1986).[5]

There were also men in the Royal Flying Corps 52 men (including four dead)
from West Belfast show up in various records as having served in the RFC and
its successor, the Royal Air Force, but those records are far from complete, so
there would have been more, possibly many more. Meanwhile, because the bulk
of the names come from Presbyterian records, the RFC/RAF evidence that we
have may disguise a further story of side-by-side service by Protestants and
Catholics. Of the four who were killed, one died without ever reaching the front.
Sergeant George Dunville of the Grosvenor Road was training in Grantham on
5 September 1917 when his aeroplane crashed. At an inquest, an eyewitness told
how Dunville, flying solo, 'had looped several times, and then ascended to about
4,000 for a spin, when the left wing of the aeroplane broke. This caused him to
lose control, and it spun to the ground.'[6]

Other deaths in England were caused by the enemy. On the night of 3 September 1917, the Germans carried out their first night-time air raid on the UK. One West Belfast man who may have thought that the navy was a safer option than the army lost his life in the raid on Chatham in Kent. Stoker 1st Class Robert Anderson of Ghent Street had served in the army in both the retreat from Mons and the Marne but had later transferred into the navy. He served on a mine-sweeper and patrol boats, and was torpedoed at least three times.[7] The raid was carried out by four Gotha IV aircraft, and the switch to night bombing came after the Gothas of the 'England Squadron' had suffered heavy losses the previous month. Their target was fully lit as an air raid warning had been ignored. Two bombs landed on a drill hall at the Royal Naval Barracks, which was being used as a dormitory. The roof of the hall was largely glass and the men asleep in hammocks stood little chance of survival: 132 were killed.[8]

However, most casualties continued to come from the Western Front. Battalions that fought at Messines had time behind the lines in July, but they were then regularly at the front and also training. From the 6th Connaughts, Captain Stephen Gwynn MP returned to speak to his constituents at Castlegar. He had a poor reception, with both eggs and stones thrown at him – a sign of how far nationalists were losing faith with the Irish Parliamentary Party and were rapidly moving over to Sinn Féin.[9] On 12 July, the anniversary of the Battle of the Boyne was marked by the 9th RIRifles with parades and sports. Meanwhile, the 6th Connaughts trained around Locre, while the 7th Leinsters did so at Tatinghem. Battalion sports proved hazardous for Rowland Feilding, who was thrown from his horse and taken to hospital on 2 July. He did not resume command of the battalion until mid-September. By the end of July, previously excellent weather had turned bad. The rain was so heavy on Sunday 29 July that it was too wet even for church parades.

This was a sign of things to come at the third battle of Ypres, better known as Passchendaele. Billy Ervine, who interviewed many veterans, says that 'During my many conversations with First World War veterans, almost all have expressed the opinion that Passchendaele was worse than the Somme.'[10] One of those veterans, Jack Christie, even said that while he had some happy times on the Somme, 'Ypres was never like that. Ypres was hell from beginning to end.'[11] George McBride of the 15th RIRifles recalled, 'It was awful, we were up to our knees in muck and water . . . I was glad to see the back of it.'[12]

When the battle began on 31 July, the 2nd and 9th RIRifles and 47th Brigade were in reserve. It was expected that the 9th RIRifles would advance once the 55th Division had gained ground, while 47th Brigade would do the same behind the 15th Division. Yet both the 55th and 15th divisions, after some initial progress, were driven back by the Germans. Due to heavy rain, a further attack was postponed. Instead, the Ulster Division moved towards the front at the Wieltje sector on 2 August. In six days there they were under constant German shell-fire. According to Cyril Falls, a member of the division's General Staff, the heavy rain on 31 July had made the area a 'sea of mud'. Wieltje was clearly seared on

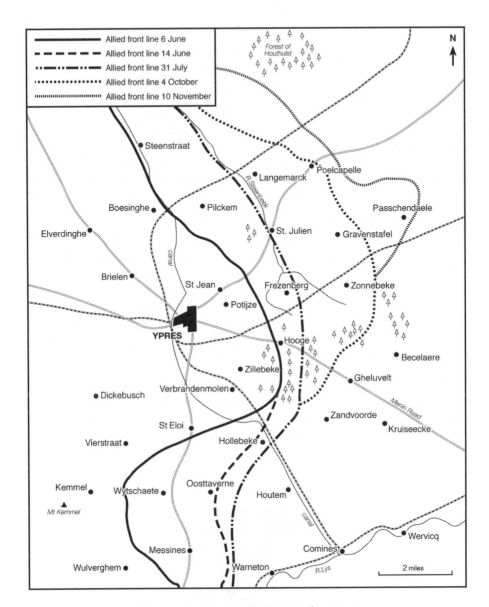

Map 7 Ypres front, June–November 1917

his memory when he wrote, 'Wieltje dug-outs! Who that saw it will forget that abominable mine, with its ... water that flowed down its main passages and poured down its wall ... its smells, its huge population of men – and of rats?' Even the paths leading back from the trenches had their share of horrors. Falls wrote that dead bodies did not affect men greatly, but that one spectacle, 'the mangled remains of a complete party of artillery carriers, six men and twelve horses ... burnt itself upon the brains of those who saw it'.[13]

Meanwhile, 47th Brigade had moved to the front in the Frezenberg sector, close to the Ulster Division. As 'the rain poured incessantly', the 6th Connaughts found all the trenches 'in a terrible condition' and worked as stretcher-bearers helping the 55th Division search for wounded men. The war diary noted on 6 August that conditions were 'as adverse as could be imagined' with 'the ground a sea of mud' and shelling constant. Twenty-four men were lost in the 6th Connaughts between 2 and 11 August. Three of these, Lance-Corporal Patrick McKillen and Privates Thomas English and James McIlwee, were Belfast recruits. Both McKillen and English came from the Falls, the former from Oranmore Street, the latter from Balaclava Street, and McKillen had received the divisional certificate for gallantry in 1916.[14]

The 2nd RIRifles joined the fray on 10 August at Westhoek, having spent the previous five days under shell-fire in the trenches. At 4.35 a.m. they advanced behind a barrage and secured two concrete dugouts, taking the Germans by surprise to gain a strong-point that might otherwise have cost many lives. The battalion then secured its next objective and consolidated. The war diary described how the Germans fled and were therefore 'annihilated' in the British barrage.[15] The 2nd RIRifles then held the line at Westhoek against successive German counter-attacks which were broken up first by artillery and then by the action of men in the trenches repelling German patrols. With the consolidation accomplished, the depleted battalion was withdrawn from the line on the night of 11 August. Although the initial advance had been relatively easy, the counter-attacks had taken their toll, as had the shelling before the advance. Forty men were killed over 10 and 11 August, and wounds accounted for hundreds more. The battalion had gone to Ypres on 4 August with 15 officers and 459 men; seven

L/Cpl Patrick McKillen, 6th Connaught Rangers, 60 Oranmore Street,
DoW 7 August 1917 (*Belfast Evening Telegraph* 26 September 1916, p. 3)

days later their fighting strength was just ten officers and 148 men. Among the dead were three West Belfast men: Lance-Corporal James Donaldson from Ton Street in the Falls, and two Shankill men, Riflemen John Greer from Weir Street and Kennedy Wilkinson from Bristol Street.[16]

Although conditions remained terrible at the front, 16 August was set for the attack that became known as the Battle of Langemarck. In the days leading up to this, 107th Brigade as a whole was in the front line, as it was to be a reserve brigade in the attack which would see the Ulster Division in the middle next to the 16th on their right. On the left of the 36th was the 48th Division. Leading the push for the 36th were 108th and 109th brigades, in the latter of which West Belfast men were best represented in the 14th RIRifles. Each battalion was to attack on a 'two-company front'. This involved each company dividing into three platoons. The first two platoons in a company would provide the first wave of the attack. The second wave would then be provided by the third platoons of each company. The remaining two companies in a battalion would provide the third and fourth waves in similar formation. The first target was designated 'green line'. Having taken that, after 20 minutes of consolidation, the third and fourth wave companies would take the final objective. Specific strong-points were identified for attack by 'special platoons' within brigades.

The infantry attack was preceded by a range of assaults on German lines including 'harassing fire', wire-cutting bombardments and gas shells. But the Germans replied in kind. At 4 a.m., the 14th RIRifles came under a heavy barrage. A direct hit on a dugout killed six and left many more wounded. Not all of these could be bandaged as the battalion had run out of dressings. The war diary noted, 'Their sufferings are terrible and we cannot move.'[17] At zero hour, 4.45 a.m. on 16 August, the men of 108th and 109th brigades went over the top behind a creeping barrage. Though the German barrage was fierce, the terrain was also a hazard, with men getting stuck in the mud of shell-holes. There at least they were safe from machine-gun fire from German lines, which seemed unaffected by the British barrage. Equally undamaged was much of the wire that had to be crossed to reach the enemy. Despite British efforts it had been cut in few places. Ensnared by mud and wire, men became sitting targets for the machine-gunners. Some soldiers reached the green line but were unable to hold on. By 10 a.m., they had all been forced to retreat, most going all the way back to British lines. The remaining men were in no fit state for another attack and the brigades dug in where they had started the day, before 107th Brigade relieved them that night. The mud, the uncut wire and countless strong-points undamaged by the British bombardment, combined with continuous heavy fire from the Germans, gave the 36th Division a torrid time at Langemarck.

The 16th Division fared little better. At Langemarck, 47th Brigade was a relief battalion. Both 48th and 49th brigades had led for the 16th Division in the battle from 4.45 a.m. on 16 August. They incurred heavy losses though some ground was temporarily gained. Among those who suffered the effects of gas at Langemarck was Francis McCann, a Boer War veteran of McDonnell Street, of the now merged 7th/8th Royal Irish Fusiliers. On the evening of 16 August, 47th Brigade moved forward to relieve others of their division. There was no question of further advance, so the 6th Connaughts acted as stretcher-bearers. On the evening of 17 August, when the brigade was relieved, they left third Ypres for good. In that first half of August, total casualties for the 6th Connaughts amounted to 249, of whom 25 were dead. The 7th Leinsters had 33 dead. The 47th Brigade as a whole had lost heavily at Ypres: total casualties were nearly 1,000 from 26 July to 19 August, including 117 killed.[18]

Among the 106 dead in the 14th RIRifles were at least 11 from West Belfast.[19] Only three of the 9th RIRifles' 25 dead came from that part of the city, including one former West Belfast UVF member, Rifleman William McComb.[20] One West Belfast man lost in another battalion (the 13th RIRifles) at this time was Sergeant William Henderson of Warkworth Street. Aged 54, he was the oldest known combat death from West Belfast during the war. Henderson was a veteran of the Zulu War of 1879. His only son, Herman, had been killed serving with the 1st Inniskillings in the Dardanelles. William Henderson's widow, Annie, was left with three daughters.[21] Two West Belfast soldiers older than Henderson also

Sgt William Henderson, 13th Royal Irish Rifles, 44 Warkworth Street, Zulu War veteran, DoW 25 August 1917, aged 54 (*Belfast Evening Telegraph* 8 September 1917, p. 6)

died, William Rosbotham (57) and John McManus (64), but Henderson was the oldest to be killed in combat.

Langemarck had broken the Ulster Division and, soon after, the 8th and 9th RIRifles were amalgamated to form a joint battalion. Some men from each unit went elsewhere, especially to the 10th and 15th RIRifles to bring those battalions up to strength.[22] A wider reorganization saw the 1st Royal Irish Fusiliers join 107th Brigade from 4th Division earlier in August, thus ensuring that when the 8th and 9th merged, there would still be four battalions in the brigade. Similar movements took place late in the year in 108th and 109th brigades, with the 2nd RIRifles joining 108th Brigade.[23] Father Gill was disturbed by this: 'The prospect of a change into a political division was not pleasant, nor did the outlook appear very bright.'[24]

One response to the transfer was an assertion of Irishness from the officers of the 2nd RIRifles. John Lucy, now risen from the ranks and returned to the battalion as a second lieutenant, was asked to bring back from leave 'a supply of Irish flags with harps only inscribed on them'. He later wrote that the Ulster Division 'was considered to be poisonously loyal by many of our southern officers, hence the flags'. But when the transfer took place, there was a dinner with officers of the Ulster Division and Lucy recorded, 'They came, and affected no surprise at our very Irish table, decorated with green flags and other national emblems, and we had a very merry evening.'[25] In the ranks, the division had already lost much of its UVF character due to casualties, drafts and mergers.

The new 8th/9th RIRifles itself had a relatively short life, only existing until early February 1918.[26] But in that time it added a further area to the list of those in which the 9th had fought: the front at Havrincourt, a few miles south-west of Cambrai. September 1917 was relatively quiet in that part of the line, with a war diary entry for 16–20 September summing it up: 'Battalion in the trenches, a very good time. 1 OR [other ranks] killed 2 wounded.' Later on 28–30 September, the notes said, 'Very quiet time, 2 OR killed and 3 OR wounded.' It is exceptionally striking, compared to the early days of the war when every death was recorded in the war diary by name, that by the autumn of 1917 a death every day or so counted as a quiet time. By the end of October 1917 the battalion's 1–0 victory over the 1st Royal Irish Fusiliers in a football match was the sort of event that deserved special mention for being out of the ordinary.

Football was a major activity for the Connaughts too. Like the rest of 47th Brigade, they spent much of late August rotating with other units in relatively uneventful periods at the front, but September saw them training behind the lines. The battalion's earlier prowess at football was maintained. The Connaughts had the measure of the 9th Royal Dublin Fusiliers who were on the end of 4–0 and 6–0 drubbings. The 6th Royal Irish Regiment provided tougher opposition, going down only 2–1 to the Connaughts, although in mid-October in the first game of a 'Brigade League', the Connaughts asserted their superiority with a 4–1 win in a return match. When the battalion eventually lost its first game 1–0 to the 2nd Royal Irish Regiment on 16 November, even though it was only a friendly, battalion pride was obviously affronted as the war diary noted that the team 'was by no means up to full strength'.

When at the front, the 6th Connaughts' trenches were in a terrible condition. In late September, Feilding described the trenches he and his men were in as 'more or less a graveyard'. One section was 'lined with tin discs with numbers on them, indicating where soldiers have been buried'. To find the bodies, 'It is not even necessary to dig, for they outcrop in places.'[27] The main engagement with the enemy at this time was through sniping, which took place on both sides. Feilding balked at picking off individual targets. He wrote, 'It is very necessary, but what a callous business it is. I have to order others to do it, but I cannot say I like the idea.' Nevertheless, the Germans sometimes responded in a jocular way to a 'miss' by 'raising and lowering a stick above the parapet'. This ironic kind of camaraderie between enemies developed to such an extent that there was at least one German at whom the 6th Connaughts would not shoot. Feilding described him as 'an exemplary sentry' because he showed no sign of movement except when being relieved. For that reason, Feilding recorded, 'He is not allowed to be shot at, because that would spoil the picture.'[28]

The training that punctuated the Connaughts' football matches was preparation for a British attack at Cambrai, and by mid-November they were rehearsing on a replica of the German trenches. Meanwhile, the 7th Leinsters maintained their reputation as effective raiders. On 16 October about 100 men from the battalion raided German lines with one of its men killed. They obtained useful information about a German position known as 'Tunnel Trench'.

The aim at Cambrai was to break the 'Hindenburg Line' of German defences built largely by Russian forced labour. It included a forward zone of around 1 km in depth, with relatively lightly manned trenches. The aim of this zone was to slow down any British attack through skirmishing, before the main defensive lines consisting of wire up to 100 yards in depth, concrete bunkers, deep trenches and strong-points for machine-gunners. It was a formidable target and so the British decided to use a formidable weapon against it: the tank. Though used as far back as September 1916 on the Somme, Cambrai was the main debut for the tank. Previously, it had only been used after an initial advance, but at Cambrai it was there from the start.

The 16th Division was also involved in the action around Cambrai from the first, but away from the main front launching a diversionary attack at Croiselles Heights. Its aim was to seize control of a 2,000-yard section of Tunnel Trench and Tunnel Support. The former, the target of the 6th Connaughts (the 7th Leinsters being in reserve), was about 30 feet underground, with ferro-concrete pill boxes at the top. The British had designated these Jove, Mars, Vulcan, Juno and Pluto. The first four were the targets of 16th Division.[29]

At 6.20 a.m. on 20 November, a four-minute barrage of the line began. One minute later, B Company of the 6th Connaughts leapt out of the British front line to make the 223-yard journey to Tunnel Trench. A further minute later, A Company left their part of the line, which was closer to the Germans, having only 75 yards to cover. The timing of the charge was dictated by previous experience, which had 'shown that the impetuosity of these men in the attack often carries them forward into our own barrage'. The timing was just right. Both companies entered the German line about half a minute after the barrage had stopped, taking it with few casualties. The men of the Connaughts found the Germans 'in a very dazed condition'. The enemy had expected a gas attack and therefore had their gas masks on. Having secured their portion of Tunnel Trench, the Connaughts attacked Jove and Mars, gaining both 'after slight resistance'. A communication wire was then established between Tunnel Trench and the old front line. In the hours to come, it was damaged on several occasions and subsequently repaired, often under heavy fire.

The trench itself was something of a maze – and in a dire condition after the barrage. Indeed, the men who reached it first 'could hardly believe it was really their objective. The place looked more like a muddy ditch, and had neither duckboards nor fire-bays.'[30] Covering the entrances into the tunnel were only curtains. Off the tunnels were rooms and alcoves from which the Connaughts rounded up 152 prisoners with little resistance. Yet the Germans behind the lines were not willing to surrender their ground so lightly and counter-attacked for several hours beginning within 40 minutes of the attack. The enemy came from German lines in tunnels connected to Tunnel Trench and fighting was 'almost hand to hand'. Heavy losses were inflicted on the Connaughts. One platoon lost its commander with 26 of its 28 men killed or wounded. When the Connaughts ran out of British bombs, they scrabbled around for German ones and kept going with those. In an incredible act of bravery, Private Kieran White moved close to the area from which the Germans were throwing bombs, caught some of the bombs in mid-air, and threw them back before they had exploded. For this, he was awarded the Distinguished Conduct Medal.

With munitions running out after an hour in Tunnel Trench, the Connaughts were forced to withdraw from Jove and consolidate at Mars. But by 8.30 a.m. supplies of bombs arrived at the front and the Connaughts consolidated their position before being relieved by the 7th Leinsters on the evening of 22 November, having suffered 34 killed and 109 wounded. Four were Belfast men: Privates Francis McCoy, Joseph McKay, John Mellon and John Short. On 23 November, the Leinsters regained Jove and found many of the Connaught dead in that area. The 6th Connaughts' war diary notes, 'One of our dead was actually found locked in grips with a dead German.' It had been a ferocious battle. Feilding's impression of the trenches in which the men had fought was that 'Each time I see this kind of thing I think it is worse than the last time.'[31] Given the tendency of people to adapt to horrific conditions, that is a telling remark on how bad life in the trenches had become.

No tanks had been involved in 47th Brigade's part of the battle of Cambrai, but they were central in the area covered by 36th Division, and there were about 200 in the battle as a whole. For the 8/9th RIRifles, the battle did not properly begin until two days after the Connaughts. On 20 November, 107th and 108th brigades had been in reserve while 109th was at the front. In that action, the 14th RIRifles lost only two men, and having advanced at 6.20 a.m., the 36th Division was in place in the front section of the Hindenburg Line in under two hours as the Germans fled in the face of the tanks.[32] However, during the course of the day, German machine-gun fire slowed down the advance to a near stalemate.

On 23 November, the attack was renewed with 107th Brigade joining the fray. At 10.30 a.m. that morning, four platoons from the 8th/9th RIRifles attacked 'Lock 5' and 'Round Trench'. Close by, men from the 10th and 15th RIRifles, supported by two tanks, renewed their attack on the Hindenburg Support Line. But one of the tanks broke down, and the other turned the wrong way and left the battalion. So while the men of the 8/9th gained their objective (helped by a fully operational tank), the 10th and 15th failed to break through.[33] The remainder of the 8/9th had been due to follow behind them, with the 1st Royal Munster Fusiliers, to take Quarry Wood. But the failure to take the entire Hindenburg Support Line meant that the 8/9th came under heavy machine-gun fire and were forced to lie down in the open having made little progress. In the middle of the afternoon they were ordered to withdraw. Meanwhile, the 2nd RIRifles had fought its way into the village of Moevres in support of the 12th RIRifles, but had been forced to withdraw because they had no support on their flanks. It was here that Second Lieutenant William Rainey, a Shankill man who had risen through the ranks, lost his life.[34] The other 12 men lost that day included Rifleman Walter Erskine from Sancroft Street who had been wounded the previous year.[35]

By the time 107th Brigade handed over their part of the front to 109th Brigade on 26 November, the weather was difficult to bear. Persistent rain changed into snow and 'swept almost horizontally before a wind that rose at times to tempestuous force'.[36] During that brief involvement at Cambrai, the 8th/9th RIRifles lost 26 men with around 150 further wounded.[37] There was, however, also a contingent of West Belfast men in the 15th RIRifles, which had received some transfers from the 9th when the latter was disbanded. They included Rifleman Isaac Burns of Brownlow Street. Burns had served with the 15th on the Somme and had been saved from a bullet by a Testament carried in his breast-pocket. However, at Cambrai, his luck ran out. First reported missing, he was not officially presumed dead until late August 1918.[38]

In the two months following Cambrai, the 8th/9th Rifles lost another 11 men, all on different days – the 'quiet' days noted in the war diary. The battalion took part in no further offensives, although it was regularly at the front around Cambrai. Much of the men's time at the front was spent clearing and repairing trenches that were in a terrible state due to the weather. They also worked on clearing roads behind the lines.[39] When the Ulster Division reorganized in January and February 1918, several regular battalions joined, and the 8/9th RIRifles was one of five battalions to be disbanded. The choice of which battalions to disband was influenced partly by a desire to ensure that as much of Ulster as possible remained represented in the division but there were also some concerns over the capabilities of the 14th RIRifles.[40] Men from the disbanded battalions filled gaps throughout those battalions remaining in the division. Two officers and 123 other ranks went into the 2nd RIRifles from the 8th/9th. Others went into three new 'entrenching battalions', in the case of the men of the 8/9th, the 21st Entrenching Battalion, where they joined the remnants of the 10th RIRifles and 10th Royal Inniskilling Fusiliers. Men from the 14th went into 23rd Entrenching Battalion.[41]

Some went into the Labour Corps. One of these, who may have transferred from the 9th, was Rifleman John B. Smyth. A former member of the West Belfast UVF and an Orangeman, he was awarded the Ulster Division certificate in January 1918 'for devotion to duty'. This award was made when a German aeroplane bombed a railway, killing the person directing the traffic over it, at which point Smyth took charge, 'got the traffic moving in both directions, and completed the dead man's tour of duty.'[42] However, most transfers from the RIRifles at this time seem to have been into entrenching battalions and eventually there were 25 such units. They were formed from early 1918 with the aim of providing a home for 'surplus' men from disbanded regimental battalions. Their main purpose was to provide labour for work on defences but they also supplied men to cover losses in front-line battalions.

The result of these reorganizations was that the Ulster Division bore little resemblance to the UVF division of 1915–16, and not only because brigades now consisted of three rather than four battalions. Of the Belfast RIRifles battalions, only the 15th (North Belfast) still existed, joined in 107th Brigade by the 1st and 2nd regular battalions of the RIRifles. The 108th Brigade retained the 9th Royal Irish Fusiliers (originally formed from the Armagh, Cavan and Monaghan UVF), and the 12th (Central Antrim) RIRifles, but it was now supplemented by the 1st Royal Irish Fusiliers, another regular battalion. Meanwhile, in 109th Brigade, only the 9th Inniskillings, formed from the Tyrone UVF, remained, joined by the two regular battalions of the same regiment. As a result, Father Gill noted in March 1918, 'A census of "religions" ... showed that in the Ulster Division ... there were between 3,000 and 4,000 Catholics.' He added with evident pleasure that whereas 'When this Division came from Ireland their boast was that there was not a single R.C. in their ranks!' they now had four Jesuit chaplains and three interpreters who were French priests.[43]

There were also major changes in the 16th Division. At the end of January 1918, five battalions were wound up, including the 7th Leinsters. Two battalions joined the division, the 2nd Royal Munster Fusiliers and the 2nd Leinsters. This allowed the division to be reconfigured, like the rest of the army, into brigades of three battalions each. The 6th Connaughts remained in 47th Brigade, joined by the 2nd Leinsters and 1st Munsters. The largest number (15 officers and 330 men) transferred in bulk from the 7th Leinsters into their regiment's 2nd battalion, so they continued to be part of 47th Brigade.[44] But 200 others went into the 19th Entrenching Battalion[45] and others found themselves moved to the 11th Hampshires. Carson's Ulster Division and Redmond's Irish Brigade now existed in name only.

12

Retreat

*There was a most unusual and dense fog, which made it impossible
to make our way. With shells falling all around, the journey was not a
pleasant one.*

FATHER HENRY GILL, 2ND RIRIFLES

In the spring of 1918, Germany nearly won the war. From late 1917 it had strengthened its forces on the Western Front as Tsarist Russia collapsed and the war in the east ended. On 21 March, Germany launched what is now known as the 'Spring Offensive', gaining 40 miles of Allied ground in their first thrust. Eventually, they came within 50 miles of Paris, putting the city within range of their artillery. Over 300 shells landed on the French capital.

The British army that faced this advance was nothing like the army of 1914–16. It was partly a conscript army, although the extension of conscription (introduced in Britain for men aged 18–41 in May 1916) to Ireland in April 1918 was vigorously opposed in an Irish general strike and was never implemented.[1] Reorganizations and casualties saw all but one of the Belfast battalions of the Ulster Division disbanded in February 1918, along with the 7th Leinsters. Recruits from Great Britain increasingly swelled the ranks of the Ulster Division.[2] Meanwhile, since the Somme, men from West Belfast were increasingly in regular battalions of the army as new recruits from Ireland were sent to regular rather than service battalions. Throughout 1917, it is likely that more men were still in volunteer battalions than anywhere else. In 1918 that changed. The 6th Connaught Rangers survived as a fighting unit until April 1918, but most West Belfast men were elsewhere. The 2nd RIRifles, which had carried the flag for West Belfast in 1914–15, did so once again.[3] Those who remained in a volunteer battalion were now with the 15th RIRifles, which had once been notionally linked to North Belfast.

They faced a German offensive that had three distinct phases. First, the *Kaiserschlacht* offensive in late March centred on Arras. That was followed by an attack in Flanders on the Lys in April, and then the Aisne in May. The initial attack deployed infiltration tactics. 'Stormtroopers' bypassed heavily defended front lines and attacked weaker rear positions. In the ensuing confusion, the regular infantry attacked the front. The advance was also aided by a heavy creeping artillery barrage, which made great use of gas shells, and the advancing soldier's natural friend, the morning mist.

The 6th Connaughts were among the first caught in the advance, alongside the

2nd Leinsters, which contained some remnants of the 7th. For both battalions, the four months since Cambrai had been relatively quiet, in and out of the front line around Lempire and Ronssoy. They faced shell-fire at night, and periodic patrols checked the enemy's wire, but little else happened. Then, on 19 March, newly captured German prisoners said that an attack was imminent. The private diary of Major Raynsford, second in command of the 6th Connaughts, noted that the prisoners 'reported all sorts of horrors impending for us'. A day later, no attack had come and Raynsford was told by divisional HQ that there was 'no likelihood' of any German attack coming on the division's front.[4] Clear plans existed for what should happen in the event of a German offensive: 48th and 49th brigades would hold the front, around the settlements of Ste Emilie and Villers Faucon, and the 6th Connaughts would counter-attack. As Feilding later noted, 'A retreat was the one possibility that had never occurred to us.'[5]

At 4.30 a.m. on 21 March, a heavy German bombardment of 47th Brigade's positions began. Feilding noted with evident satisfaction that there were no casualties, 'and though on one occasion a large shell hit a field kitchen, throwing the cook, the latter picked himself up and continued cooking the men's breakfast'. However, the bombardment did make communications between brigades and battalions exceptionally difficult.[6] When, soon after 1 p.m., Feilding was ordered to report to 49th Brigade HQ, disaster ensued. On the way there, he met the Commanding Officer of the 1st Royal Munster Fusiliers, Lieutenant-Colonel Kane, who said that his battalion and Feilding's were to launch a joint counter-attack. This was confirmed when Feilding reached his destination: their aim was to regain Ronssoy, which had been lost in the first wave of the German offensive. Feilding's instincts told him that a precise time for the attack was necessary but 49th Brigade HQ said that the two battalions should operate semi-independently and Feilding was told to return to the Connaughts as soon as possible and order the attack. One of the battalion's officers, Second Lieutenant Desmond McWeeney, subsequently questioned the logic of the order, arguing that any ground regained would be 'no more than a line of outposts which had been completely obliterated'.[7] At 3.45 p.m. the battalion advanced. C Company spotted soldiers to their right, where the Munsters should have been, but they were Germans and a fight ensued. All of C Company's officers and most of the men became casualties and those left standing were forced to retreat to their starting-point. The Connaughts might have feared that the Munsters had been wiped out, but in fact they had never advanced, neither had two tanks that were supposed to assist. Later that evening, Feilding discovered that the entire counter-attack had been cancelled and the tanks sent elsewhere. While the orders had reached the Munsters, they had not arrived in Feilding's hands. Commenting on the orders that had made the Connaughts advance, Desmond McWeeney later said, 'Such rigidity of mind was worthy of the Crimean War and this, combined with an inability to see that the situation was long past a local solution, ensured the destruction of the Battalion.'

Like the 6th Connaughts, the 2nd RIRifles had also received hints of an offensive. Fr Gill noted that two soldiers came over from German lines on the afternoon of 20 March and said that an attack would begin at midnight.[8] They were not far wrong. In the battalion's part of the line near Saint Quentin, there was a bombardment throughout the night, intensifying from 6 a.m. Being ordered to move to the front, Gill wrote later, 'There was a most unusual and dense fog, which made it impossible to make our way. With shells falling all around, the journey was not a pleasant one. Soon we had to put on our gas masks, which made things much worse.'[9] By early afternoon on 21 March, the battalion had dug in and was ordered to recapture the village of Contescourt. As with the 6th Connaughts, the order to attack was countermanded without reaching the battalion in time, and following heavy losses, the battalion retired to defensive positions overnight.

Close to the 2nd RIRifles were their 107th Brigade comrades the 15th RIRifles. Having been bombarded from 4 a.m. on 21 March, they were attacked and surrounded at an area known as Ascot Redoubt at around 9 a.m. The battalion held off the attack for much of the day. Second Lieutenant Robert Sprott from Woodvale Road was a former sergeant in the 11th RIRifles but had become an officer in mid-1917. He was one of those who held off the Germans, but later told how the enemy had forced their way into the centre of the redoubt making it impossible to defend. The garrison surrendered, and for Sprott and others a prison camp beckoned.[10]

The Connaughts dug in overnight like the 2nd RIRifles, but faced a heavy barrage again the next morning (22 March). By this time it was becoming difficult for Feilding to keep track of events elsewhere at the front as runners were coming under heavy fire. When information did eventually reach battalion HQ it was often hours old. The Connaughts desperately tried to hold a line near to the road between Villers Faucon and Ste Emilie, alongside battalions as diverse as the 1st Munsters, the 11th Hampshires, the 13th Royal Sussex and 1st Hertfordshires. Divisional boundaries and organization had thoroughly broken down. Later, both the 16th and 36th divisions would be criticized for not performing well at this time, although circumstances were against both of them.[11]

For the Connaughts, steady retreat and hard fighting continued. Officer casualties had been heavy and by 5 p.m. on 22 March Feilding was left in command of a makeshift battalion consisting of 6th Connaughts, 1st Munsters and 2nd Leinsters. Two men were lost through friendly fire on 23 March – an enemy aeroplane dropped a flare on the retreating soldiers, which the British artillery mistook for one of its own markers and fired shrapnel on the target. Yet again, Feilding did not receive up-to-the-minute orders: when he was told that the Munsters had received an order to retreat he believed a mistake had been made. Only later did he learn that Major Raynsford had been sent with orders for the Connaughts but had been injured on the way. Though Feilding had actually met Raynsford after the orders had been issued, the latter 'had just been severely wounded and was being carried back under considerable difficulties on a ground sheet'.

By this time, the 21st Entrenching Battalion, full of men from the former

8th/9th RIRifles and attached to 107th Brigade, had entered the fighting. It was
in reserve when the offensive began.[12] From the village of Villeselve (south-west
of St Quentin) the battalion moved to plug the gap between the 36th and 30th
divisions at the front line. On the morning of 23 March, under the cover of more
thick fog, the Germans broke through at the side of the battalion. Despite making
a counter-attack, the battalion was driven back further. The next day, a British
cavalry attack regained the line lost the day before, but the men then came under
heavy fire from new German machine-gun positions. Over the next four days the
battalion fought hard, sometimes losing ground, sometimes gaining it, generally
digging in somewhere new each day. Ultimately, this willingness on the part of the
entire British line to counter-attack despite heavy losses surprised the Germans
and slowed down their advance.

The defence against the German offensive also depended on the determined
holding of positions by battalions such as the 2nd RIRifles. They held their line
over 22 and 23 March, but on 24 March came under heavy attack close to Cugny
where the battalion was struggling to maintain contact with other units. Cyril
Falls described how, in these circumstances, 'The salient held by the 36th Division
suddenly caved.' But before this, he noted that the 2nd RIRifles had 'enacted a
drama truly heroic which has never been recorded, because, in the days when
reports were written, there was no survivor to tell its story.' Captain J. C. Bryans
later told that story. At about 2 p.m. on the afternoon of 24 March, artillery and
machine-gun fire, supported by low-flying aeroplanes, attacked the battalion.
By the time the German infantry attacked, many men had only their bayonets
left having fired all their rounds. Thus 'a desperate hand-to-hand fight' ensued,
after which the battalion was surrounded. Of the 150 who had faced the attack,
92 were killed.[13] The dead included 13 West Belfast men.[14] Over the next week,
the remnants of the battalion continued to retreat, working with other units
wherever they found them, before being taken away from the front at the end
of the month. At that point, there was great confusion over the precise nature
of casualties. Among the battalion's other ranks, there were 628 missing, ten
confirmed dead, and 64 wounded. In time, it became clear that 128 had been
killed between 21 and 31 March, with most 'missing' actually prisoners.

The rapidity and depth of the German advance can be seen in the positions
of the 15th RIRifles over 23 and 26 March. During that time they held the line
at successive villages as they sought to slow the German advance: Brouchy,
Guiscard, Guerbigny and Erches.[15] That meant a retreat of over 20 miles in just
four days. By the time the battalion was resting behind the lines on 29 March,
71 of its members were dead in a week of hard fighting, including six men from
West Belfast.[16]

In the 6th Connaughts' part of the line, as the Germans attacked, French vil-
lagers hurriedly evacuated villages in the German path. Feilding realized that no
orders had been given to police the abandoned houses 'many of which contained
large stocks of wine'. So he stepped in to provide order 'with the gratifying result
that I neither observed a sign nor heard a single case of looting or drunkenness

throughout the day'. In the early hours of 27 March, word came that French reinforcements were about to pass through British lines to counter-attack the Germans. They did not, however, arrive, and at daylight on 27 March a large German force had broken through a gap between the Connaughts' position and the River Somme. By this time, enough men had regrouped to start to reorganize original battalions and the 6th Connaughts fell back. They set up a new position from which machine-gunners had a clear sight of the Germans. From this position, the Germans were held up for several hours, until fresh British troops began to force them back. Here ended the Connaughts' involvement in the Spring Offensive, and the 2nd Leinsters were also back in billets by 30 March. Just before the fresh troops arrived, Feilding had accidentally fallen over a hidden trip-wire while going forward to issue orders to a Lewis gun company. He dislocated his elbow and had to relinquish command. By the time he was fit again, in August, the 6th Connaughts had been disbanded. Feilding resumed service with the 1/15th London Regiment in August, surviving until the armistice.[17]

Casualties had been heavy in the retreat. In the 2nd Leinsters, approximately 69 men[18] were killed between 21 and 31 March, including one West Belfast transferee from the 7th, Private J. McGrath of Irwin Street.[19] Ninety of the 6th Connaughts were killed, with over 500 more wounded. The dead included the last three Belfast men in the 6th Connaughts to be killed in action: Privates Andrew Bloomer of Norfolk Street, Hugh Malone of the Falls Road[20] and Alexander McCloskey of Currie Street. McCloskey already had three children, Lizzy, Mary and Alex. His wife, Susan, gave birth to a fourth, Brigid, ten weeks after her husband's death.[21] A fourth private, William McConnell of Scotland Street, died of wounds incurred on 24 March a day later.[22]

When the battalion assembled at Aubigny on 31 March with a new Commanding Officer, just five other officers and 150 other ranks remained. The battalion was decimated. Its losses came close to those of the 9th RIRifles on 1 and 2 July 1916 on the Somme. As the army reorganized itself in the wake of the retreat, such a small battalion was an obvious one to be disbanded. That effectively happened on 13 April, when most of the officers and 281 men – numbers swelled by the return of the wounded – joined the 2nd Leinster Regiment, meeting former 47th Brigade comrades who were once in the 7th Leinsters, although that battalion was soon (on 23 April) transferred to 88th Brigade in 29th Division. A small body of HQ officers and transport staff remained in the 6th Connaughts to form a training staff that was attached to American troops at Doudeauville. The small band of men remaining in the 6th Connaught Rangers Training Staff had much expertise to pass on to their new comrades, yet the Americans were all at the front from early July and the training staff became redundant. On 31 July 1918, the 6th Connaughts received the order that they were formally disbanded.

Ultimately, the first phase of the German counter-attack was halted because the Allies cooperated as never before. The French Marshal, Foch, was given command of all Allied forces on 26 March. He sent French troops towards Amiens, the main German target. This, along with a British, Australian and Canadian counter-attack in Moreuil Wood on 30 March, stopped the Germans in their tracks.[23] Meanwhile, the Allies continued to supply their front line with food, munitions and reinforcements, and British soldiers remained confident in their ability to win.[24] Though the Germans made significant gains, they did not sweep all before them. Despite the fact that earlier the Ulster Division had been driven around 20 miles west towards the Montdidier area, their resistance was an important part of the effort that stopped the Germans in their tracks. On 5 April the German offensive was called off after they had failed to take Amiens. Five days before the tide had already turned enough in the Allied direction for the remnants of the 36th Division to be sent north to the coast to rest. In so doing, the 21st Entrenching Battalion was broken up, with its men distributed between the 2nd Royal Inniskilling Fusiliers and the 1st, 2nd and 15th RIRifles.

The German offensive had only just been held back. Thousands of British soldiers had been taken prisoner. What they faced was down to the nature of the Germans who captured them. George McBride of the 15th RIRifles described how 'we were put into a big field which was surrounded by barbed wire, we were then given a bath, had our clothes fumigated and our heads shaved. Then we were given a meal.' He was then taken to Germany, eventually reaching Giessen, where businesses took prisoners for work. For the remainder of the war he worked in a stone quarry in the Black Forest.[25] Another Shankill man, Sergeant Samuel Marshall of Ambleside Street, serving with the Royal Irish Fusiliers, was twice captured and twice escaped.[26] But for many captives, grim conditions beckoned and some died. That fate befell Rifleman Ashley Milne of the 15th RIRifles who was captured in April. He had enlisted underage (at 16) and was in his 19th year. At the end of June, he wrote to his brother that he was working in a salt mine. Possibly to get the letter through the censor he wrote, 'It is a very good job. I get a rate of 4/- per week. It keeps me in fags.' Three weeks later he was dead.[27] In late August, George Tully of the 15th RIRifles died while a prisoner in Limburg. His brothers David and William had been killed on the HMS *Hawke* and at Passchendaele.[28]

Meanwhile, as with an unsuccessful advance, a rapid retreat meant that remains of many dead were never identified and relatives clung on desperately to small hopes. As late as April 1919, the mother of Lance-Corporal William O'Neill of the 2nd Leinster Regiment was still seeking news through newspapers from her home on Bombay Street in the Falls.[29] O'Neill never returned as he had been killed on 26 March 1918. His body was never found, so he is one of those commemorated on the Pozieres memorial. Other families received news much more quickly. Lance-Sergeant William Manning had been born in Ardglass, County Down, and was a prominent hurler and Gaelic footballer. He served with the 10th Royal Dublin Fusiliers, and his mother lived on Kashmir Road in the Falls. In mid-April, she received news of her son's death from an officer who wrote, 'I don't think I ever felt so knocked out about anyone's death. He had applied for his commission, and I can't help thinking that if he had been spared he would have made one of our finest officers.'[30]

Cpl William O'Neill, 2nd Leinster Regiment, 13 Bombay Street, still thought missing in April 1919, KIA 26 March 1918 (*Belfast Evening Telegraph* 19 April 1919, p. 4)

Rfn Ashley Milne, 15th Royal Irish Rifles, 107 Roden Street, captured 21 March 1918, died as PoW 19 July 1918 (Somme Heritage Centre)

The Germans continued to try to win the war with a swift blow at the Allies. Having stalled by early April, they made another effort, which became known as the Battle of the Lys, from 9 April. By this time, it was difficult to find any concentration of West Belfast men in any unit beyond small clusters, even in the Ulster Division. For example, among the 80 lost in the 12th RIRifles (once the Central Antrim Volunteers) on the Spanbroek Ridge between 11 and 17 April, were 13 Belfast men.[31] Among them were six from West Belfast.[32] Writing of 17 April 1918, Cyril Falls of the Ulster Division said that to many observers it 'appeared the blackest day they had seen' as 'Huge slices of territory on which the Germans had never stood, or over which they had never been hustled in retreat, were now in their possession.'[33]

Despite their gains, the Germans sustained heavy casualties in the Lys offensive and came to a halt by the end of April. In May, as the fighting ground on, the pattern of fatalities with West Belfast connections shows how far men were dispersed throughout units. Indeed, no more than two fatalities can be identified in any one unit for the whole month. Private Samuel McAllister of Fallswater Street had been serving with the Royal Army Medical Corps attached to 109th Brigade, but was a prisoner of war when he was killed in an 'aircraft raid'. Gunner Lee Adderley, who died of sickness, served with the Royal Garrison Artillery, and Lance-Corporal James Robinson was killed in action with the 1st Royal Dublin Fusiliers. Company Sergeant-Major William McIlveen was killed in action with the 15th RIRifles, while Rifleman Samuel Hooks died accidentally on a railway line serving with the 990th Area Employment Company.[34]

The final German effort came on 27 May, at the third Battle of the Aisne, which lasted until 6 June. None of the Ulster regiments were drawn into this. As with the previous offensives, the Germans gained a swathe of territory, reaching as far as the Marne. But the previous barriers to advance – Allied counter-attacks, supply problems and, of course, losses in the German ranks – prevented them once more from capitalizing on their gains. When the advance ground to a halt, the Germans would go no further. In fact, the tide was about to turn once and for all in the Allies' favour.

13

Victory

... the spirit of victory, the bright-hued prospect of deliverance, spread among all ranks ...

CYRIL FALLS, ULSTER DIVISION

It is easy to forget that the Allies won the First World War on the battlefields. In the end, the German army was exhausted and dejected as it faced the Allies' superior resources and manpower.[1] Yet military 'victory' is at odds with the images of slaughter and of lions led by donkeys that are so ingrained on public memory.[2] There had been successes in the past, at Messines and Cambrai, which showed that the generals were not quite the plodders they have been held to be by popular history, but the public still resists the rigorous work of revisionist historians.[3] Having narrowly survived defeat in March 1918, the Allies turned the lessons they had learned into a military rout of Germany on the Western Front. From April there were signs that the Germans could be dealt small blows, for example with the raid on Zeebrugge in which several Belfast men took part.[4] But from July 1918, the German army as a whole was driven back towards its homeland. Little more than six months after threatening Paris, the German empire collapsed.

The West Belfast men who drove forwards to victory were dispersed throughout many units. Several of the battalions featured in earlier chapters saw it through to the end and retained links with West Belfast, especially the 1st and 2nd RIRifles, now part of the Ulster Division, alongside the 12th and 15th RIRifles. But there were also small groups of men in other units in the Ulster Division: the 1st Royal Irish Fusiliers, which had transferred there, and 9th Royal Inniskilling Fusiliers, which had always been in it. Meanwhile, the 2nd Royal Irish Regiment, part of 49th Brigade in the 16th Division since October 1916, saw out the war in the 63rd Division. Finally, there was a continued West Belfast presence in the 2nd Leinsters (by now in 29th Division), which had absorbed the two battalions earlier associated with nationalist Belfast. All eight battalions represented West Belfast in some way as the Allies drove forward to victory.

That victory began with two failed German efforts to break through French lines: at the Matz on 11–13 June, and at the Marne on 15 July–3 August. In the latter, the Germans suffered considerably higher casualties than the Allies, which made it difficult for them to consider another offensive in the short term. Meanwhile, from May 1918, the American Expeditionary Force had been working closely with British and French troops, adding much to Allied strength. By summer 1918, the Allies were therefore in a strong position to regain the initiative, and on 8 August they launched the Amiens offensive. General Ludendorff, who had planned the Spring Offensive, later described that day as 'the black day of the German army' as Amiens was captured by Allied forces that advanced as far as five miles in some places. Units from across the British Empire were involved in this initial stage. Serving with the 7th Canadian Infantry (British Columbia Regiment) was a West Belfast émigré, Private Andrew Carson, whose mother lived in the Shankill Road. He died on 10 August of wounds sustained in the advance.[5] But on 12 August, the attack ground to a halt as the Germans reinforced their lines.

Another advance came at Albert on 21 August. The 2nd Royal Irish Regiment was part of an effort to gain ground in the area. Their target was a railway cutting west of Achiet-le-Grand, a few miles north-west of Albert, while other units would take the town itself. The battalion advanced at 4.53 a.m. on 21 August. But they faced thick fog, which made it difficult to maintain a sense of direction. When it lifted, around 10 a.m., strong German resistance was met and the battalion consolidated 500 yards short of its objective. However, reflecting the growing tendency of German soldiers to surrender, 70 prisoners were captured during the daytime advance and a patrol rounded up eight others in the evening. The next day, a strong counter-attack by the Germans was held off, and the line was handed over on 23 August to the 37th Division, which made further advances on Bâpaume. The town was occupied on 29 August, bringing to a close the second Battle of Albert and this phase of the Allied advance.

The 2nd Royal Irish Regiment lost 50 men over two days at Albert, nearly half of whom (23) were from the south of Ireland. Eighteen were English transfers, but among the handfuls of men from Scotland and Wales, there were also five from Ulster, two of whom were from West Belfast. Private Christopher Toner was from Ligoniel Road, part of Shankill ward but on the greenfield edge of West

Pte Christopher Toner, 2nd Royal Irish Regiment, 374 Ligoniel Road, KIA 21 August 1918 (*Belfast Evening Telegraph* 18 January 1919, p. 4)

Belfast. The other man, Private Thomas Waugh, of Ninth Street, had transferred from the 5th RIRifles, a reserve battalion, based in Ireland, earlier in the war. He was missing and not confirmed dead until the end of 1918. His body was never identified.[6]

During July and most of August the Ulster Division was in the relatively quiet Messines Ridge area, and it was not in the earliest Allied advances. On 22 August the 15th RIRifles captured a quarter of a mile, partly because of a successful ruse that fooled the enemy. Instead of using poison gas, which would prevent an advance by British troops until it had cleared, a non-poisonous but similar-smelling substance was sent over German lines. Some Germans retreated, while others were encumbered by respirators when the 15th arrived at their lines. Following this, on 24 August, the 1st and 9th Royal Irish Fusiliers gained further ground, which put the Ulster Division within a thousand yards from the ruined town of Bailleul. The division had expected not to advance further and was due to be relieved. However, on the morning of 30 August, news came that the Germans were withdrawing, and by the afternoon patrols of the division were in the town. The division's relief was shortlived, however, as they received orders for 109th Brigade to advance to take Ravelsberg Hill and the village of Neuve Eglise. In later years, Cyril Falls wrote about the mood of the men at this time. He said it was not true that by this time, the horror of war 'had robbed men of their stores of latent enthusiasm'. While 'defeat and retirement had bred melancholy and bad temper', the prospect of an advance created a new mood. 'Like a flame', he said, 'the spirit of victory, the bright-hued prospect of deliverance, spread among all ranks . . . To go forward, to strike, to make an end – those were the impulses and the hopes that swept through the waiting ranks.' Such good morale seems to be in line with patterns across Irish regiments at the time.[7]

The 36th Division certainly made considerable gains during August to October. The 109th Brigade, supported by the 108th Brigade, took control of their targets on 1 and 2 September. Then on 5 September the Germans retaliated with mustard gas. By this time, many of the advancing soldiers had been fighting for several days with little rest and it was necessary to relieve them.[8] So on 6 September, 107th Brigade was in position at the front and ready to advance. This Brigade included West Belfast men in all three battalions: the 1st, 2nd and 15th RIRifles, and nine fell in the two regular battalions in a successful action to advance in the Hill 63 area under heavy shell-fire and then hold on to it.[9]

By mid-September the Allies scented a decisive victory.[10] On the Western Front, the Hindenburg line was breached on 2 September, and American forces made their numbers tell. Elsewhere, there were advances from Salonica and in Palestine. By the end of the month an armistice was signed with Bulgaria, and the German Chancellor, Hertling, had resigned. To push home their advantage, the Allies planned an attack involving British, French and Belgian troops, with the Ulster Division playing its part from a few miles east of Ypres. The operation became known as the Battle of Ypres 1918. On 28 September, the 29th and 9th divisions, plus the 8th Belgian Division, drove all before them as they advanced behind a creeping barrage, despite heavy rain making the ground difficult. It was in the 29th Division that the 2nd Leinsters took their role. They had endured heavy losses since joining that division on 23 April, with 175 fatalities between then and the end of the war. Most of those were from the south of Ireland, and some were Scottish or English, but there was still a body of men who had enlisted in Belfast (11 of the dead), and some of these were from West Belfast. One was Private Thomas Mullan of Sultan Street[11] who died on 17 September of wounds, probably incurred in action on 4 September when the battalion was in fierce fighting near Ploegsteert. Mullan was one of the men who had transferred from the Connaughts. Others who had transferred from both the Connaughts and the Leinsters took part in the advance on 28 September when the battalion marched to its assembly point near Hooge 'pipers playing and flag flying'. They then also took part in the Battle of Courtrai, specifically at Ledeghem on 14 October, and saw their last action at Staceghem, six days later.

The 109th Brigade joined the battle on 1 October, with the 1st Royal Irish Fusiliers losing 48 men in one day. These included Private William Douglas of Theodore Street in the Falls and Lance-Corporal J. Herron from part of the Crumlin Road on the edge of Shankill ward. The day before, in the 9th Royal Irish Fusiliers, Second Lieutenant Francis Hall of Lonsdale Street was killed. He was a teacher before the war and a graduate of Queen's University, Belfast, who had gained his commission only in June having been a sergeant in the RIRifles.[12]

However, the Germans had not entirely given up, and when 107th Brigade was

Second Lieutenant Francis Hall, 9th Royal Irish Fusiliers, 13 Lonsdale Street, rose through ranks, KIA 30 September 1918 (*Belfast Evening Telegraph* 9 October 1918, p. 4)

moved up to relieve 109th Brigade, both the 2nd and then the 1st RIRifles came under heavy machine-gun fire. The 2nd escaped with eight fatalities on 1 and 2 October, although it lost the same number while in reserve over the next three days. But the 1st lost 43 men and another ten while holding the line during the next two days. Among them was Rifleman David Burdge of Battenberg Street. He was only 19 years old but had been serving for four years, having enlisted in the 14th RIRifles at the outset of the war aged just 15 when working for an engineer. He had earlier been wounded on the Somme on 1 July 1916. The next-of-kin of two of the other fatalities were in the same street in Woodvale ward: Warkworth Street. The parents of Rifleman William Croft lived at no. 7 and the aunt and sisters of Company Sergeant-Major Thomas Bell Willis were at no. 15.[13]

The Ulster Division was again on the advance a week later in the Battle of Courtrai, with the 1st RIRifles entering Moorseele with relatively light casualties on 14 October, taking its German occupiers entirely by surprise. The next day, the 2nd RIRifles captured Heule and entered Courtrai to find that all the bridges crossing the Lys had been destroyed as the Germans left.[14] Over the next two weeks, the Division played its final part in the advance in several key actions. These included the crossing of the Lys on pontoon bridges and advances on villages east of the river. All the battalions of the division took some role, with West Belfast men losing their lives in the 1st Irish Fusiliers, 9th Inniskillings and the 12th and 15th RIRifles.[15] Some of the casualties, like Private Charles Grundy of Disraeli Street serving in the 9th Inniskillings, succumbed to gas which the Germans were deploying heavily. He died of the effects of gas on 27 October, having been wounded twice previously.[16] One of those killed in action was another man who had risen through the ranks through the duration of the war: Second Lieutenant Hubert Victor Jones of Bedeque Street serving with the 12th RIRifles, but once a private in the 14th.[17] One man who survived was a double-medallist, John Dickson of Dover Street, and a sergeant in the 9th Inniskillings, who had enlisted in 1914. He had already won the Military Medal in September 1918 at Neuve Eglise for taking command of a platoon when its officer was lost and going on to capture an enemy position. His bravery was rewarded for action at Heule on 15 October. This time winning the Distinguished Conduct Medal for 'the greatest gallantry and leadership', the medal citation said:

> Time and again he rallied his Platoon, and led them on against heavy machine gun fire, enabling the whole company to get forward.
>
> With only five men left, he succeeded in reaching his objective, and establishing posts on the railway outside the Village and with a Lewis gun put an enemy machine gun out of work. He did fine work.[18]

Dickson's bravery was typical of the actions that ultimately won the war for the Allies, as they were repeated along the front. There was even a West Belfast medal for action in the air at this time, as Lieutenant Robert Sterling of the Royal Air Force, a resident of Glen Eden in Woodvale Park, won the Distinguished Flying Cross.[19]

Lieutenant Robert Sterling DFC, Royal Air Force, Glen Eden, Woodvale Park
(*Belfast Evening Telegraph* 2 November 1918, p. 4)

On 21 October, the Ulster Division's final engagement with the enemy began, as part of the successful effort to cross the River Lys. Among six men killed that day was Rifleman Samuel Reid of the 1st RIRifles, a shop assistant from the Shankill. Aged 23, he had fought throughout the war with the Ulster Division, arriving in France in its first wave in October 1915, and serving in both the 9th and 14th RIRifles.[20] He missed survival by less than a week, for the Ulster Division's war effectively ended on 27 October when its troops were relieved at the front line by 101st Brigade of the 34th Division. Behind the lines, battalions trained and were supplemented with new drafts. Men of the Division continued to die of wounds, but there was no more fighting. Elsewhere the influenza that accounted for millions of lives across Europe started to bite. Lance-Bombardier James Gilliland of Milner Street, serving with V Anti-Aircraft Battery of the Royal Garrison Artillery in Italy, succumbed on 2 November. So did Private Archie Ussher of Jersey Street, serving with the 6th Inniskillings in France.[21]

The last West Belfast man killed in action was probably Sergeant William Stewart of Malt Street on the west's southern edge. A member of the Royal Army Medical Corps' 92nd Field Ambulance, he was killed by a land-mine on 9 November. On 10 November the war diary of the 1st Royal Irish Fusiliers noted 'Rumour peace declared'. On the next day, when news of the armistice came through, the battalion's officers played the 12th RIRifles at rugby. The divisional

Samuel Reid, c. 1915, 1st, 9th and 14th RIRifles, KIA 21 October 1918

history later described the mood about the armistice at the front as being 'without that wild hilarity, wild almost to hysteria, that greeted it in London', speculating that men who had been alert to avoid death so often could hardly believe it was all over.[22]

Despite the armistice, 20 men of the British army were killed in action on 11 November.[23] Another 475 died of illness or wounds. They included Corporal Robert Johnston of Legland Street, Ligoniel, in Shankill ward, a member of the 15th RIRifles.[24] The 2nd Leinsters, though not losing men in doing so, continued to march forwards to the last. Because one condition of the armistice was that the line reached at 11 a.m. on 11 November would be the front line, 88th Brigade tried to secure as much ground as possible. The battalion war diary noted that 'By a dashing exploit' the brigade commander 'with a few cavalrymen' crossed the River Dendre at Lessines, adding, 'Our troops were everywhere received with the greatest enthusiasm.'

Belfast was less able to celebrate the armistice than other cities. The *Belfast Telegraph*, which carried news of the armistice on the evening of Monday 11 November, also included a front-page notice headed 'INFLUENZA OUTBREAK'. The notice, issued on 7 November, stated that the Public Health Committee advised all schools and places of public entertainment to close for ten days. It also advised people to avoid crowds, a warning that remained in place until December.[25]

Despite this, Belfast still greeted the armistice with rejoicing that was, according to the *News Letter*, 'without parallel in the history of the city'. Cheers rang out in shipyards and factories, and workers downed tools to join crowds assembling in the city centre, many singing patriotic songs. Flags and bunting were draped on memorials and from houses. There was a parade of troops stationed at the Victoria Barracks. Celebrations continued into the next day. In the Falls, the *Irish News* said that 'there was a remarkable outburst of enthusiasm', while 'Irish flags of green and gold mingled with the Stars and Stripes and the flags of the Allies in a most effective colour display.' However, there were also incidences of rowdiness (which does not appear to have been sectarian), including the smashing of the interior of a picture house in High Street by shipyard workers, which culminated in the mob demanding a picture show.[26]

Two gatherings on Monday 11 November were more sombre. On the Saturday before, the family of Private John Lynas, a member of Woodvale Cricket and Lawn Tennis Club, placed a small newspaper notice advising that his funeral would be on 11 November, leaving his Woodvale Street home at 2.30 p.m. for Belfast City Cemetery. Lynas, once of the Inniskillings, was a member of a labour corps when he died of pneumonia in a military hospital in Oswestry on 4 November.[27] As the mourners progressed across the Falls to the cemetery, his wife, Harriet, may have had mixed feelings about an armistice that had come too late for her husband to return home alive. In the Shankill graveyard, Ambrose Sterling, a North Belfast resident, was also being buried. He had twice tried to enlist underage but been refused. But even though he was just 14 when he enlisted in the Royal Flying Corps in 1918, he was well over six feet tall and had been shaving since he was 12. While serving in France, it was flu that felled Sterling and led his family to the Shankill graveyard on the day war ended.[28] For many other families the armistice was only the beginning of anxiety over whether or not their loved ones had survived.

14

Peace and Partition

He was sent for a medical and was asked by someone to jump over a chain. My Dad . . . told them he had been jumping over barbed wire fences for four years and flatly refused.

MARY CLOSE ON THE PENSION APPLICATION OF HER FATHER, JOHN DICKSON, EX-ROYAL INNISKILLING FUSILIERS

. . . he was wont to say 'so much for the land fit for heroes'.

MARIE TONER MOORE ON DANIEL MCKEOWN, EX-ROYAL IRISH FUSILIERS

He is an ex-soldier, but, unfortunately the experience here is that many ex-soldiers with good war records became I.R.A. criminals.

POLICE FILE ON PATRICK BARNES, EX-ROYAL IRISH RIFLES

The war's impact on some families was devastating. The three Quinn brothers of North Boundary Street never returned.[1] George and Susannah Tully of Bristol Street in the Shankill lost three sons, David, George and William, with only Joseph returning. He had served in the RAF.[2] Margaret Conlon of Omar Street in the Falls had lost two sons: James, who died of tuberculosis in 1918 after long service in the 6th Connaughts; and Owen of the 6th RIRifles, who died at Gallipoli in 1915. Her husband, also Owen, had enlisted in the 6th Connaughts and also served in the Leinsters. It appears that he survived his service, and was out before the end of the war, but by the time James died, he was the 'late' Owen Conlon in the *Irish News*.[3]

Yet there were certainly plenty of ex-soldiers back in Belfast. We forget that across Britain and Ireland, most soldiers did return. Probably 722,785 men were killed of (again, probably) 6,146,574 British and Irish who served in the war. That makes 87.1 per cent survivors (including 27.27 per cent wounded), and 11.76 per cent dead overall.[4] Estimates for the precise number of dead across Ireland range from as many as 49,000 to as few as 25,000, from between 172,000 and 210,000 serving. Across Ulster, the fatality rate as a percentage of those eligible to serve was probably only around 3 per cent.[5] However, if Ulster matched the rest of the UK, and there is no reason why it should not have, the losses were more marked in particular age groups. In England and Wales, nearly 37.15 per cent of the deaths came in the 20–24 age range, accounting for 15.1 per cent of those of that age who actually served.[6]

Margaret O'Connor,	Owen Conlon Jnr	Owen Jnr and
Owen Conlon Snr and Jnr		James Conlon
Margaret Conlon		

The Conlon family of 8 Omar Street. Centre Private Owen Conlon Jr was killed with the 6th Royal Irish Rifles at Gallipoli on 10 August 1915. Sgt James Conlon died in June 1918 after discharge from the 6th Connaughts. It appears that this also happened to Owen Conlon Senior.

In the years that followed the war's end, ex-soldiers returning to Belfast lived through tumultuous times. They witnessed the partition of Ireland and the creation of the Northern Ireland state. They saw the 'Troubles' and 'Pogroms' of the early 1920s on the streets of Belfast. Some of the veterans would be active participants in the policing of these episodes, whether as regulars or 'Specials'.[7] Some joined paramilitary groups, including the Irish Republican Army, deploying their military training against the British state they had once served. Others simply suffered whether through illness, wounds or unemployment. Few found that the land to which they had returned was fit for heroes.

As survivors began to return home, the country was plunged into a general election campaign as Lloyd George sought a mandate to continue the wartime coalition government. Boundary changes saw Joseph Devlin's West Belfast seat carved up into smaller units. Although the new Falls seat was theoretically safer for Devlin, he was challenged by Sinn Féin's Eamon de Valera, the future President of the Republic of Ireland. In the Shankill seat, Unionism presented itself as 'The Soldiers' and Workers' friend', with Samuel McGuffin standing as 'The Labour Unionist Candidate'.[8] Three issues dominated: a desire to punish Germany, the needs of ex-servicemen and Home Rule. On the latter, Nationalists and Unionists used the sacrifice of the war as part of their case for either backing or defeating Home Rule. In Devlin's case, Home Rule was popular: he polled 8,488 to de Valera's 3,245.[9] But across Ireland, Sinn Féin won 73 seats to only seven for the Nationalists. Even for some who had joined the British army, both the consequences of the Easter Rising and postwar events in Belfast had a radicalizing effect, which drove them away from nationalism towards republicanism.

However, for many veterans peace did not mean the end of military service. The records of the Royal Irish Fusiliers, which had relatively low numbers of West Belfast men compared to other Irish regiments, show at least 46 West Belfast men with postwar service in the regiment.[10] Consequently, the war's end did not mean the end of deaths in service. Belfast soldiers had already been lost in Russia: one was Sergeant John Agnew, who was serving with the American army, having joined it in Michigan, and though buried in France is remembered on the family headstone in Belfast City Cemetery.[11] After the armistice, British forces continued to fight in Russia for the 'White' Russians against the Bolsheviks. Private John Harvey of the Royal Army Medical Corps had served with the Ulster Division, and after the war was attached to 238th Infantry Brigade serving in north Russia. His mother lived in Carlow Street and in October 1919 was desperately seeking information after he was posted missing from 11 August.[12]

Meanwhile, the former front was still a dangerous place to be and illness was rife. Corporal Thomas Shields of North Boundary Street died of influenza in Dar es Salaam (in part of German East Africa now covered by Tanzania) on 8 December 1918 while serving with the Royal Engineers.[13] Sapper W. J. Wilkinson of Barton Street drowned on 26 December while serving in an Inland Water Transport unit of the Royal Engineers.[14] Another Royal Engineer, Sapper John Ritchie of Silvio Street, died at Courtrai in an accidental petrol explosion on 13 February 1919.[15] Sergeant Thomas Stephenson from Cupar Street, a DCM winner and Boer War veteran, had served with both the 14th RIRifles and a battalion of the Royal Irish Fusiliers. He died on 2 March 1919 of pneumonia.[16] There were also men who succumbed to wounds well after the end of the war. One was Arthur Hill of Enfield Street, declared dead on 1 July 1916, but actually alive as a prisoner. He returned to Belfast after the war but only lived until August 1919, when he was given a full military funeral with his coffin carried on a gun carriage to Belfast City Cemetery.[17] It was not until 4 August 1921 that Gunner William Dunlop of Wilson Street, once of the Royal Field Artillery, died aged 27 of sickness resulting from the effects of gas poisoning five years before.[18]

For some families, peace meant a continued agonizing wait for news, or the safe return of prisoners of war. The parents of Samuel Reid, of the 1st RIRifles, knew that their son had gone missing on 21 October 1918. They travelled to southern England to search hospitals there, in the hope that their son might be unable to identify himself but still alive. It was another year before they were able to confirm his death.[19] Survivors like David Spence of Matchett Street,

Sapper John Ritchie, 554th Coy, Royal Engineers, 87 Silvio Street, died accidentally
13 February 1919 (*Belfast Evening Telegraph* 11 March 1919, p. 4)

who had been captured on 21 March 1918 when serving with the 1st RIRifles,
were released before the war ended: August 1918 in his case.[20] But most awaited
Germany's collapse. Systematic searches for the missing were made by the War
Office and the Red Cross, both through hospitals and searches of battlefields.[21]
Unwelcome news reached many families in late 1918 and early 1919, but by that
time many other families had been overjoyed at the return of prisoners. Woodvale
Road resident Second Lieutenant Robert Sprott of the 15th RIRifles was typical
in returning from Karlsruhe, Germany in December 1918.[22]

The family of Second Lieutenant Robert Moore of the 1st RIRifles received
news in a more roundabout way. He was mentioned in earlier chapters as a
winner of the Military Medal while a sergeant in the 9th RIRifles, and for rising
from private to officer. In April 1918 members of his family were told by the War
Office that he was wounded and missing in the retreat of late March 1918. They
then heard nothing until the day of the armistice when they received a postcard
from the Queen Victoria's Jubilee Fund Association suggesting that he was alive.
However, two days later, a letter and photograph arrived from the Red Cross in
Switzerland. The photo was of Moore's grave and it had been sent to the Red
Cross by a German officer who had found an address for Moore's parents on his
body, and wished them to know that their son had been properly buried. The War
Office was unable to locate the grave and it was not until April 1919 that Moore
was officially declared dead. In November, the grave was found and the remains
moved to a British cemetery at Mezieres.[23]

For those who did return to Belfast, their arrival was often as part of a large
contingent. But for the remnants of the Ulster Division, the War Office gave little
notice to the city authorities when they arrived in Belfast on 13 June 1919. The
Belfast Telegraph, worried that the soldiers would feel unappreciated, made it

Sgt Thomas Stephenson DCM, Royal Irish Fusiliers, Boer War veteran, 280 Cupar Street, died of pneumonia 2 March 1919 (*Belfast Evening Telegraph* 7 March 1919, p. 4)

clear that had even 24 hours' notice been given 'the entire city would have been present to meet them' instead of the much smaller crowd which gathered.[24] More formal opportunities for a welcome home were part of the process of remembering the fallen and celebrating victory, and are discussed in the next chapter. But the key consideration for most soldiers on their return was to find work.

Doing so was a challenge. Very little was ever done for ex-soldiers in terms of housing in Belfast, except for limited building in the Cregagh area of East Belfast.[25] Ex-soldiers living with wounds faced a life of discomfort and disability, but they got on as best they could. Sergeant John Dickson of Dover Street in the Shankill, who had won both the DCM and the Military Medal in the final Allied advance, had been hospitalized earlier in the war. His daughter recalls, 'His health was never very good as a result of his wounds and gas poisoning . . . He had shrapnel in both arms and legs, and developed a serious cough which lasted a number of years.' However, John Dickson was one of many who did not qualify for a pension. Again, his daughter recalls, 'He was sent for a medical and was asked by someone to jump over a chain. My Dad . . . told them he had been jumping over barbed wire fences for four years and flatly refused.' He did, however, find work as a commercial traveller. He worked both in England and Scotland, before later settling in Bangor with his wife, whom he married in 1924, and four children. Having moved back to Belfast in the 1950s, he died in 1967.[26]

Veterans were afflicted by a range of health problems, neurasthenia (as shell-shock was classified from 1917) and 'valvular disease of the heart', the most common symptoms of which included rapid heartbeat, shortness of breath, fatigue and dizziness.[27] As in the wider population, tuberculosis was rife. Samuel Boyce of Whiterock Road and the 16th RIRifles was just 19 when diagnosed

Sgt John Dickson DCM MM, 9th Royal Inniskilling Fusiliers, Dover Street,
pictured in 1960s

with 'tubercle of lungs' in July 1918, which he attributed to burying men who
had died of gas poisoning. He missed seeing peace by just five days, as he died
on 6 November 1918.[28] Daniel McKeown was another tuberculosis sufferer. He
had helped to train the 5th Royal Irish Fusiliers and was wounded at Gallipoli,
before serving from late 1916 to 1918 in his regiment's 2nd Garrison Battalion
in Salonica and being discharged in May 1918 as no longer fit. Life after the war
was hard and he died in 1927 from tuberculosis. His granddaughter, Marie Toner
Moore, was born after his death, but due to the death of both her parents while
she was a child, Marie was brought up by her grandmother and was therefore

told much about her late grandfather. Eligibility for a war pension and the amount that could be awarded depended on the degree to which an ex-soldier was prohibited from working. McKeown was entitled to a pension, having been discharged as medically unfit for further service, and he received 44d per day from 1 April 1919, which was increased by 5d per day when he reached the age of 55 in 1925.[29] However, at £66 per year this was well below the average wage for a skilled worker and he was keen to find a job. He had qualified as a gym instructor in his first period in the army and had exemplary references. Marie recalls her grandmother's account of his life after the war, applying for many positions that he did not obtain and doing work as a cobbler from his house in Forfar Street:

> My granny also told the story of how she had to pawn his 'great coat' which they had been using as a blanket during his last illness to feed his children. My grandmother believed that it was because of his Catholicism that he was denied work and I understood from her that he believed this too. She often remarked that he was wont to say 'so much for the land fit for heroes'.[30]

Corporal Thomas Fleming was a neurasthenia sufferer. He had enlisted in September 1914 into the Ulster Division, having been a member of the West Belfast UVF Special Service Company. He had earlier served in the Boer War with the Grenadier Guards, and went through the war with the 9th RIRifles and then the Labour Corps. He won both the DCM and the Russian Order of St George (4th Class) for his actions on 1 July 1916.[31] After the war, he managed to obtain temporary work at Harland and Wolff, but faced long periods of unemployment due to ill health before his death in 1949, aged 70. At various points in his life his family was helped by grants from the Ulster Division Patriotic Fund, which had been formed originally to help ex-UVF members, but was later expanded to the Ulster Division as a whole.[32]

Another former member of the West Belfast UVF Special Service Company was Sergeant John Alexander Verner of Canmore Street. Like Fleming, he enlisted in September 1914 after Boer War service, and won the DCM. After service with the 9th Battalions of both the RIRifles and the Royal Irish Fusiliers, Verner returned home with gunshot wounds in both arms. He could do light work only, and consequently, he endured long periods of unemployment.[33]

Of course, many soldiers did manage to find work. Joseph Hewitt of Canmore Street, once of the West Belfast UVF and a corporal in the 9th RIRifles, worked in a printers prior to the war. After 1918 he worked in the shipyards, but died in 1925 when he fell 55 feet from a gantry.[34] George McBride of the 15th RIRifles went back to Mackie's where he had worked prior to the war, and later lectured for the National Council of Labour Colleges. An active trade unionist, he joined the Labour Party in 1924 and met Winifred 'Winnie' Carney whom he later married. They shared politics then, but had very different pasts, McBride in the UVF and Carney as a prominent figure in Sinn Féin. Imprisoned with Countess Markiewicz for their part in the Easter Rising, she had been James Connolly's secretary at that time and was the Sinn Féin candidate in the 1918 parliamentary

Cpl Joseph Hewitt, 22 Canmore Street, died in 1925 in a workplace accident

election for the Victoria division of Belfast. Carney died in 1943, outlived for 45 years by her husband.[35]

For some who were fit and healthy, finding a job could be just as hard as for the wounded and, like Daniel McKeown, they believed religion to be a factor. One drew attention to his plight by committing a crime, or at least attempting to do so. A former Connaught Ranger, John Loftus was charged with loitering to commit a felony in the city centre after presenting himself to a police officer claiming to have broken a poster frame in Royal Avenue with a stone. When the officer investigated, he found a small stone beneath an undamaged frame. Loftus said:

I meant to break a window so that I would be arrested and have public attention drawn
to the unfair way I have been treated by the War Pensions Committee. I was employed
in the Durham Street Flax Spinning Coy, and was not taken back after the war because
I suppose I was not in the Ulster Division.

Loftus was told in court that he could have applied for an 'out-of-work dona-
tion', but he replied that it was work he wanted. He was discharged without
punishment, having got his wish for publicity.[36]

The desperation of others was seen in the uses to which they put tangible
'prizes' of the war: medals. Desy Brennan's father, Michael, served in the 6th
Connaughts, and Desy has recently been involved with his niece, Siobhán Deane
in researching the family history. Desy himself left school aged 14 in 1941 and
went to work in a pawnshop in the Carrick Hill district on the edge of the
Shankill. He remembers a pile of medals in the shop window from, he estimates,
at least 50 individuals, many of whom had more than one medal. He has a strong
memory of 'the poor people in desperation coming in to pledge war medals, or
boots' and said, 'There was a massive amount of war medals, not the most unique
ones, but good service medals.' These medals did not remian in Belfast after the
Second World War, however, because American soldiers based there bought them
up as souvenirs.[37]

Aside from the necessity of feeding their families, soldiers also had to tackle
psychological problems. James Vinter, a discharged soldier, was being treated
for 'nerve trouble' when he struck his wife Bridget in the face after a quarrel in
her sister's Norfolk Street house. When the wound became infected, she died of
septicaemia in the Belfast workhouse on 1 January 1919. Vinter was convicted of
manslaughter, and given three months in prison, although he had already served
his time in advance of the verdict. The court seems to have been sympathetic
to the medical evidence, which pointed out that Vinter had been 'buried' by an
explosion in March 1916 and that he had spent most of the time since then in
various hospitals. It was argued that 'Men suffering from shell shock were more
liable to act on impulse than others. They had not such strong self-control.'[38]
Such arguments had found little favour with military courts when men deserted,
but a civil court was more impressed. They may have been more sympathetic to
soldiers' plight, but they may also have simply reflected contemporary attitudes
to domestic violence.

Other soldiers tried to adjust to life back in Belfast through organizations that
maintained wartime comradeship, while also giving soldiers a voice on practical
issues confronting them. 'Comrades of the Great War' was launched in August
1917 and established in Belfast in June 1918. By that time the grievances of unemployed ex-soldiers who believed the city was doing little to help were being
aired publicly.[39] Prior to its merger with three other organizations to form the
British Legion in 1921, the Comrades of the Great War made representations to
bodies such as the local War Pensions Committee to help soldiers get the assistance they were due. It began work in July 1918, and by March 1919 it had lobbied
on 1,200 grievances and was in the process of tackling 500 more. Membership

was 2,000 and the Comrades also held social events.[40]

However, perhaps because the Comrades of the Great War saw themselves as 'a centre of loyalty and patriotism' there was another organization in Belfast that found favour with nationalists. The Irish Nationalist Veterans' Association (INVA) held its first general meeting in Dublin on 22 May 1919 and declared that it was a betrayal of promises to John Redmond and the men who went to France that Home Rule had not been implemented.[41] When the Belfast branch was established in July 1919 its founders argued that the organization was needed because other veterans' organizations avoided politics, whereas nationalist ex-soldiers had fought in the war explicitly to advance Home Rule.[42] The group also had a social function organizing both dances and boxing, but many Belfast branch meetings were used to rally support for Home Rule, and the organization supported Nationalist candidates in Belfast municipal elections.[43] A similar role was later played for Unionism by the Ulster Ex-Servicemen's Association, which broke from the Comrades of the Great War in 1920 and later campaigned for Unionists in elections to the Northern Ireland parliament.[44]

As it became clear that Home Rule was not going to happen in the form backed by Nationalists, the INVA's focus changed. In 1920 it took part in political events such as a May Day labour rally in Belfast,[45] but it was increasingly concerned with representing its members. In particular, it lobbied the local War Pensions Committee. There are examples of the committee working hard on individual cases, for example by helping disabled ex-soldiers to get access to free treatment from doctors.[46] However, there was a widespread feeling that it was not giving ex-soldiers a fair deal and was not aware of their concerns. One consequence of these sentiments was that in April 1920, bodies such as the INVA gained representation on the committee.[47]

Such grievances of ex-soldiers fed into wider unrest in Belfast in 1920. As far back as 1915 families of soldiers were vulnerable to local politics. In July of that year, 135 families were served notice to leave the Hamill Street area of West Belfast, notionally under plans to improve living quarters. But Nationalist politicians alleged that this was a plot to remove Nationalist voters from an area with tight election results and pointed to the deadline to quit being the day before the deadline for inclusion on the electoral roll. Most of the families, it was said, had a member serving in the forces. After a week of uproar, the notices were withdrawn.[48]

Where people lived became an issue in the Belfast Troubles of 1920–22, which saw more violence in Belfast than any other part of Ireland except Cork in 1917–23.[49] The most comprehensive analysis of the period puts Belfast deaths between July 1920 and October 1922 at 498. Catholics suffered particularly: in a city where they were only around 25 per cent of the population, 60 per cent of the fatalities were Catholic. In the more recent Troubles only one year – 1972 – was more intensive in terms of killing than 1920–22.[50]

The Troubles were fed by several political and economic factors. The Anglo-Irish war of 1919–21 saw the IRA carrying out operations against British targets in a fight for independence. In Belfast, paramilitary groups on both sides organized vigorously: the IRA was growing and Carson had threatened a year before 'to call out the Ulster Volunteers' if Home Rule was enforced.[51] In July 1920, with Unionists sensing that they could defeat Home Rule and at least secure partition of Ireland, the UVF was being reorganized and ex-soldiers played a role in that. Another loyalist paramilitary organization, the Ulster Imperial Guards had also been formed.[52]

Meanwhile, across the UK an economic depression was setting in, and there was bitterness from ex-soldiers over their claims to reinstatement in jobs they held prior to enlistment. This was a UK-wide phenomenon, with a mass protest organized by the National Federation of Discharged Sailors and Soldiers in London's Hyde Park in May 1919. That ended in a riot in Parliament Square.[53] In Belfast, in July 1919, there was an orderly protest at City Hall when about 300 veterans marched on the building and successfully demanded a meeting with the Lord Mayor over veterans' treatment by the local Pensions Committee. The unnamed leader of the group said that the men 'were not Bolshevists or Socialists, God forbid!' but that they wanted 'justice which was due them'.[54]

One year on, these sentiments contributed to violence on the streets of Belfast. Returning from their Twelfth of July holiday, militant Protestants evicted Catholic workers from shipyards. The militants also ejected those Protestants, mainly socialists, who refused to sign an 'oath of loyalty'. The tension of the shipyards spilled into the streets of East Belfast, and then into the west and north of the city, with crowds gathering in the Shankill and the Falls on the evening of 21 July 1920, joined by the military. The role of employment grievances in the violence was seen at a meeting on 30 July at the Deacon Memorial Hall in McTier Street, chaired by former Company Sergeant-Major Selby, once of the 9th RIRifles. Selby reminded those present (as many as 440) that their employers had assured them in 1914 that 'the men who went would be reinstated in their jobs'. Selby claimed that 'men from other parts of the country, many of them Sinn Feiners' had filled the jobs and he linked the street violence to disgruntlement among ex-servicemen. A resolution was passed calling on employers in the city to find work for an estimated 3–5,000 unemployed ex-servicemen.[55]

The first night of violence in the Falls saw two deaths, one of which was that of an ex-soldier: Bernard 'Bertie' Devlin, a resident of Alexander Street West and a member of the INVA. He was shot on 21 July when soldiers opened fire on a rampaging crowd in the Falls Road. The *Irish News* was adamant that all of those killed on 21 July 'were respectable members of the community, and not one of those amongst them can be regarded as being capable of participating in a riot under any conditions'.[56] The United Irish League joined the INVA, and the Ancient Order of Hibernians at the joint funeral procession of Devlin and five other Catholic victims of the violence which made its way up the Falls Road to Milltown Cemetery on the afternoon of Saturday 24 July.

On the night of 22 July 1920, William Dunning of Bellevue Street had 'practically the left side of his head blown off'. He died instantly as a result of, according to the *Belfast Telegraph*, 'intense firing . . . by a Sinn Fein element' at the junction of Kashmir Road and Bombay Street. Dunning had served with the 9th RIRifles but had been discharged as unfit for further service in 1916. Meanwhile, Joseph Giles of Kashmir Road, another ex-soldier, 'was on the street when the military replied to the fire of the Sinn Feiners' and was killed after being hit in the abdomen.[57] The next day, an unnamed man claiming to be an ex-soldier who had lost two fingers in the war was given a 'rough handling' by a crowd on the Shankill Road having 'voiced disloyal sentiments'. He received a scalp wound but was saved by the police. He claimed to have gone to the Shankill 'to see what it was like' and the *Telegraph* took pride in saying 'He now knows that disloyal sentiments are not popular there!'[58] With violence continuing over the weekend, David Dunbar, who had served with the Mechanical Transport Section of the Royal Engineers from 1916 and later the 7th Buffs (East Kents), was killed early on Monday 26 July. A resident of Silvio Street, he had trained as a taxi driver on a government-sponsored scheme after the war. At 2.30 a.m. that morning, he failed to stop his taxi when challenged by a sentry at a military post on the Falls Road end of Northumberland Street. He had almost hit the barbed wire across the road when the sentry fired. It was speculated that as an ex-soldier he would have understood the importance of a command to 'Halt!' but that the noise of the taxi might have drowned out the demand.[59]

Such events were repeated over the next two years. Victims fell both to specific targeting by gunmen and more random acts of violence. In July 1921 a number of ex-soldiers or the families of war dead had their homes burnt out.[60] There were also evictions, with the main pattern being the driving of Catholic families from homes in Protestant areas, and the boundaries of Catholic areas pushed back. In both 1920 and 1921, the violence was at its peak in the summer months of July to September, when people were more likely to be out on the streets at night. However, there was violence on Armistice Day in 1920 when there were clashes in the city centre as workers marched back to the shipyards from the two minutes' silence.[61] In 1922 the first six months were the most violent before the fighting petered out. The virtual end of the violence was partly due to the increased success of the security forces at dealing with disorder but also because the IRA almost ceased operations in Belfast as it became divided and distracted by the Irish civil war.[62]

During these two years, at least 12 further ex-soldiers were killed in West Belfast. Six are known to have been Catholics, four of whom died on an especially violent night, 10 July 1921. They included Daniel Hughes of Durham Place and a former corporal in the 7th Leinsters. Two were former members of the Inniskillings: Alexander Hamilton of Plevna Street, once of the 6th battalion, shot in Cupar Street, and James Lenaghan of Locan Street. A fourth Catholic ex-soldier killed that night was Frederick Craig in Clonard Street.[63] Two ex-soldiers known to be Protestants were William Mitchell of Downing Street, killed on 16 October 1920, and William Allen of Sackville Place, who died on 9 March 1922.[64] An ex-soldier of unknown religion, but in the Royal Ulster Constabulary, was Constable James Glover of the Springfield Road barracks. He had been part of a batch of 200 police who had joined the Irish Guards at the start of the war, and had been wounded twice.[65] He was shot by the IRA on 10 June 1921 while on patrol in Cupar Street. He had been targeted by the IRA, which suspected him of being one of the 'rogue cops' of the Nixon gang, alleged to have carried out sectarian killings.[66]

The most harrowing story was that of Joseph Walshe a victim of the 'Arnon Street massacre' on 1 April 1922.[67] Taking revenge for the killing of a policeman, uniformed men in an armoured car toured predominantly Catholic streets close to the Brown Square Barracks. They killed two men in Stanhope Street and Park Street, before moving to Arnon Street. A 70-year old man was killed at no. 16, and the raiders then moved next door to no. 18. In bed with two of his children, Michael (7) and Brigid (nearly 2) was Joseph Walshe, an ex-soldier. Walshe's wife, Elizabeth, described how men burst through the front door and went upstairs. Shots followed. Elizabeth Walshe came upstairs to find her husband dead on the bed having been shot, while the two children were also injured. Michael died subsequently on 4 April.[68]

Among the evictions were Patrick O'Hare and his family in Urney Street. O'Hare had served for 13 years, eventually becoming a sergeant, and opting to continue service after the war for two more years from September 1919.[69] The *Irish News* reported on 21 June 1921 that he had been home on leave from the Connaught Rangers the previous week. One of 'the Orange mobs'

> ... armed with revolvers, numbering over a hundred, rushed down Urney Street, and commenced to smash the windows and doors of O'Hare's home. They got into the house, and proceeded to smash the furniture in the kitchen. O'Hare, who was in uniform at the time, had his wife and children upstairs. Not content with smashing the furniture, the gang of rowdies went one better in cruelty and terrorism. They surrounded O'Hare and his family, dragged them downstairs, and then told Mrs. O'Hare that they were going to shoot her husband.

The newspaper said that from the mob's point of view, despite his uniform, 'he was a Catholic, that was sufficient crime'. Mrs O'Hare apparently ran screaming into the street and feared the worst when her husband was taken into the yard and she heard a shot. But the attackers had not killed him and the family was allowed to leave, although they never went back to their home.[70]

There is a slightly different account of this story from Seán O'Hare, a grandson of Patrick O'Hare. Intriguingly, he said that in the O'Hare version

> ... they said that he [Patrick O'Hare] had been saved by British regulars, that ... my grandmother had sent one of her daughters ... running down to a British army peaceline ... which must have been down near the Falls, with his paybook and said that they were going to kill a soldier and that when they saw the paybook they came up and got him released.

As Seán himself points out, 'It's not something that would be made up because

. . . they didn't have any love for the British army but they said that they had saved him and that they actually took him.' To explain quite how unlikely it was for the family to have added that side of the story, one needs to note that Seán's father, also Patrick, was active in the IRA in the 1930s, and spent some of his time in its unit in London, before being interned in the Second World War.[71] Seán himself was later associated with the Official IRA and was interned in Long Kesh in 1972. Whatever did actually happen in June 1921, the family went to England for some time in the 1920s, but they later came back to Belfast with Patrick O'Hare working on the production side of the *Irish News*.

The response of the authorities to such violence tended to focus on republicans rather than loyalists. They saw the IRA as being at the root of disorder and

Sgt Patrick O'Hare (right), Connaught Rangers, pictured with Shankill veteran
Billy Wilkie outside Beehive Bar, Falls Road, c. 1930

introduced internment in the Special Powers Act of 1922. This allowed detention without trial to protect public order, and it was used for 728 men throughout Northern Ireland between May 1922 and December 1924, many of them ending up on the prison ship *Argenta*.[72] At least 105 of the internees had West Belfast addresses and at least ten of these were former British soldiers.

Internment was a blunt tool and mistakes were made even within the terms of the Special Powers Act. There were cases of individuals being interned even though they had no republican connections and no involvement even in nationalist politics. What made them targets for internment was their military expertise, which, if they were Catholics, meant that the Royal Ulster Constabulary feared they would use their skills in the IRA. The general attitude of the authorities to ex-soldiers was summed up in one case when it was noted, 'He is an ex-soldier, but, unfortunately the experience here is that many ex-soldiers with good war records became I.R.A. criminals.'[73]

But there were often major mistakes. In South Belfast, one such case was that of Peter Murray, whose family are clear to this day that he had nothing to do with the IRA. He had served with the RIRifles from January 1917, was gassed at Ypres and was later captured by the Germans, spending some time as a prisoner of war working on a German farm. He remained in the army after the war, eventually being discharged in May 1921 after service with the 2nd Royal Ulster Rifles in Mesopotamia. One relative was a known republican, but when police raided the family home in July 1922 they were nowhere to be found and Peter Murray was arrested instead. The RUC said that Murray was a bomber and machine-gunner in the IRA. Writing from Crumlin Road gaol on 3 August 1922, Murray cited his war and postwar service as evidence that he was not connected 'to any Organisation operating in opposition to the powers of the Northern Government'. Murray was eventually released in July 1923 and what makes his family's view of his non-involvement so compelling is that instead of holding a grudge against the British, he re-enlisted in the British army in 1940, aged 41, serving with the Cheshire Regiment until July 1945. Moreover, his granddaughter, Kate McNeill, remembers how he always bought poppies for Remembrance Sunday and wore them with pride at a time when many Catholics regarded them as a symbol of unionism. Kate remembers him saying, 'These poppies are your poppies. I fought for them for you.'[74] This was not the stance of a man who had been in the IRA.[75]

Francis McCann of McDonnell Street experienced different attention from the authorities. He had served in the Boer War and had enlisted in 1915 in the 8th Royal Irish Fusiliers, remaining in the army after the war. When he was home on leave, an RUC raiding party arrived at his house. His grandson tells the family story of how the police, fearing that he would assist the IRA with his military skills, 'brought him out into the backyard and put a gun to his head and threatened to shoot him if he became involved in such actions. My grandmother had to plead for his life.' Francis McCann survived, although when he died in 1931 aged 54, his family was so hard-up that he was buried in the poor ground at Milltown Cemetery.[76]

Peter Murray, Royal Irish Fusiliers and PoW, Roden Street, interned in 1920s

More complicated was the case of James Davey of Baker Street, a Gallipoli veteran of the 6th RIRifles, who was wounded in August 1915 and discharged a year later.[77] The police believed he was a member of the 'Red Gang' that was responsible for armed hold-ups and robberies. He had at one point informed on the IRA to the police and on 22 April 1922 'was pursued by a number of Sinn Feiners who tried to capture him in his house'. But he was later interned because the RUC concluded that despite fleeing to England at government expense, he had returned and was not therefore afraid of the IRA. Aside from this possible connection, it was concluded that Davey was 'a dangerous man'. Released after only a few months on condition that he left Northern Ireland, Davey was unable to find work in England and was imprisoned for two months having been found back in Belfast in September 1923. On his release, the authorities seem to have taken pity on his claim that he could best find work in Belfast in order to support his wife and children. He was allowed to remain under a restriction order that included regular reports to the police.[78]

A former soldier who said that he was vehemently opposed to Sinn Féin was Thomas McCrory, who was wounded on the Somme in September 1916, probably serving with the 6th Connaughts. When arrested in July 1922, he stressed his military service, but was interned on the *Argenta* and later at Larne Workhouse 'on the grounds that he is a person suspected of having committed outrages and likely to continue to do so'. This was despite doubt over whether he had been confused with other McCrorys. When he protested against his internment in March 1923, he said that he had been a member of the Ancient Order of Hibernians for the past 13 years, was a strong supporter of Joseph Devlin and 'loyal' to 'the Northern Government'. The authorities may have accepted his case for he was released on bail in August 1923.[79]

Many other men protested their innocence, even though the police had more evidence against them. Although ex-servicemen could be targets for the IRA,[80] their military expertise was highly valued. Two cases against ex-soldiers were substantial and involved those accused of taking part in a December 1921 IRA arms raid on the Balmoral barracks. One was Hugh Harper of Omar Street, accused of leading the raid. Alleged to be with him was George Hamill who had served with the Royal Irish Fusiliers in Egypt. He was not somebody who settled into internment easily, twice going on hunger-strike over disciplinary matters, before being released in early 1923 on condition that he went to Canada. He never did go, and instead turned up on a Ministry of Pensions training course in Maidstone in Kent. A two-week visit to Belfast in July 1924 was on condition that he reported to the RUC every three days, although he did not do so.[81]

David McKinstry of Leeson Street, a veteran of the Royal Naval Air Service, was one of the few who admitted to IRA membership. When arrested in October 1921 in possession of a revolver he said that he was protecting Catholics who were working on the tramways and had been attacked. He was sentenced to seven years but served only two, following internment for one month. Released on bail in January 1924, he was rearrested on suspicion of IRA membership in December 1925. However, the police concluded that while he clearly held republican views, they did not believe he was active and 'has learned a lesson'.[82]

Perhaps the most senior alleged West Belfast IRA member to be interned – although he denied his membership – was Patrick Barnes, who ran a second-hand clothes shop on the corner of Cullingtree Road and Brooke Street with his wife Jane. He had been a soldier before the war, serving ten years in the 1st RIRifles, but had re-enlisted at the outbreak. After action in France in 1914 he was later wounded at Ypres. The police alleged he was involved in bomb-throwing and the burning of a tram in Divis Street. He was described as 'a prominent gunman and firebug' and the police claimed to have documents showing him to be a captain in E Company of the 1st Battalion of the IRA's 3rd Northern Division. This led to his internment on the *Argenta* and later in prison in Belfast, before release on bail in December 1923. Throughout, Barnes protested that he was not in the IRA and was loyal to the Northern government.[83]

Only one of the West Belfast internees was accused of anything other than IRA activity. Samuel Ditty of Carlow Street was a loyalist and part-time policeman as a 'B Special'. He had served in the RIRifles, first in the 5th battalion, and was in Dublin for the Easter Rising, before being sent to France. He was arrested in December 1922 on suspicion of being involved in 'one of the most dangerous armed hold-up gangs in the City'. He had powerful supporters in the police, including District Inspector John Nixon.[84] Nixon said that Ditty was innocent of all crimes and the police officers who had given evidence against him were unreliable. Despite Nixon's support, Ditty was interned for six months until June 1923.[85]

Aside from the men interned, other ex-soldiers joined the IRA yet evaded prison. In the Bone area of North Belfast, James Cassidy, who had served both before and during the war, lost an eye defending the area against a loyalist mob.[86] Robert Brennan, an early enlistee in the Connaught Rangers in 1914, was a staunch supporter of Redmond. Brennan did not serve abroad and was discharged in June 1916 through ill-health. His younger brother, Michael, had been in Dublin in hospital during the Easter Rising, but took no part in politics after the war, except for returning his medals. Michael ran a chip shop, pursued his interest in boxing as a referee, and attended church on a daily basis. Robert was also a shopkeeper, but was radicalized either during or after the war, and in 1921 he was in command of an IRA unit in Carrick Hill in West Belfast. While he was away from his Alton Street home (a family story has it that he was away with the leading IRA figure Dan Breen) his wife Mary was arrested for being found with two revolvers (one loaded) in her blouse. She said that two men who ran into her house had made her hide the revolvers, and was eventually released after agreeing to testify against them.[87]

Another case was that of A. J. P. 'Pat' Stapleton of Forest Street in the Falls. Stapleton served as a sergeant in the Royal Irish Regiment in the Balkans and rose to second lieutenant in the 3rd Battalion of the RIRifles, one of the reserve battalions. After the war, he enlisted in the 'A Specials', which made him an un-likely recruit for the IRA. But despite this part-time police work his day-jobs, first in the filing office of the Royal Army Service Corps at the Victoria Barracks, and then in the Military Adviser's office, made him a source of useful information. Stapleton was a Catholic and his sisters were said to be 'out-and-out Sinn Feiners'. When he disappeared in August 1922, the RUC believed that he had been passing information to the IRA. Although the 14 files found missing when Stapleton stopped turning up for work were not regarded as especially important, the matter was significant enough for James Craig, then prime minister of Northern Ireland, to be alerted.[88]

Perhaps the most remarkable case is that of Seán Cunningham.[89] When he died in 1963, one newspaper headed his obituary 'Fought in four armies'. He first enlisted in September 1904, claiming to be over 18, but one record suggests he was actually 15. Cunningham served for eight years until March 1912 when he was discharged to the army reserve. During this time, he became active in nationalist politics, enlisting in the Irish Volunteers in May 1914, at which point he was living in Gibson Street in the Falls. However, as a reservist at the outbreak of war, Cunningham was called up and served through to March 1920. His time in his first army saw service with both the Royal Inniskilling Fusiliers and Dragoon Guards. Soon after his discharge, he joined the East Belfast IRA, serving as a captain in 1920–21. On backing the Anglo-Irish Treaty, he then joined the army of the Irish Free State, and was briefly a policeman in the Garda Síochána. In 1936 he joined his fourth army, Eoin O'Duffy's pro-Franco brigade which went to Spain. He served as captain of a machine-gun company, meeting Franco himself. Cunningham campaigned against conscription in 1939, by which time he was living in Harrogate Street in the Falls. He visited Spain several times, including attending the opening of Franco's civil war memorial, Valle de los Caidos (Valley of the Fallen), after its completion in 1958. For many years he led the annual Easter Sunday parade of IRA veterans to Milltown Cemetery.[90]

One final case of an ex-serviceman has eluded the usual research. In a British army skirmish with an IRA unit on Lappinduff Mountain in County Cavan in May 1921, Seán McCartney was killed. McCartney grew up in Norfolk Street in the Falls, and is buried in the Republican plot at Milltown Cemetery. In the newspaper reports at the time there was no mention of his past. Thorough searches of British military records have failed to find any record relating to McCartney, even when multiple variations of his name are used, especially bearing in mind that 'Seán' was almost always anglicised to 'John' in British army records. However, Philip Orr is clear (on the basis of an oral history source) that McCartney served at Gallipoli in the Connaught Rangers, which would have meant the 5th battalion. McCartney's British military past has been forgotten, but he has been immortalised in a Republican song which laments:

> On Cavan's Mountain, Lappinduff
> Fought one with bravery,
> Until the English soldiers killed
> Brave Seán McCartney.[91]

Such stories of ex-soldiers illustrate something of the lives of hundreds if not thousands of war veterans in Belfast. Some are notable because they tell a largely forgotten story. Others, like Seán Cunningham, stand out simply for being so unusual. Yet many of the other stories are tips of icebergs. John Dickson represents all those who struggled to live with wounds. Daniel McKeown also represents the wounded, plus all those who struggled to find work.

Of course, there were other soldiers who were not wounded badly enough to cause them postwar problems, so they were able simply to get on with their day-to-day lives as best as they could, aided by a stable job. Harry Donaghy, who grew up in the Falls in the late 1950s and 1960s, remembers one such soldier: his grandfather, Patrick Donnelly, who served at different times with both the Connaught Rangers and the Royal Irish Fusiliers. Patrick died in 1964 when Harry was 7 and, as a child, Harry remembers, 'I used to sit at the fireside and look in fascination at his big strong arms with the regimental tattoos, one the Connaught Rangers, the other the Royal Irish Fusiliers.' An unexpected outcome of the war for Patrick Donnelly was a loathing of camels. He had been strapped to one having been wounded and transported to a first aid station somewhere in Palestine. Consequently he acquired a strong dislike of their smell. This manifested itself when he took his grandchildren to Belfast zoo and stayed as far away from the camels as possible. More happily, he had acquired a taste for spicy food while serving in the Middle East. Harry believed this was common for men who had served there or in India, a point that was also made by Seán O'Hare about his grandfather. Harry remembers,

> We always knew when he came into the house because if a pot of stew or soup was on the stove he would help himself to a bowl. From his pocket he would produce a small packet of curry powder or spices, which at the time you could only buy in chemist shops, and sprinkle it into the bowl and you could smell this aroma all around the house.

This was one of the more tolerable ways in which the war changed forever the lives of the men who served in it.[92]

Patrick Donnelly, Royal Irish Fusiliers and Connaught Rangers, Inkerman Street, pictured after war

15

Remembrance

Thiepval emblazoned on our flags shall flame
To all the winds unfurled.
'COMMEMORATIVE ODE', BELFAST EVENING TELEGRAPH,
30 JUNE 1917

We would have thought that anybody in the British army then would
have been a traitor to Irish nationalism/republicanism. But many of us
have come to realise that's not the case, it's just that they were as much for
Home Rule as anybody else.

SEÁN O'HARE

It is difficult for people from outside the island of Ireland to understand why remembrance of a war that ended over 90 years ago is politically controversial. Yet, as so often in Irish history, as the Ulster poet Robert Greacen wrote, 'The past invades the present, the present lives in the past.'[1] While in England people wear poppies on Remembrance Sunday without regard to contemporary political divides, it is very different in Belfast.[2]

The first acts of remembrance took place well before the armistice, indeed, in the first weeks of the war, when individuals were marked by their families and friends. They often did so through newspaper notices, sometimes chosen from a range of options available to those placing an 'In Memoriam' message. A popular Catholic text was 'O! Immaculate Heart of Mary/Your prayers on him extol/O! Sacred Heart of Jesus/Have mercy on his soul.' This was placed by Sarah Sweeney of Stanhope Street in memory of her husband, John, killed with the 6th Connaughts in January 1916.[3] The parents of James Close, 2nd RIRifles and Eastland Street, chose the thought that 'He gave his life for his country, What braver deed could he have done.'[4] Other notices expressed a political message. John Mailey's widow, Sarah, marked her lance-corporal husband's death in the 9th RIRifles on the first day of the Battle of the Somme with words including these: 'For King and Country well he stood/Unknown to coward's fears/In battle strife he shed his blood/With the Ulster Volunteers.'[5] Other messages reflected sorrow. Sarah Shearer, wife of William Shearer drew on a standard range of texts offered by the *Belfast Evening Telegraph* in marking her husband's death: 'O, could I see you now, my dear/As fair as in olden time/When prattle and smile made home a joy/And life was a merry chime.'[6]

The focus for collective remembrance in Belfast after 1916 was the Somme.

One year on, the newspapers carried lists of the dead and the *Belfast Evening Telegraph* included a large picture of J. P. Beadle's painting of the Ulster Division attacking at the Somme, offering copies for sale to readers.[7] Friday 29 June 1917, was 'Forget-me-not Day' when the flowers were sold in memory of the fallen, with the money raised going to the UVF Patriotic Fund.[8] Meanwhile, on 1 July itself, services in Protestant churches in Belfast focused on the sacrifice at the Somme.[9] The anniversary of 1 July 1916 would continue to be a central point for marking the city's contribution to the war effort, and by 1918 it was fully incorporated into the Orange Order's activities for July of each year. In 1918 and in 1919 it became tied up with 12 July commemoration.[10]

There was also activity outside Somme commemorations, often not linked to any military anniversary. There was a collection for the Lord Roberts' Memorial Workshops for Discharged and Disabled Soldiers and Sailors around Christmas 1918. The envelopes were distributed before 25 December by Boy Scouts, in the hope that people would fill them on Christmas Day itself, with the envelopes collected before the new year.[11] In the summer of 1919 a series of events drew a line under the war, and also celebrated the return of soldiers. On 29 July an event was held at Celtic Park for veterans of the 16th Division, including sports and the St Peter's Brass Band. The meeting was also infused with the politics of the day. Joseph Devlin MP argued that Ireland had made a great contribution to the war effort, but that while 'She kept her faith . . . faith has not been kept with her.' Yet Devlin also saw hope in the shared experience of war, saying that he had not abandoned his hope that the good relations between the Ulster and Irish divisions could play a role in building a peaceful future in Ulster.[12]

Saturday 9 August 1919 was Peace Day in Belfast, marking the signature of the Treaty of Versailles.[13] Elsewhere in the UK it had been celebrated on 19 July, but in Ulster, other than a small march-past in Belfast,[14] it was not held then to avoid clashing with annual Orange marches. Estimates of how many veterans took part ranged from 20,000 to 36,000. The day included the unveiling of a temporary Cenotaph at City Hall and a march from the Antrim Road in North Belfast to Ormeau Park in the East. In the Ulster Division section of the parade, 107th Brigade marched in its original format of the 8th, 9th, 10th and 15th RIRifles.[15] Many streets were decorated, with Glenwood Street off the Shankill covered from end to end with lanterns and bunting, and the pavements coloured red, white and blue. Parties for children were held in a number of parks, including Woodvale Park, where children played games and were given sweets.[16]

Many nationalists avoided Peace Day. Even during the war nationalist remembrance of the dead was problematic. Catholic churches did not produce lists of the dead in the way that many other organizations did, although in October 1916 there was a Requiem Mass at St Mary's, Belfast, for the souls of Belfast Catholic soldiers and sailors who had lost lives in the war. It was a major event at which the Bishop of Down and Connor presided.[17] Later, while many Catholics were not ashamed of their ancestor's service, their remembrance was private. The *Irish News* argued that Peace Day celebrated militarism and that 'there is absolutely no difference between the manner and temper of a Red Indian victory carnival and the gorgeous processions arranged to celebrate the triumph over Germany'.[18] However, the *Irish News* could not criticize one of the final events of the peace celebrations – entertainment, food and gifts given to 1,000 adult poor in St George's covered market.[19] Nationalists commemorated their dead formally in an INVA parade of Belfast's nationalist ex-soldiers at 7.30 a.m. on Sunday 12 October 1919. They marched to St Peter's in the Falls where a Requiem Mass was said for Catholics who died in the war.[20]

One further anniversary in 1919 was crucial. On 11 November the first commemoration of the armistice was held across the UK. In Belfast, at 11 a.m., all work in shops and factories, and all traffic, stopped for two minutes. The same applied to post offices, fire stations and police courts. The signal to begin and end the mark of respect was given by guns fired in Belfast Lough and sirens sounded at shipyards and mills. This contrasted with Derry City where there was no mass observance despite an appeal by the Lord Mayor.[21]

From 1919 onwards, 1 July was the key commemorative event in Belfast.[22] But remembrance in Belfast in the 1920s should be seen in the context of wider remembrance, both in the rest of Ireland, and in Great Britain. From 1919 to 1938, 11 a.m. on 11 November was marked by two minutes' silence across the UK. Suspended during 1939–1945, it was reinstituted in 1946, but in subsequent years the dead of both world wars (and subsequent conflicts) have been remembered on Remembrance Sunday, the second Sunday of November. The focus of UK remembrance is the Cenotaph in London and the Tomb of the Unknown Warrior in Westminster Abbey, both of which were unveiled in 1920 (in the case of the Cenotaph, replacing a temporary structure). Meanwhile, the British Legion's poppy has been sold since 1921.[23]

Other specific memorials and symbols are more resonant in Belfast, especially the memorials to specific divisions. On the site of the Ulster Division's advance on 1 July 1916 stands the Ulster Tower, a replica of Helen's Tower in grounds of Clandeboye estate in County Down where volunteers had trained in 1914–15.[24] This was initially conceived of and opened in November 1921 as a memorial to the Ulster Division. Trees were planted on the pathway leading to it, mainly funded by men from specific parts of the division.[25] Meanwhile, the 16th (Irish) Division is commemorated in France and Belgium with stone Celtic crosses at Guillemont and Wytschaete, replacing an earlier wooden one at Ginchy. A similar cross in Salonica honours the 10th (Irish) Division.[26] The Belfast Cenotaph was unveiled in November 1929. In the Shankill Road is a Garden of Remembrance which pays tribute to the dead of both world wars and later conflicts, especially the Troubles, and is the site of annual parades in November.[27]

In an all-Ireland context, work on a memorial at Islandbridge in Dublin began in 1931, and was effectively complete in 1938. From 1940 to 1970 the British Legion held ceremonies at Islandbridge, but unease among the leadership of first the Irish Free State and then the Republic of Ireland meant that it was not formally opened until 1994 when Bertie Ahern, later Taoiseach but then Finance

Ulster Tower, Thiepval

Minister, represented his government at the ceremony. At this time, Islandbridge had in fact been open only for six years after closure between 1971 and 1988 due to fears over Troubles-related action against ceremonies. It had only reopened as part of a process of responding to criticism of the Republic's government's attitude to remembrance in the face of the Enniskillen bombing in 1987.[28]

That there were such delays at Islandbridge was largely due to the identification of remembrance with expressions of Britishness and militarism, as the INVA had said of Peace Day. There is some debate over how far unionists consciously appropriated remembrance of the war. Meanwhile, the government of the new Northern Ireland state did not feel any need for 'national' remembrance in Northern Ireland, leaving London as the centre of remembrance, and other ceremonies as matters for local communities.[29] However, as Gillian McIntosh argues, the story of the Somme became absolutely central in the creation of inter-war unionism, with many unionist writers pointing out the contrasts between the activities of loyal Ulstermen on the Somme in 1916, and the rebellion in Dublin in the same year.[30] Meanwhile, regardless of whether unionists intended to make commemorations unionist in tone, any nationalist attending would be surrounded by the flags and symbols of a country to which they felt no allegiance, in a crowd singing songs that had nothing to do with nationalists' national identity.

There was no overt Catholic presence in most parades. The unveiling of the Belfast Cenotaph in 1929 was notable for the absence of Catholic organizations. Although two fascist groups laid wreaths in the formal ceremony, 16th Division veterans only did so after the official proceedings, although they were included a year later.[31] More comfortable for Catholic ex-soldiers were events such as a September 1934 pilgrimage to Lourdes, organized by the French Association of former Priest-Combatants. Twelve Belfast men took part in a group of around 400 from Britain and Ireland, on a journey that aimed to promote peace and reconciliation and included veterans of opposing armies.[32]

Nationalist and republican hostility to commemoration was strong from 1918 until recent times. In 2006 former republican prisoner Jim Gibney wrote, 'The First World War was an imperialist conflagration which claimed the lives of more than five million soldiers with 23 million casualties. The scale of the human loss is incomprehensible. It was a pointless and futile war.'[33] It may surprise republicans that this is little different to the popular version of history that prevails in Great Britain. However, it is markedly different from the unionist account, which emphasizes sacrifices 'for King and Country'. Moreover, what was uniquely problematic for nationalists and republicans was that, in Gibney's words, 'It was after all a British-sponsored war at a time when all of Ireland was occupied and that occupation in part continues today.' He added, 'Unionists used the Somme sacrifice as a badge of loyalty to their new state and still do. Wrapping their ceremonies in the Union flag and British military regalia, intentionally or otherwise, diminishes the memory of nationalists who fought and died there.'

These attitudes meant that the First World War became an untold and

16th (Irish) Division Cross at Guillemont

Shankill Memorial Garden

eventually forgotten story for nationalists and republicans. When the 7th Leinsters were disbanded, they were told: 'Your children, grand-children, unto the last generations, will tell with pride not only of the great and noble deeds of the 7th LEINSTERS, but of the brilliant and heroic deeds of the individuals of the BATTALION.'[34] In fact, their story was soon forgotten, as many of their descendants shied away from telling it.

Meanwhile, unionists were as enthusiastic about the 36th Division as nationalists were reticent about the 16th and marked their remembrance with the display of British symbols. George and Margaret Mabin of Crosby Street lost two sons on the Somme. From 1917, they put out a Union flag annually on 1 July. Even in 1941 when the house was struck and badly damaged by a German bomb, a neighbour put up a flag on the roof of the empty house. Philip Orr, who interviewed members of the family in the 1980s, said that a belief in it being worthwhile to die for your country has 'enabled the Mabins and many other families to make sense of their loss, down through the years'.[35]

Veterans' visits to the battlefields and cemeteries took place from the 1920s, but as the years moved on, the events became more formalized. In August 1936 a group of former regular soldiers, including members of the 2nd RIRifles, visited the Mons area. They were not marking a special anniversary, but they were visiting at the same time of year in which some of them had taken part in the retreat of 1914. Twenty years on, there was a sizeable pilgrimage to Thiepval to mark the 40th anniversary of 1916, including up to 100 veterans. In 1966 about 200 veterans, many well into their seventies, marked the 50th anniversary. Two former officers and five other ranks represented the 9th RIRifles.[36] James Colville, once of the 15th RIRifles, was able to visit the grave of his brother

Sammy who had been killed towards the end of the war. A few days later, Queen Elizabeth inspected 840 veterans at Balmoral Showgrounds in Belfast on 4 July.[37]

By the time of the 60th anniversary of 1916, most veterans were dead. The membership of the Old Comrades Association of the 9th RIRifles shows how many members had died. A minute-book survives for the 1951–1976 period. During this time the association organized social events as well as commemorative activities, including a presence at Remembrance Sunday and 1 July marches. But in the membership list for 1971, only eight names remained undeleted and when the organization handed over its standard to the Royal Ulster Rifles Museum in 1976, there were probably only five members surviving.[38] By 1996, there were only two veterans from the whole of Northern Ireland at Theipval for the 80th anniversary (Harry Currie from Belfast and James Taylor from Kircubbin, County Down).[39] Because nationalist memorial of the war was surreptitious and private, where it happened at all, we have no idea of the last Falls veteran to die. The last two Shankill veterans had both originally enlisted underage: James Colville died in 1989 aged 92 and Abraham 'Abie' Kirkpatrick died in 1996 . He had enlisted in 1915 aged just 15, and had initially been 'claimed out' by his parents for being too young, but had successfully re-enlisted in the Royal Flying Corps soon after without their objection.[40]

As these men departed, their service in the war was increasingly marked by a new generation as the Somme became ever more central to Loyalist identity. For people in the Shankill, visits to the graves of their ancestors are important and profound acts, which are displayed publicly. In many cases, it is only recently that people have been able to travel to the graves. Rifleman Henry Jones of Urney Street and the 9th RIRifles died of wounds in August 1916. His son, Albert Jones, who was just 3 when his father died, paid his first visit to his grave in Bailleul 86 years later. The trip was an 89th birthday present from his daughter, and it was the first time that any family member had visited.[41]

Meanwhile, the Somme is important to many Orange lodges which include references to it on their banners, particularly Thiepval Memorial Loyal Orange Lodge 1916, which was founded in 1996.[42] The Somme is also claimed by the Ulster Volunteer Force, which was formed in 1966 (using the name of the earlier organization) and engaged in some of the earliest killings of the Troubles. As Graham and Shirlow have shown in an important article, which draws particularly on East Belfast, the Somme has been used to assert both the masculinity and the local links of the UVF.[43] That organization puts its role after 1966 in an historical context running from resistance to Home Rule in 1912, via the Somme in 1916, to the Troubles of the late 1960s onwards. That lineage is seen most clearly in two Shankill murals. One, at the corner of the Shankill Road and Glenwood Street, depicts a 1914–18 soldier mourning his dead comrades alongside a contemporary masked UVF paramilitary. Loyalist symbolism and the poppy are both present, and the mural painters have equated sacrifice in 1914–18 in the British army with UVF deaths post-1969. Another mural, a little down the

Corner of Shankill Road and Glenwood Street. A soldier in a First World War uniform is shown alongside a contemporary masked UVF member, equating the deaths of 1914–18 with those of the Troubles. Poppies are shown around gravestones.

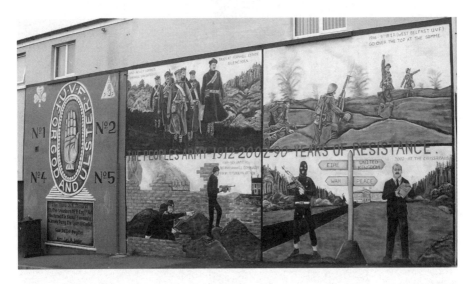

Corner of Shankill Road and Canmore Street. The top left of the four oblong pictures shows the West Belfast UVF training in 1912, followed by the 9th RIRifles (describes the West Belfast UVF) on the Somme. The bottom left image says '1969 – Volunteers defend Shankill community against Republican attack'. The continuity that is claimed between the UVF of 1912, the 9th RIRifles and the later UVF is striking.

Island of Ireland Peace Park, Messines

Shankill Road on the corner of Canmore Street, shows this even more starkly with the label 'The People's Army, 1912–2002: 90 years of resistance', picking out 1912, 1916 and 1969 as key moments in a continuous story of UVF organization in the Shankill.

The place of the Somme in loyalism is continuing to develop and has been argued to be helping loyalists move away from a 'balaclavas and assault rifles' heritage.[44] The Ulster Defence Association has not traditionally asserted an identity informed by the Somme but its South-East Antrim Brigade (which broke from the rest of the UDA in 2006) has been doing exactly that through a group called 'Beyond Conflict'. This group is led by Tommy Kirkham who has been involved in issues around remembrance for many years. He once ran the Fernhill House Museum, which opened in 1996 and contained exhibits relating to the Shankill until its closure in 2006.[45] Among Beyond Conflict's other activities, this group has organized visits to battlefields for members of its community.[46]

These developments within loyalism have taken place while attitudes have been changing even more significantly throughout the island of Ireland. One of the first of these significant developments was at grassroots level, as such moves often are, through the Farset Youth and Community Development Project. This was launched in 1982, primarily to tackle unemployment in West Belfast, but since the mid-1980s it has been taking cross-community groups of young people to visit sites associated with the war. The first visit was unplanned, in 1983, when travelling back from a trip to Paris that had no connection with the war. The group detoured to Thiepval and found the Ulster Tower in a bad state of repair and a range of initiatives followed involving Farset and many others. That led both to the reopening of the Ulster Tower and the formation of the Somme Association which established the Somme Heritage Centre at Conlig in County Down. In 1989 the Tower was re-dedicated by the Duchess of Gloucester, and a visitors' centre was opened in 1994, with Thiepval Wood purchased for the association in 2004.[47]

Underpinning this work has been a mission to tell a new story of the war, encouraging a cross-community approach to the past. A key statement of Farset's approach was a short but important publication produced in 1993, which told the story of the Somme as a battle involving both the 36th and 16th divisions, and also placed it in the context of later collaboration at Messines.[48] It was not the first time this had been done. A booklet produced in 1919 by Belfast City Council had covered both divisions and the 10th, but this approach had been lost in time and the Troubles.

From grassroots initiatives, state involvement followed. The Island of Ireland Peace Park at Messines was opened in 1998 by the UK, Republic of Ireland and Belgian heads of state. It had been initiated by Glen Barr, a leading figure within Loyalism, and Paddy Harte, a Fine Gael politician in the Republic. The park consists of an Irish round tower and memorials to the 10th, 16th and 36th divisions, close to the site of the 16th and 36th divisions' collaboration at Messines in June 1917. Meanwhile, a nearby Peace School has provided a venue

Reconstructed trench in Thiepval Wood

for the activities of the Messines Association, which was formed in 2002 to bring together former combatants of the post-1969 Troubles. During visits to Messines, former paramilitaries and members of the security forces have explored issues around the First World War to try to reach some shared understanding of them. One should not pretend that this has allowed peace and love to break out among all parts of Belfast. In a pamphlet produced in 2007 to reflect on the success of the project, one participant said:

> ... just last week I got a shock. I was organising a group of Loyalists to go to Messines, and some of them said, 'We'll not be going, because we hear there's Republicans going too.' And I said, 'Why not?' 'We're not walking on that sacred ground with Republicans, not a chance.'[49]

However, the participant went on to say that 'I really believe that this is now only a minority viewpoint.' Another participant argued that the grassroots reconciliation that has flowed from the Messines Association is crucial in building long-term stability: 'the peace process is not the outcome of a couple of days ... away at a hotel somewhere by a group of politicians. The peace process is a manifestation of what has gone on in the community over the years.'[50]

Among Belfast's nationalist political parties, one opportunity for change was after the IRA bombing of Enniskillen's Remembrance Sunday service in 1987.

There was cross-community revulsion, and in the aftermath, for the first time ever, boys from Enniskillen's Catholic grammar school, St Michael's, attended a Remembrance Day service at the town's predominantly Protestant Portora Royal School.[51] A year on, there were some unionist calls for the SDLP to attend Belfast's Remembrance Sunday service. Dr Joe Hendron, the party's leader on Belfast city council, said that he had visited the Belfast Cenotaph after both the Enniskillen bombing and the deaths of Corporals David Howes and Derek Wood in Andersonstown in March 1988. However, of the formal Remembrance event, he said, 'While we have nothing but respect for the dead of the two World Wars, Poppy Day over the years has been associated with the Unionist-British tradition.' In a recent interview, the SDLP's Alban Maginness said of remembrance, 'It was alien to our political tradition and to what we were comfortable with.'[52] There was no formal SDLP presence at a Remembrance Sunday event in Northern Ireland until 1992, when the leader of Omagh District Council, Paddy McGowan, laid a wreath at his town's ceremony. He did so again in 1993, in which year Mary Robinson, became the first Irish President to attend the Remembrance service in Dublin's Protestant cathedral, St Patrick's.[53]

In Belfast, there had been some informal Remembrance Sunday attendance by SDLP councillors over a number of years. In particular, Dorita Field, who had herself in the South African forces in World War Two, often attended. However, she used to wear both a red poppy and a white poppy (a peace movement symbol), and was one of those in her party who said that she was not an Irish nationalist, but was in the SDLP as a socialist. The first engagement from the Belfast SDLP as a group came in 1994 as Alex Attwood, an Upper Falls councillor, and the party's leader on the city council, attended with four of his party colleagues. Like Dorita Field, Attwood wore both red and white poppies. This was the first Remembrance Sunday event in Belfast since the IRA ceasefire in 1994, and Attwood said, 'In the environment in the city at the moment, we felt that it was important that a further symbolic step be made.'[54] In the same year, the SDLP also took part in ceremonies in Armagh, Enniskillen and Omagh.[55] In 1995, Attwood attended again, with two other SDLP councillors, and laid a wreath. Meanwhile, the SDLP mayor of Derry, John Kerr, was his city's first mayor to lay a wreath at the 1995 service, at a time when there was a live public debate about the role of the poppy.[56] This had been provoked by BBC Northern Ireland presenter Donna Traynor refusing to wear a poppy on air, having earlier in the year refused to wear a shamrock on St Patrick's Day. In 1997, Belfast gained its first Nationalist Mayor, Alban Maginness, who took a full role in the city's remembrance events. In the first place, that involved laying a poppy wreath during the Somme commemoration on 1 July. The Lord Mayor of Dublin also attended, and Maginness said afterwards that he hoped unionists would see his attendance as 'a genuine act of reconciliation.' He added, 'There has recently been a discovery of the history of the Great War, in terms of how it affected Ireland and the Irish people and how there should be a recognition of the fact that people from both political traditions died in the battle of the Somme.' Recently, Maginness described the evolution of the SDLP's position. Speaking of both attending ceremonies from 1994 and his formal role, he said that the SDLP in Belfast wanted 'to show respect for a Unionist tradition'. He added that it was hoped that this would 'create better relations politically within the city hall and between communities in Belfast'.[57] Later in the year, on Remembrance Sunday, Maginness wore a poppy as he became the first Nationalist to lead the ceremony. His comments later focused on the symbolism of the poppy. He said that, 'Under the history of division the poppy has been seen as a unionist symbol and nationalists have difficulty embracing it because of what they see it standing for.' However, he hoped that it could now become 'a symbol of reconciliation rather than recrimination' while recognising that this would take time. Before the event, there had been some discussion within the SDLP about whether or not he should wear a white poppy, but this was rejected. He describes his colleagues' attitudes as, 'Don't be doing something that would spoil the whole impact of doing this. Do it properly. Do it well.'[58]

Both the SDLP and the Dublin government have a moved a long way on remembrance. By 1997, Dublin had announced funding for the memorial at Messines, and members of the SDLP were taking a full part in remembrance ceremonies, although its party leader (by this time, Mark Durkan) did not take part in an event until 2002. None of this means that SDLP members are completely comfortable with the nature of the ceremonies. Alban Maginness would like to see the Britishness of the ceremonies less overt, and has told this to the Royal British Legion. However, it was a striking to see another SDLP Lord Mayor of Belfast, Pat McCarthy, leading the 90th anniversary of the Somme event in the city in 2006.[59]

There were also big movements in Sinn Féin, which had their origins as far back as 1995.[60] Since the 1980s, the party has adjusted a number of historic positions, taking seats in the Dáil in Dublin and contesting elections for the Westminster parliament. The first person to signify a shift in attitudes to remembrance was Tom Hartley, a Sinn Féin councillor for Lower Falls since 1993, and a former chairman and general secretary of the party. In 1995, with the approval of his party's *ard chomhairle* (executive), he attended a Second World War commemoration at Islandbridge, which included both war veterans and Holocaust survivors.[61] It was not a First World War event in any way, but Hartley's presence at Islandbridge opened a door by engaging with a place and process Sinn Féin had once boycotted.

The next step from Sinn Féin came in 2002 when Belfast gained its first Sinn Féin Lord Mayor, Alex Maskey. A leading republican for decades, Maskey had been twice interned in the 1970s. Like many other republicans, he had a relative who had served in the British army in 1914–18, in this case his maternal grandfather, Patrick McClory, in the Army Service Corps.[62] The Lord Mayor, who remains in office for one year only, is integral to Belfast's Somme commemoration as the city's chief representative and ceremonial figure, and Maskey pledged to work with all on becoming Mayor. His analysis was that 'The history of the people of this island is complex, layered, has many strands and indeed, many versions of those strands.' He added that it was necessary for all 'to recognise the worth and the integrity of the individual soldier as perceived, honoured and commemorated by those he or she left behind'.[63]

Yet the republican tradition dictated against parades with British military connotations. Meanwhile, some unionists told Maskey that if he attended the commemoration at the Belfast Cenotaph many people would walk away. Maskey came to the conclusion 'that the bolder the step I chose to take, the more damaging it could have been for everyone'. So he decided to lay a wreath at the Cenotaph at 9 a.m. on 1 July 2002, two hours before the main ceremony. Instead of a wreath of poppies, which Maskey said were 'too closely identified with the symbolism of British militarism', he laid a laurel wreath. Meanwhile, he agreed to chair a special meeting of the city council, which was central to events. This involved him reading a tribute to the British monarchy and Commonwealth, and to British soldiers who died at the Somme. Although he felt it ignored the Irish nationalists who died there, he read the motion so as not to be accused 'of being disrespectful to the war dead. That was something which I could not allow to happen.' So, in a short ceremony joined by a dozen other Sinn Féin councillors, Maskey laid the wreath, bowed his head at the Cenotaph and took part in a minute's silence. In so doing, as his biographer says, 'he had rewritten one of the unspoken tenets of Irish republicanism'. The move was far from universally supported within Sinn Féin, and some unionists took offence. But Maskey had avoided any unsavoury counter-demonstrations from either side, and had taken a step which the Secretary of State for Northern Ireland, John Reid, described as 'a sign of encouragement and hope for the future'.[64] Maskey's approach was repeated by Tom Hartley when he became mayor in 2008, by which time Sinn Féin had also taken part in the 90th anniversary of the Somme commemoration and Islandbridge.[65]

Belfast Catholics and nationalists/republicans generally, and republicans in particular, now feel able to show an interest in the war service of their ancestors in a way that simply was not possible when British soldiers were on the streets of Belfast. But their approach is clearly different from that of unionists. While the latter feel pride in their forebears fighting for King and Country, republicans honour the men but not the cause. Máirtín Ó Muilleoir is a former Sinn Féin councillor in Belfast. His great-grandfather was Boer War veteran John McManus, who died in 1916 aged 64 while training the 18th RIRifles. Ó Muilleoir also had relatives in the IRA in the 1920s and he is clear that while he feels 'pride' for their past, as regards John McManus, 'we are not proud of him. We do respect him though.'[66] Ed McCann describes himself as coming from 'a strong Republican background'. His grandfather Francis McCann was gassed at Langemarck, and Ed has spent much time researching men from the Falls. He puts it in a similar way to Ó Muilleoir, saying that while he has no love whatsoever for the British army, he holds the individuals who served 'in the highest regard. They were the cream of that generation without a doubt.'[67]

Such republican attitudes are making it possible for remembrance of the war to play some role in cross-community reconciliation in a way that would have been difficult even to imagine a decade ago. Martin Meehan, once a leading figure in the IRA in North Belfast, visited his grandfather's First World War grave in France in 2002, making arrangements in conjunction with the senior loyalist, Gusty Spence. Before his death in 2007, Meehan was involved, with loyalists such as Winston 'Winkie' Rea in the R-PAST project, which brings together young people from across Ireland in the study of the military history of the island. At the launch, Meehan said, 'People fought for all sorts of reasons, from political beliefs through to economic survival.' Rea argued, 'By understanding other people's experiences we will hopefully avoid the mistakes of the past.'[68]

Activities that reach into these hidden histories are now commonplace. In June 2007 the Falls Community Council, which among other activities runs an oral history project, organized a public meeting in Cultúrlann McAdam Ó Fiaich in the Falls Road. This Irish cultural centre was once a Presbyterian church for which there is no longer any demand following population movement since the 1960s. The meeting came out of a conversation I had with Tom Hartley earlier in the year. Aside from his political activity, Tom is a knowledgeable local historian who has written a book about Belfast City Cemetery, a profoundly unionist space in the heart of the republican Falls. Tom told me that it was increasingly common for people in the Falls to show him memorabilia and medals from the First World War and to ask him to put them into context. While in the Shankill such material and stories are readily available, in the Falls it was necessary to stage an event involving community representatives to access such information. Tom Hartley, and Sinn Féin's Upper Falls councillor, Paul Maskey (brother of Alex and now a Member of the Legislative Assembly at Stormont) and I all spoke at the meeting. The aim was to provide a forum in which it was possible for people to discuss this lost history.

Around 20 people attended, including three loyalists from East Belfast who are involved in cross-community work. It was an incredible occasion. Those who came brought with them stories, medals, photographs and records of internment from the 1920s. This brought to my attention a number of individuals whose stories have featured to greater or lesser degrees in this book. One case was that of Patrick McKillen of the 6th Connaught Rangers, whose great-nephew, Robert McKillen, arrived with some information and a photograph, but has since found out more in parallel with my own research.

Two of those attending have undergone a very personal reassessment of their own view of history and their own family stories. For Seán O' Hare, whose grandfather was discussed in the previous chapter, a lifetime of commitment to republicanism did not sit easily with an interest in the British army record of his ancestor. I asked Seán whether Patrick O'Hare's treatment at the hands of the loyalist mob had influenced the family's political views. Although his grandfather's politics were not affected by events, references to Patrick O'Hare's British military service were not a popular subject in the family in later years. According to Seán, the general view would have been that 'grandfather was mistaken in joining the

British army and he was kind of written out of family history', but his attitude has now changed:

> It's only when you get more mature that you realise that things aren't that black and white. We would have thought that anybody in the British army then would have been a traitor to Irish nationalism/republicanism. But many of us have come to realise that's not the case, it's just that they were as much for Home Rule as anybody else.[70]

The practical outcome of this has been involvement in the Connaught Rangers Research Project, which was launched through the *Irish News* in 2006 and which invited people whose relatives had served in the Connaught Rangers to meet to discuss the past.[71] Partly because of the absence of the word 'Royal' from the Connaughts' name, this regiment is particularly accessible to nationalists and republicans. In discussing this aspect of their past they are helping to inform definitions of Irishness in 1916 that go beyond the Easter Rising, allowing recognition of the diversity of experiences among Irishmen at that time. The project has now published a booklet, which has been hailed by Roy Garland writing in the *Irish News* as something that might 'help liberate our people and their memories from slavery to divided histories'.[72]

A central figure in that project and another attendee at the Cultúrlann meeting is Harry Donaghy. Harry's grandmother Elizabeth regularly talked about her two brothers, Johnny and Dominick Adams, who had been killed within a week of one another in 1915. She also lost her sweetheart, Private Thomas Donnelly, who was killed at Gallipoli serving with the 5th Royal Irish Fusiliers in August 1915. Having lost Thomas, she later married his brother, Patrick, a veteran of the Connaught Rangers and the Royal Irish Fusiliers. Harry Donaghy says his grandfather was 'an ardent Redmondite . . . until the day he died. He never switched and went over to republicanism.' Harry himself did make that switch and later served five years in Long Kesh as a member of the Official IRA. However, despite that, he remembers the attitude in the family being unlike many nationalist households. He told me, 'It wasn't "don't be talking about this" that might have been the general response to nationalists who had fought in the war.'

How did Patrick Donnelly himself remember the war? Harry recalls him being happy to show his medals and talking about the 'awfulness' of war. But he was also clear that his grandfather was only really comfortable talking about the war when other veterans were around – a point made by a number of people who have sent me details of their ancestors who served. In Patrick Donnelly's case, when he collected his pension each week, he met for a drink with former soldiers from all over Belfast, including the Shankill: 'They were more prepared to engage in conversations and stories about their experiences when they were there together, but you had to push them sometimes to go into any detail.'

The quest for understanding of the stories of his relatives who served has given Harry a significant personal commitment to his now full-time work on the Messines Project, in which he works closely with members of the loyalist community. Meanwhile, his approach to why men fought represents an understanding which neatly summarizes what is now becoming an orthodox republican assessment of why men joined the British military in 1914–18. He said:

> Redmond and Devlin . . . called on their supporters to enlist . . . they had the assurances from the British government [that] at the end of hostilities that Ireland would be granted Home Rule . . . That was the political leadership of Irish nationalism at the time . . . and they [army recruits] took that pointer from their political leadership and went and did what they did.[73]

This understanding is leading to an approach to the war among former foes of the Troubles that was once impossible to imagine. It has also led to a revolution in the republican approach to the war, which has been part of the peace process.

Like much of Belfast since the 1990s, the story of its role in the war has changed dramatically. This book has sought to add substance and detail to the many grassroots initiatives that have tried to tell a broad story of the war. The ways in which that story is told will continue to develop as individuals come to terms with pasts that previously they did not wish to address, or did not know they had. There is a danger in assuming that simply because Protestant and Catholic soldiers went through the same war experiences, they or their descendants should be able to live together peacefully. As others have pointed out, wartime unity was 'suspicious and conditional'.[74] Forgetting that would gloss over the very real differences they had both during the war and soon after. However, in communities where divisions have been more apparent than similarities, recognition of a common or shared past can help to build bridges. Such recognition can help to tell the new stories, which are already having positive impacts on community relations in the city. I hope that they continue to do so.

Appendix: Methods and Patterns of 'Military History from the Street'

This book rests on a new approach to the study of the First World War which involves taking a specific area and locating those from it who served.[1] It can be described as 'military history from the street', beginning with where men were from, rather than the units in which they served. The use of that method was determined by a desire to understand as much as possible about the military service of men from West Belfast, including but also going beyond those units (such as the 9th RIRifles and 6th Connaughts) specifically associated with the area. It began from a sense that the stories of the 'volunteer' battalions told a very partial story of the service of West Belfast men.

Three types of source are central to the method. First, newspapers have been analysed in a way that they are not commonly used, drawing on the extensive biographical material contained in Belfast newspapers for soldiers of all ranks. Second, soldiers' individual pensions and service records are now online and can be searched by place name which was never before possible. Third, church memorial rolls have also been used. These sources have been supplemented by a range of other smaller sources which are discussed below. This Appendix explores the methodology to establish what quantifiable conclusions can or cannot be reached about West Belfast's service in 1914–18? In so doing it outlines a methodology that could be applied to mapping service in other areas.

One qualification needs to be made about one source. As is discussed in depth below, pensions and service records available online from www.ancestry.co.uk have been extremely valuable. However, service records for surnames O to Z have yet to be released.[2] Despite that, it is possible to make estimates of how many individuals this tranche of records will include for West Belfast, based on what we already now about the distribution of surnames in the fully-released pensions records. In total, from all sources, as many as 8,484 individuals have been found, although possible duplication may mean the number is as low 8,176. To these totals, it is expected that among the O-Z service records, there will be approximately 421 more West Belfast individuals in total, of whom approximately 319 will not have been found in any other source.[3] Added to the 8,176–8,484 individuals, this extra 319 would result in a total of approximately 8,495–8,803. Because the 319 yet to be analysed constitute only 3.6–3.8 per cent of the expected total, the author believes that the overall patterns found in the other 96 per cent of the records will retain their value. In some places below, the possible impact of these extra 319 on sub-total figures is set out, and it is anticipated that once all the records are released, an article will be published in an academic journal setting out the full statistics so that the most accurate figures possible are in the academic domain.

To return to the mechanics of studying a specific local area, one challenge in any such project is boundary-drawing. Belfast is easier to deal with than many cities because politics has made people unusually conscious of where boundaries are. To an extent, that has meant that electoral ward boundaries do relate in some way to real communities. The area analysed in this book is broadly described as 'West Belfast'. That exists in at least two forms today, both as a parliamentary constituency and in the popular imagination as the area comprising the Falls and the Shankill, and some linked areas. In this book, the bulk of the area included is certainly covered by what were and are seen as the Falls and the Shankill, and it was tempting to use just these two words to describe the geographic scope instead of 'West Belfast'. However, there were two problems with that. First, both words defined specific electoral wards in 1914–18 and these were rather narrow. For example, much of the area thought of as 'the Shankill' was in Woodvale or Court wards, and there were similar problems with 'the Falls' and St Anne's ward. Second, a number of areas which are not strictly Falls or Shankill were part of the wider social and cultural connections of that part of the city: the areas we now call Ligoniel, Glencairn, Springmartin, Woodvale, Ballymurphy, Turf Lodge and Andersonstown.

Consequently, 'West Belfast' is a suitable label but it needs some caveats attached. First, in 1914–18, the West Belfast constituency stretched right into the city centre. Some of that area needs to be included as it was not separated from the Shankill or the Falls by today's 'Westlink' road, but not all of it should be included as it is clearly 'city centre'. Second, the Shankill area was and is divided between the North and West Belfast parliamentary constituencies. In 1914–18, the entire northern side of the Shankill was in the North Belfast seat. The lines are further blurred by the fact that men living in the Shankill electoral ward who joined the Ulster Volunteer Force in 1912 seem to have gone into the North Belfast UVF. Yet when the Ulster Division was formed in 1914, those same men went into the West Belfast battalion, the 9th Royal Irish Rifles. The boundary is further complicated on the Falls side because some of the roads off the Falls Road, such as Thames Street and Fallswater Street, and indeed the whole of the Royal Victoria Hospital and parts of the Grosvenor Road, were in South Belfast in 1914. That also applies to the area around Celtic Park which was central to the political life of West Belfast nationalism, and must be included in any such study. Third, areas like Roden Street in South Belfast were more linked to the Falls than they are now. In 1914, indeed until the 1960s, the whole of the Donegall Road down to the railway line, which today we think of as South Belfast, was more closely connected with the Falls than it is today.

So, the following boundaries have been adopted as having some formal basis, but also representing the communities lived in by people at the time (see Map 1, p. xiii). The basis of the area is five electoral wards: Shankill, Woodvale, Court, Smithfield and Falls. Also included are sections of the Donegall Road and Grosvenor Road west of the railway line. These were in St Anne's ward, but formed part of what we might call Greater Falls in 1914 in terms of living, working and socialising. Broadly speaking, that means an area bounded by the Crumlin Road to the north, the Donegall Road and railway line to the south, Upper Library Street and Smithfield Market to the east, and the city boundary to the west. It is an area that is not perfect, but has met with great satisfaction in the author's discussions among people who have knowledge of Belfast before the Westlink, and also in discussions with many academics. Meanwhile, sticking as far as possible to ward boundaries enables comparative studies of other parts of Belfast at a later stage. It results in an area with around 118,000 residents, of whom about 60 per cent were Church of Ireland, Presbyterian or Methodist, 37 per cent Catholic, and 3 per cent members of another or no faith, principally smaller Protestant denominations.[4]

With an area defined it was possible to start establishing which of its residents served. Sources traditionally used for studying service in 1914–18 are all hugely problematic in determining who served from a specific area. For the British military as a whole the Commonwealth War Graves Commission website (www. cwgc.org) is the most useful because it often includes the address of the deceased's next-of-kin, although this is sometimes a post-war address. The CWGC is willing to provide researchers with downloads of their data searched for place name and the value of that is discussed below. There are also *Soldiers Died* and *Officers Died* listings and *Ireland's Memorial Records* which were originally books but are now available on CD-Rom. However, the *Soldiers Died* records never included an address, and *Ireland's Memorial Records* is focused on Irish regiments, which means it includes many non-Irish soldiers and misses out many Irishmen in other regiments, and in any case rarely contains addresses. Meanwhile, all these sources, by definition, only cover the dead.

However, a number of recent developments have revolutionised research. The digitisation of pensions and service records by the National Archives with ancestry.co.uk is nearing completion. In the case of service records, up to 75 per cent were destroyed in the London Blitz in 1940, and many of those remaining are badly damaged so that key information is missing. These records were previously only available on microfilm, and the author once calculated that it would take 27 years of full-time research to go through them one-by-one to search for Belfast men. But online, they can be searched by place name. It is now possible to search the records for a keyword such as 'Belfast', along with other words such as 'Falls' and 'Shankill' (including its mis-spelling Shankhill which correctly relates to a parish in County Armagh but was often written on Belfast records). There are problems with the transcribing of street names,[5] but Belfast is hard to mis-read and simply searching for that word in the pensions records finds 2,968 individuals, and in the service records another 4,204 with a Belfast address. When other terms are also searched for the totals become 5,129 pensions records and 7,325 service records (with another 2,313 of the latter expected to be published as explained earlier).[6] Each of these 12,454 has been read, with the result that 1,506 West Belfast individuals were found in the pensions records and 1,339 in the service records. The reason for fewer individuals from West Belfast being found in the larger number of service records than in the smaller number of pensions records is that there is much duplication in the service records with many individuals having two files due to copies being kept.

Meanwhile, as this book was being completed, an invaluable listing of 9,279 soldiers' wills appeared on CD-Rom for Ireland as a whole, researched by Kiara Gregory and produced by Eneclann. Of these 1,558 were from Belfast. That includes addresses and could be narrowed down to 518 from West Belfast, although the vast majority of those can be found in other sources as is discussed below. Two memorial rolls have been used, both of which contain the names of those who served rather than only the dead. The Presbyterian Memorial Roll, which the author had digitised to make it searchable, contains 9,835 names for the city as whole. A roll for the St Michael's Church of Ireland congregation included names and addresses for 767 who served. Only one nominal roll for a battalion has been found, for the 14th Royal Irish Rifles which included at least 2,000 names, of whom 287 were from West Belfast. Duplication between sources, and the extent to which each source provides unique data is discussed below.

Other than a small number of names (22) which only came to light from individually-held records such as family papers and 21 from early 1920s Troubles-related material, the final sources, and major ones at that, were local newspapers. For each day of the war (and several months after), the following were consulted: the *Belfast Evening Telegraph* (which dropped *Evening* in April 1918), *Belfast News Letter* and *Irish News*. The first two contained detailed biographical information for not only the dead, but also the wounded, missing, prisoners, medallists, and sometimes those who just wrote an interesting letter home. Such information included a minimum of name, address, regiment and, until the middle of 1916, battalion. Often there is much more such as next of kin, place of work, or membership of an organisation. Sometimes there is an account of the moment of death, wounding, capture or heroic act. When specific battalions were not mentioned for the dead, such information could usually be found by cross-referencing to sources such as CWGC website or medals rolls. It is important to note that newspapers included significant details for both officers and other ranks. In the *Telegraph* there were often photographs. The *Irish News* did not include lists of the dead, but it did contain family 'In Memoriam' notices and many individual stories.

There are other newspapers that were considered. In particular, key Dublin newspapers (*Irish Independent* and *Irish Times*) were suggested to the author because they might have had a different readership to the Belfast papers and were to some extent, all-Ireland. Therefore, sampling was carried out of copies from seven months over 1915, 1916 and 1917 when Irish regiments were reporting high casualties. Unfortunately, the value of both is limited by their focus on officers. Moreover, the overall result of the sample was that of more than one thousand family death notices in the two newspapers over a seven month period, there were only seven individuals referred to as having a Belfast connection, six of whom were not connected with West Belfast, and one of whom contained just a general reference to the city. There were two West Belfast officers whose pictures appeared in the *Independent*, but as much or more biographical information on both men was in the Belfast newspapers, and a picture for one of them can be found in the same source.

Two other newspapers were also considered: the *Northern Whig* and the Irish Parliamentary Party's organ *Freeman's Journal*. The *Journal* however simply did not carry biographical information on casualties, except the official British lists which contained no addresses. Meanwhile, although the *Whig* did carry much detail, it was not as comprehensive as that in the other newspapers and all the samples found that the information was already revealed in my searches of either *Telegraph* or *Newsletter* except for one reference to two soldiers from the same address.

Before assessing the relative value of these sources, it is important to state their limits. Service in the Royal Navy or RFC/RAF will be understated in overall figures because records for these services are not yet searchable in ways which allow them to be searched by place of residence. Only around 25 per cent of service records have survived. Obviously, church memorial rolls do not pretend to contain anything other than members of their own congregation, although there is some possible duplication between Presbyterian and Anglican records, perhaps explained by both rolls showing men who were in 'mixed' marriages. As rolls were not produced by Catholic churches any effort to assess the relative service of Protestants and Catholics is hampered. Meanwhile, there were biases in the newspapers. In particular, whereas the *Telegraph* and *News Letter* would mention if someone had been in the UVF, they would often report the death of an INV veteran without mentioning the INV. Only through the *Irish News* does one find that side of the story. However, it is clear from the nature of religious references to Mary and the 'Sacred Heart of Jesus' that Catholics were regularly using the *Telegraph* for 'In Memoriam' notices, even if we cannot conclude anything about their politics. But overall, the weight of the Protestant memorial rolls and unionist newspapers means that there is a strong bias against Catholics and nationalists in the overall numbers.

This is problematic because the levels of service according to denomination were much debated at the time. There have been efforts to assess them since which suggest marginally higher recruitment rates among Catholics than Protestants in Belfast as a whole.[7] However, methods which have been used are extremely unreliable as is recognised by those using them. For example, making judgements about people on the basis of a surname poses problems from the first letter of the alphabet: what does one do with an Adams? First names can help further, but the pensions and service records for six West Belfast John Murphys, illustrate the problem: two were Catholics, one Presbyterian, one Church of Ireland, and the other two of unknown denomination. It might be hoped that some estimates would be possible using only the service and pensions records because they do not have the same bias as other sources. However, information on religious denomination is not contained in all of these records. A particular problem is that denomination is lacking for some battalions more than others. For example, it is included for 88.2 per cent of the 9th RIRifles, compared to only 30.5 per cent of the 6th Connaughts and just 18.9 per cent of the 7th Leinsters. In many cases, denomination is not recorded simply because among the various enlistment forms used in different offices and at different times, one type did not include space for denomination, although a section was sometimes added by hand. In other cases the relevant pages are missing from the service records which survived the Blitz. However, the disparity between information recorded in different battalions is highly problematic when it is suspected that some battalions began with different religious compositions. There could be many reasons for this. It might be that the staff compiling records for the Leinsters and Connaughts were simply not very diligent. However, it might also be that most or all of those in the Leinsters were Catholics and it was simply not considered necessary to write that down. In contrast, those making records for the RIRifles might have felt that while most/all volunteers would be Protestant, it was important to know what type of Protestant they were.

Despite that, there are methods for filling in the gaps, yet the figures are far from conclusive.[8] They lead to results which put the Catholic proportion of volunteers at anything between 30.8 per cent and 37.6 per cent in an area where they comprised 35.9 per cent of the population. Moreover, although all methods show members of the Church of Ireland enlisting at higher levels than their share of population, and Methodists lower, results for Presbyterians are higher or lower than their population share depending on the method.[9] Consequently any effort to assess levels of recruitment according to denomination is fraught with difficulty. Furthermore, even though we can be sure from the data available that regular battalions and non-political volunteer battalions were far more mixed than volunteer battalions of the 16th and 36th divisions,[10] the amount of information regarding denomination is small enough to be problematic. That is especially so when one notes that the extent to which a battalion was 'mixed' or not depended also on its recruits from beyond West Belfast, for whom this project has not gathered information.

However, more clarity is possible on the extent of service in specific units in terms of total numbers, and we can gain some idea of the minimum number of men who served from specific parts of West Belfast. Any such statements must be prefaced with 'minimum' because of the destruction of service records, the limits on information about Catholics, and the fact that newspapers tended not to carry any information on those who served without anything remarkable happening to them.

The overall figures are that at least 8,176 to 8,484 individuals from West Belfast served, at least in so far as getting beyond the initial medical check. The range is explained by possible duplication of a limited number of records. Of these, at least 1,990 were killed during the war[11] or died in service (with queries over a further 162). Had 75 per cent of service records not been destroyed in 1940, we might expect to find records for around 4,000 others who were not mentioned in any other source, meaning that the overall number of West Belfast men who served at some point in 1914–18 could be over 12,000.[12] It is difficult to be accurate about what percentage of the male population of West Belfast served at some point, partly because we cannot be clear of the age breakdown of the population for specific wards in the city, but also because the age of men is not always known or accurate. However, the 1911 Census shows that men between 18 and 40 were around 17 per cent of the population of the city as a whole, which would mean approximately 20,060 of that age range in West Belfast. If we assume that most recruits were in this age range, then records have been found for about 42 per cent of them, and the figure may be nearer 60 per cent.[13]

Leaving such uncertain figures behind, the figures of which we can be more sure dramatically alter our understanding of levels of service by West Belfast men. But before turning to these, it is worth reflecting on the key point that a wide range of sources must be used to gain a comprehensive picture: of 8,484 total records, 82 per cent were *only* found in *one* source. However, no single source dominates the rest. Of the records found in only one source, Presbyterian records were marginally the most important with 1,796 (21 per cent) closely followed by the newspapers with 1,670 (20 per cent). Pensions and service records provided 1,452 and 1,016 unique records respectively, the St Michael's Memorial Roll 580, and a Belfast search of the war graves records 273. Smaller finds were in the 14th RIRifles Nominal Roll (177), *World War I Irish Soldiers* CD (133) and a handful in other sources. The other 18 per cent of records could be found in more than one source, over half of these in the newspapers combined with either the Presbyterian or CWGC records. The key lesson from this is not so much the relative value of the various sources, but the fact that any historian looking at a similar area must use a similar wide range of sources to obtain comprehensive coverage. The recently discovered Red Cross records, which are not yet in an easily accessible format, may add even more names.[14]

Taking all sources combined shows where these men were from (see Table 1). Where no house number is given, and in the few cases where the road is a boundary of a ward, there is uncertainty, but we can be clear of the numbers below. It is important to recognise that both the Shankill and Falls were mixed in terms of religion in a way that they have not been since the Troubles. So, there are Catholics (135) in the figures for the Greater Shankill, and Protestants (219) in the Greater Falls, while twenty-six in total (four of whom were dead) are in roads that border wards and are harder to place in either the greater Falls or Shankill areas.

We can also learn about the units in which men served (see Table 2). From the data gathered, we can link 89.7 per cent of men to a regiment or other such as the Royal Navy, and 65.1 per cent to a specific unit, such as a battalion or ship. This means that more than ever before we can make some judgements about where men were serving.

Figures for units of the 16th (Irish) Division are much lower than for those in

Table 1 Total number by ward of individuals who served in army, navy or air force in 1914–18

Ward	Total served	Number dead
Court	1,874	314 (and 50 possible)
Shankill	2,318	537 (and 46 possible)
Woodvale	1,979	468 (and 38 possible)
Indeterminate Shankill area	58	9 (and 2 possible)
Total 'Shankill' area	*6,228*	*1,354 (and 136 possible)*
Falls	1,025	312 (and 10 possible)
St Anne's (part)	600	151 (and 9 possible)
Smithfield	589	169 (and 6 possible)
Indeterminate Falls area	14	4
Total 'Falls' area	*2,228*	*636 (and 25 possible)*

Note: If all possible duplicates are duplicates, then the 'Total served' figures would be reduced by an average of 3.6 per cent. We can also expect those figures to go up, coincidentally, but the same percentage when the O-Z service records are released, although the impact of these records on the number of dead will be minimal as a much lower percentage of the dead are found only in service records. A further 28 men cannot be linked to a specific part of West Belfast.

the Ulster Division. What does this mean for these units? For example, do these figures undermine the Falls connection of the 6th Connaughts or 7th Leinsters? The author's view is that it does not simply because of the bias of the sources. At the time, and extremely unusually, both the unionist and nationalist press were agreed that 600 men left Belfast to join the 6th Connaughts. The main reason we cannot document them individually (apart from the fact that some would not have been from West Belfast) is that from early on, the one nationalist newspaper was less detailed and enthusiastic about reporting 'their' soldiers than the unionist press. In any event, it simply is not possible to find all the names for any units, especially for ones that Catholics tended to join, due to the lack of Catholic rolls of honour and the destruction of the majority of service records.

In contrast, it is unsurprising that the largest figure is for the 9th RIRifles which was the most self-consciously 'West Belfast' unit and recruited much of the West Belfast UVF. It may be more surprising that the total for the 14th RIRifles is so high, but that figure is influenced by the survival of a nominal roll for the battalion. Such a valuable source exists for no other battalion discussed here, and if we were to use only sources available for all units, then the 14th RIRifles figure falls much lower, to 197. That would put it below the 2nd, 1st and 15th RIRifles and the total for non-infantry units in the Ulster Division, which probably more accurately reflects its place in the ranking of West Belfast recruiters.

The case of the 2nd RIRifles is especially interesting. Much of the service by these 333 men was in the early part of the war. In the 2nd RIRifles, there were 188 confirmed West Belfast deaths during the war. Well over half (102) were before the end of 1915. So in the case of the first year and a quarter of the war, if one is

Table 2 Total number of individuals who served in specific units in 1914–18 where total is 15 or more

Division or type of unit	Battalion	Number serving
36th (Ulster) – Infantry	9th Royal Irish Rifles	497 to 499
36th (Ulster) – Infantry	14th Royal Irish Rifles	369 to 372
36th (Ulster) – non-infantry troops	Divisional units of: Royal Engineers, RAMC, Royal Field Artillery, Army Service Corps and Machine Gun Corps	352
Regulars	2nd Royal Irish Rifles	332 to 333
36th (Ulster) – Infantry	15th Royal Irish Rifles	250 to 252
Regulars – Infantry	1st Royal Irish Rifles	229
Regulars – Infantry	2nd Royal Inniskilling Fusiliers	174 to 176
Regulars – Infantry	1st Royal Inniskilling Fusiliers	161
10th (Irish) – Infantry	6th Royal Irish Rifles	157 to 158
36th (Ulster) – Infantry	10th Royal Irish Rifles	140
16th (Irish) – Infantry	6th Connaught Rangers	125
16th (Irish) – Infantry	7th Leinsters	121
Regulars – Infantry	1st Royal Irish Fusiliers	86
36th (Ulster) – Pioneers	16th Royal Irish Rifles	84
36th (Ulster) – Infantry	8th Royal Irish Rifles	58
36th (Ulster) – Infantry	9th Royal Inniskilling Fusiliers	50
36th (Ulster) – Infantry	12th Royal Irish Rifles	43
10th (Irish) – Infantry	6th Royal Irish Fusiliers	38
36th (Ulster) – Infantry	9th Royal Irish Fusiliers	35
Regulars – Infantry	1st Irish Guards	32
10th (Irish) – Infantry	5th Royal Irish Fusiliers	27
Royal Navy	HMS *Hawke*	19

Note: 36th (Ulster) Division as configured in 1914. We can expect army figures to go up by approximately 3.6 per cent when the O-Z service records are released.

looking for a 'West Belfast Battalion', then it is not one of the volunteer battalions, but the 2nd RIRifles. There are also high totals in the 1st battalion of the same regiment, and the 1st Inniskillings.

Both the 1st Inniskillings and the 6th RIRifles illustrate the impact of Gallipoli, which is not a central part of the popular West Belfast story. We can then look to smaller clusters in, for example, the Royal Navy. When HMS *Hawke* went down in October 1914, it took with it at least 17 men from the Falls and Shankill, with another two surviving. The existence of such clusters, though small, add new layers to a story that has previously begun with volunteers joining the Ulster Division and culminated with those volunteers going over the top at the Somme in July 1916, but has had little room for the vast array of stories from different parts of the war. As Adrian Gregory has argued, understanding the timing of fatalities is crucial to assessing the impact of the war on specific areas.[15]

The statistics also illustrate the extent to which the local connections of battalions were reduced as the fighting wore on. This is widely assumed, but little work has been done on the details of specific units. Three snapshots of the 9th RIRifles illustrate the point, although they each carry the health warnings that must be attached to any small sample of data.

The first of the snapshots comes from the night of 5/6 June 1916, when the 9th was under heavy fire, having moved to the front at Thiepval a few days before. That night, all of the seven dead had West Belfast addresses, and six lived in the Shankill. It is a small sample, but it signifies something about the nature of the battalion, or at least companies within it, at this stage of the war. Moving to 1 and 2 July 1916 for the Somme, between 99 and 107 other ranks died. Of the 75 for whom an address has been found, 61 had a West Belfast address.[16] But by Messines on 7 June 1917, the situation had changed with only six of the 22 dead having West Belfast addresses. Ten were post-Somme transfers from English battalions.[17] There was still a Shankill connection, but it was weaker than that of July 1916, and illustrates what had happened to the local connections of the volunteer battalions in general by 1917.

For an explanation of why the local component of units was declining we need to look no further than the monthly recruitment figures (see Table 3). Following the pattern of Irish recruitment generally, West Belfast's volunteering levels fell away after 1916. Data on 2,664 men whose date of first enlistment is unambiguous in pensions or service records shows the decline clearly. Of those from West Belfast who served in 1914–18, 3.9 per cent were regular soldiers already in the army. Just over 14 per cent joined in each of August and September 1914. Of the 382 in August, 152 were reservists. The other 230 would have been the most enthusiastic to volunteer at the outbreak. The large number for September reflects the rush to join the 36th (Ulster) Division, while the November increase on October followed John Redmond's call to enlist. The slight increase in February 1915 was influenced by a renewed Nationalist focus on recruiting, while the increase in May 1915 came at a time when the Ulster Division was making new efforts to recruit. Otherwise, the story is one of steady decline. Nearly half of those who fought had joined up by the end of 1914, and over 80 per cent by the end of 1915. By the end of September 1916, approximately the mid-point of the war, 90.6 per cent of enlistments had already taken place.

One potentially interesting point to emerge from the figures on recruitment is that the Easter Rising may not have had any negative effect on Catholic recruitment in Belfast compared to Protestants. Among those who have a pensions or service record, the date of enlistment is recorded in 1,933 cases, the vast bulk (1,775) coming before the end of April 1916. Among these, Catholics represent 28.9 per cent. However, from May 1916 onwards, Catholics comprised 41.1 per cent, although the small sample size (65 Catholics from 158 soldiers) means caution must be taken in reaching firm conclusions.

Table 3 Recruitment

Year – month	Number	Month per cent	Quarter per cent	Year per cent
Pre-war	105	3.9		
1914 – Aug	382*	14.0		
1914 – Sep	381	14.0	31.9	
1914 – Oct	89	3.3		
1914 – Nov	240	8.8		
1914 – Dec	112	4.1	16.2	48.1
1915 – Jan	107	3.9		
1915 – Feb	138	5.1		
1915 – Mar	60	2.2	11.2	
1915 – Apr	63	2.3		
1915 – May	178	6.5		
1915 – Jun	85	3.1	12.0	
1915 – Jul	43	1.6		
1915 – Aug	54	2.0		
1915 – Sep	44	1.6	5.2	
1915 – Oct	47	1.7		
1915 – Nov	81	3.0		
1915 – Dec	35	1.3	6.0	34.4
1916 – Jan	50	1.8		
1916 – Feb	26	1.0		
1916 – Mar	24	0.9	3.7	
1916 – Apr	0	0.0		
1916 – May	17	0.6		
1916 – Jun	28	1.0	1.7	
1916 – Jul	20	0.7		
1916 – Aug	35	1.3		
1916 – Sep	21	0.8	2.8	
1916 – Oct	21	0.8		
1916 – Nov	9	0.3		
1916 – Dec	12	0.4	1.5	9.7
1917 – Jan	20	0.7		
1917 – Feb	24	0.9		
1917 – Mar	19	0.7	2.3	
1917 – Apr	15	0.6		
1917 – May	17	0.6		
1917 – Jun	12	0.4	1.6	

(continued)

Year – month	Number	Month per cent	Quarter per cent	Year per cent
1917 – Jul	16	0.6		
1917 – Aug	14	0.5		
1917 – Sep	5	0.2	1.3	
1917 – Oct	7	0.3		
1917 – Nov	10	0.4		
1917 – Dec	5	0.2	0.8	6.0
1918 – Jan	3	0.1		
1918 – Feb	5	0.2		
1918 – Mar	5	0.2	0.5	
1918 – Apr	7	0.3		
1918 – May	2	0.1		
1918 – Jun	4	0.1	0.5	
1918 – Jul	5	0.2		
1918 – Aug	9	0.3		
1918 – Sep	2	0.1	0.6	
1918 – Oct	7	0.3		
1918 – Nov	2	0.1		2.0
Total	2,722			

* Of the August 1914 recruits, 152 were reservists (79 Army Reserve and 73 Special Reserve).

Note: This table covers 2,722 enlistments, by 2,664 individuals, 57 of whom enlisted twice, and one of whom enlisted three times. Because this table is based only on service and pensions records, rather than all the other sources used, the O-Z service records will add about another 14 per cent to the overall number of records which contain an enlistment date, rather than the 3.6 per cent which they add to other totals. It is expected that the numbers should rise broadly uniformly by that about 14 per cent, so there is no evidence to suggest that this will lead to a different spread of recruitments over the war.

Taking all these figures combined enables us to look at West Belfast's story in a fresh light. There is a loyalist story that is told about the men of the Shankill: it has been included on websites and leaflets aimed at tourists, and is also used in a tourist information board provided by Belfast City Council outside the Shankill Memorial Garden. It says that 760 men from the Shankill fought in the war in the Ulster Division, and that only 76 came back.[18] These figures are problematic, partly because (see Table 1) they seriously understate the total number of Shankill dead in the war, but also because many more than 76 men came back.

That loyalist story is likely to have come from a particular reading of what happened on the first two days of the battle of the Somme, which can be found in the memoirs of Percy Crozier, the 9th RIRifles' commanding officer in 1916. He wrote about: 'seven hundred men of the West Belfast battalion of the Royal Irish Rifles' proving that they could 'subordinate matter to mind'; that after 1 and 2 July 1916 'only seventy men' remained to 'carry the torch'; that he had trained 'seven hundred men to kill or incapacitate at least an equal number before 'going west' themselves'; and spoke of 700 'dead and destroyed'. 'Going west' was well known at the time for meaning 'dead', but in another section of his memoirs he talked about 600 who would 'go West or to Blighty'.[19] This latter statement, about some of these men receiving a 'Blighty' wound which sent them back to England, rather than being killed is a hint that his figure of 700 dead was greatly exaggerated. In fact, as already stated, official records show that a maximum of five officers and 107 other ranks were killed in the 9th RIRifles on 1 and 2 July 1916. This makes sense within a widely accepted figure of 5,500 casualties in the Ulster Division as a whole on those two days, with perhaps 2,000 of these being killed.[20]

Yet overall, the loyalist story actually understates the Shankill's service in the war, even if one only looks at figures for the Ulster Division (as configured in 1914) in which nearly 1,900 served. Many more than 684 men from the Shankill area were killed: at least 1,354. Not 760 but over 6,000 served. Consequently, many more than 76 returned, thousands in fact. Meanwhile, most of that service and death was outside the 9th RIRifles, the Ulster Division and the Somme. Thus many more served and were killed than the story suggests, but they served in different places and at different times than in some versions of the popular story which is closely focused on 1 July 1916. Of the dead, 173 of those were killed on 1 and 2 July 1916. There is no doubt that 12.7 per cent of the entire war fatalities for a small area, on just two days (12.7 per cent on 0.1 per cent of the days of the war) is a massive proportion. That explains why the Somme is so significant to the loyalist story of 1914–18, and why it should remain so. But with over 87 per cent of Shankill fatalities coming at other times and in other places, the story also needs to factor in many other major engagements, from the Retreat at Mons, to Gallipoli, to Ypres, to the final offensive, and the battle on the seas and in the air.

For the nationalist and republican story of the war, the implications of this research are less dramatic in numerical terms, but perhaps ultimately more profound. By documenting the men of the Falls who served not only in the 6th Connaughts and 7th Leinsters, but many other battalions, it is possible to reach some understanding of their backgrounds and experiences, by providing names, faces and details of where they lived. This helps to open up new territory for people from the Falls, to understand that service in the British Army did not necessarily represent a desire to fight for King and Country, but perhaps a belief that such service would advance Home Rule. They can also understand that service provided a job in times of hardship, or simply that people joined because so many of their friends and neighbours were doing the same thing, and because their political leaders urged them to do so.

For everyone though, there is another story produced by researching in such detail. It is a story of the other West Belfast battalion, the 2nd Royal Irish Rifles. In this battalion, though men might have joined for different reasons and with different hopes, they shared an experience of war. In this battalion, men like William Shearer and Michael McGivern, who had been in rival armies before the war, served side-by-side.

Acknowledgements

I have benefited from the wisdom, support and knowledge of many. My first thanks go to Tony Morris who commissioned this book for Hambledon in 2005 and had a huge impact on its shape. Professor Keith Jeffery of Queen's University Belfast provided encouragement and advice throughout. Dr Tim Bowman of the University of Kent was generous with his time and provided incisive comments on a full draft of the book. Professor Andrew Thompson at Leeds helped me realize that the project was possible, which was essential advice.

I am grateful to my colleagues in the Department of Politics at Goldsmiths for comments in a seminar on my research. Dr John Reardon provided valuable contacts and Dr Bernadette Buckley gave probing and thoughtful comments on a full draft. Thanks to Ruth Daglish and Elaine Webb on administrative matters relating to the book. Students on my third-year course 'Northern Ireland's Politics and Political Cultures' have been persistently thought-provoking. Among them, special thanks go to Joanna Crossfield and Bethany Torvell, both of whom provided helpful comments and queries on a full draft.

Elsewhere in academe, Jane Leonard asked testing and influential methodological questions. Others offered pointers which may have seemed small to them, but were invaluable: Professor Joanna Bourke, Professor Richard English, Dr Denis O'Hearn, Professor Liam Kennedy, Eddine Khaoury, Professor Jim McAuley, Dr Eamon Phoenix and Dr Dan Todman. Dr Marie Coleman organized a seminar through the Ulster Society for Irish Historical Studies. Financial support came from the British Academy in a Small Research Grant, and the University of London Central Research Fund provided money to digitize some records at the Centre for Data Digitization and Analysis at Queen's.

This book would not be what it is without the enthusiasm of people in and around Belfast. Ed McCann has provided valuable material about Falls men over several years. I am very grateful to him for that. Colonel Derek Smyth of the Belfast Book of Honour Project has been a great source of advice and contacts and also read a draft of this book. Tommy Kirkham, then of Fernhill House Museum, was interested from an early stage and allowed my Dad and I to follow a Beyond Conflict pilgrimage to France/Flanders. A number of his colleagues are listed for thanks below. Billy Ervine was generous with his time and knowledge, while Jackie Hewitt, Cllr Dr Ian Adamson and Michael Hall discussed the Farset project. Claire Hackett (Falls Community Council), Lord Mayor Cllr Tom Hartley and Paul Maskey MLA were crucial in making contact with people in the Falls. Special thanks are due to Harry Donaghy, Seán O'Hare,

Siobhán Deane, Robert McKillen and Seamus Colligan. Through the Connaught Rangers Research Project they have provided much material, and I am grateful to Harry and Seán for inviting me on their visit to the Connaught Rangers Museum. Both Robert and Siobhán have been generous in finding material when my time in Belfast was limited.

Carol Walker of the Somme Heritage Centre has provided much advice. I would also like to thank her colleagues Craig McGuicken, Gemma Farry, Noel Kane and Matthew Gamble. Thanks are also due to Teddy and Phoebe Colligan (Ulster Tower); Valerie Adams, Margaret McPartland and Heather Stanley (PRONI); Gerry Healey (Linen Hall Library); Peter Dawson (Ordnance Survey of NI); Simon Moody and Kate Portelli (National Army Museum); Amanda Moreno (Royal Irish Fusiliers Musuem); Major Jack Dunlop (Royal Inniskilling Fusiliers Museum); Captain Jaki Knox and Terence Nelson (Royal Ulster Rifles Museum); Pól Wilson (Irish Republican History Museum); Derek Butler (Commonwealth War Graves Commission); Dr Paul McHugh, Danny Tiernan and Oliver Fallon (Connaught Rangers Association); Siobhán Pierce (National Museum of Ireland); Sharon King and Sharon Robinson (Council for the Curriculum, Examinations and Assessment); Orna Somerville and Lisa Collins (UCD); Ellen O'Flaherty (Irish Jesuit Archives); Brian Donnelly and Gregory O'Connor (National Archive, Dublin); Ciarán Barnes (*Andersonstown News*); Pete Bleakley (*Northern Visions*); Gráinne McCarry (*Belfast Telegraph*) and the staff of the National Archives, Kew (particularly Caroline Kimbell and Alan Bowgen) and the Imperial War Museum.

Kiara Gregory and Eneclann's Brian Donovan generously allowed pre-publication access to the *World War I Irish Soldiers* CD. I wish I had space to thank all the following in more detail: BBC Radio Ulster *Talk Back*; Joe Bowers; Desy Brennan; Willie Cameron; Keith Campbell; David Capper; Desmond Cassidy; Mary Close; Brian Courtney; Colin Cousins; Joanne and Paul Creasey; Jenny Davies; Justin Davin-Smith; Cathal Donaghy; Rita Duffy; Sarah Empey; Terry Enright; Marie Fallon; Stephen Farry MLA; Joe Ferguson; David Ford MLA; Bobby Foster; Mark Gallagher; Davina Gibney; Adrian Gilbert; Janet Hanson; Erskine Holmes OBE; Ian Kirk-Smith; Pam and Ken Linge; Michael Lyness; Alban Maginness MLA; Davy McCrea; Jim McDermott; Teresa McNally; Eric Mercer; Pat and Roísín O'Donnell; Máirtín Ó Muilleoir; Marie Toner Moore; Philip Orr; Brian Reid; David Robertson; George Robinson; Stephen Sandford; Charles Smith; Jane Suiter; James W. Tayler; Paul Taylor; Jim Watson; Bob White; Sam White; Avril Williams; and Carole Zandvliet.

I am grateful to all the staff at Continuum who have produced the book with great enthusiasm, and to David Appleyard for his assistance with maps. Thanks also to Matthew Taylor, Zena Elmahrouki, Ben Hardy and Joanna Crossfield for twice acting as an impromptu focus group when I needed comments on the all-important cover.

I am grateful to David, Julie and Linda McIlrath for providing a home from home on a number of visits, and to Jennie and Chris Barrett for guidance on

Excel. Thanks to my parents for their love and support over 40 years, and more specifically, my Dad, Donald Grayson, for joining me on the battlefields and my Mum, Jannat, for commenting on a full draft. Finally, my deepest thanks are to my wife, Lucy, and son, Edward, for their love and support, and also their tolerance of time spent researching and writing. As the three of us combined a holiday in France in 2006 with a visit to the Somme, it was humbling to be around Thiepval on a hot summer's day among memorials to men who were deprived of a full life with their family.

Notes

Notes to Preface

1 Irish regiments in general are covered in Tom Burke, *The 16th (Irish) and 36th (Ulster) Divisions at the Battle of Wijtschaete – Messines Ridge, 7 June 1917* (Dublin, 2007); Henry Harris, *Irish Regiments in the First World War* (Cork, 1968); Tom Johnstone, *Orange, Green and Khaki: The Story of the Irish Regiments in the Great War, 1914–18* (Dublin, 1992) and Steven Moore, *The Irish on the Somme: A Battlefield Guide to the Irish Regiments in the Great War and the Monuments in their Memory* (Belfast, 2005). On the 36th (Ulster) Division, see Cyril Falls, *The History of the 36th (Ulster) Division* (Belfast, 1922) and Philip Orr, *The Road to the Somme: Men of the Ulster Division Tell their Story* (Belfast, 1987). On the 16th (Irish) Division, see: Terence Denman, *Ireland's Unknown Soldiers: The 16th (Irish) Division in the Great War* (Dublin, 1992). The 10th (Irish) Division is covered by Bryan Cooper, *The Tenth (Irish) Division in Gallipoli* (Dublin, 1993); Philip Orr, *Field of Bones: An Irish Division at Gallipoli* (Dublin, 2006) and Jeremy Stanley, *Ireland's Forgotten 10th: A Brief History of the 10th (Irish) Division 1914–18, Turkey, Macedonia and Palestine* (Ballycastle, 2003). Relevant regimental or battalion studies are: W. J. Canning, *A Wheen of Medals: The History of the 9th (Service) Bn. The Royal Inniskilling Fusiliers (The Tyrones) in World War One* (Antrim, 2006); Frank Fox, *The Royal Inniskilling Fusiliers in the World War* (London, 1928); H. F. N. Jourdain and Edward Fraser, *The Connaught Rangers: Vol. III* (London, 1928); Rudyard Kipling, *The Irish Guards in the Great War, Volume 1: The 1st Battalion* and *Volume 2: The 2nd Battalion* (London, 1923); James W. Taylor, *The 1st RIRifles in the Great War* (Dublin, 2002) and *The 2nd RIRifles in the Great War* (Dublin, 2005); Stuart N. White, *The Terrors: 16th (Pioneer) Battalion RIRifles* (Belfast, 1996); Frederick Ernest Whitton, *A History of the Prince of Wales's Leinster Regiment (Royal Canadians), Volume II* (Aldershot, 1924).

2 For important academic studies see Thomas Bartlett and Keith Jeffery (eds), *A Military History of Ireland* (Cambridge, 1996); Timothy Bowman, *Irish Regiments in the Great War: Discipline and Morale* (Manchester, 2003); Adrian Gregory and Senia Pašeta (eds), *Ireland and the Great War: 'A War to Unite Us All'?* (Manchester, 2002); Keith Jeffery, *Ireland and the Great War* (Cambridge, 2000). For the Irish element in the literature on individual soldiers' 'voices', see: Richard Doherty and David Truesdale, *Irish Winners of the Victoria Cross* (Dublin, 2000); Myles Dungan, *Irish Voices from the Great War* (Dublin, 1995) and *They Shall Grow Not Old: Irish Soldiers and the Great War* (Dublin, 1997); and Stephen Walker, *Forgotten Soldiers: The Irishmen Shot at Dawn* (Dublin, 2007).

3 See Chs 9 and 16 for a discussion of this.

4 Important academic studies are Mark Connelly, *Steady the Buffs: A Regiment, a Region and the Great War* (Oxford, 2006) and Helen B. McCartney, *Citizen Soldiers: The Liverpool Territorials in the First World War* (Cambridge, 2005). For Pals, see for example, John Sheen, *Tyneside Irish* (Barnsley, 1998).

5 For example, Belfast Book of Honour Committee, *Journey of Remembering: Belfast Book of*

Honour (Belfast, 2009); Robert Thompson, *Bushmills Heroes 1914–18* (Coleraine, 1995; 2nd edition 2003); Robert Thompson, *Portrush Heroes 1914–18* (Coleraine, 2001); Colin Moffett (ed.), *Newry's War Dead* (Newry, 2002); *County Donegal Book of Honour* (Letterkenny, 2002); James S. Kane, *Portadown Heroes* (Portadown, 2007).

6 Jeffery, *Ireland and the Great War*, p. 155.

Notes to Chapter 1: Civil War?

1 Henry Patterson, 'Industrial Labour and the Labour Movement, 1820–1914', in Líam Kennedy and Philip Ollerenshaw (eds), *An Economic History of Ulster, 1820–1940* (Manchester, 1985), pp. 158–83, see p. 178.

2 *Irish News (IN)* 8 February 1912, p. 5.

3 *Belfast Evening Telegraph (BET)* 8 February 1912, pp. 6–7.

4 *IN* 9 February 1912, p. 6.

5 Eamon Phoenix, *Northern Nationalism: Nationalist Politics, Partition and the Catholic Minority in Northern Ireland, 1890–1940* (Belfast, 1994), pp. 2–6.

6 *IN* 9 February 1912, p. 7.

7 *Belfast News Letter (BNL)* 9 February 1912, p. 8; and *IN* 9 February 1912, p. 12.

8 Patrick Maume, 'The *Irish Independent* and the Ulster Crisis, 1912–21', in G. George Boyce and Alan O'Day (eds), *The Ulster Crisis, 1885–1921* (Basingstoke, 2006), pp. 202–28, see p. 208.

9 *IN* 16 September 1912, p. 5; *BET* 16 September 1912, p. 6; *BNL* 16 September 1912, p. 9; National Archive, Kew, Colonial Office Papers (CO) 904/88: Monthly Report, September 1912, Royal Irish Constabulary (RIC), Belfast, p. 1.

10 CO 904/88 and 89: Monthly Reports, October 1912 and April 1913, RIC, Belfast, pp. 2–3 and p. 3.

11 www.proni.gov.uk/index/search_the_archives/ulster_covenant.htm, accessed 1 December 2008.

12 *IN* 30 September 1912, p. 5.

13 Alvin Jackson, *Home Rule: An Irish History, 1800–2000* (Oxford, 2003), p. 123.

14 *BET* 17 January 1913, p. 6.

15 *BNL* 1 February 1913, p. 8.

16 Timothy Bowman, 'The Ulster Volunteer Force, 1910–20: New Perspectives', in Boyce and O'Day (eds), *Ulster Crisis*, pp. 247–58 (see p. 249); Timothy Bowman, *Carson's Army: The Ulster Volunteer Force, 1910–22* (Manchester, 2007), pp. 53–4 and 62; CO 904/91: Monthly Report, September 1913, RIC, Belfast, pp. 4–5; A. T. Q. Stewart, *The Ulster Crisis: Resistance to Home Rule 1914–14* (Belfast, 1967), pp. 69–71 and 128.

17 Timothy Bowman, 'The Ulster Volunteers 1913–14: Force or Farce?', *History Ireland*, 10, 1 (2002), pp. 43–7; CO 904/90 and 93: Monthly Reports, June 1913 and May 1914, RIC, Belfast.

18 *BNL* 23 April 1914 p. 8; CO 904/93: Monthly Report, Apr. 1914, RIC, Belfast, p. 7; Stewart, *Ulster Crisis*, p. 200; *BET* 25 April 1914, p. 7; *BNL* 27 April 1914, p. 7 and 8; *BET* 4 May 1914, pp. 3 and 5.

19 CO 904/91, 92, 93 and 94: Monthly Reports, December 1913 and February, April and July 1914, RIC, Belfast.

20 Joseph Devlin MP, cited in *BET* 7 November 1913, p. 6.

21 *BET* 26 November 1913, p. 7.

22 Matthew Kelly, 'The Irish Volunteers: A Machiavellian Moment?', in Boyce and O'Day (eds), *Ulster Crisis*, p. 69; *IN* 26 November 1913, p. 5; CO 904/92 and 93: Monthly Reports, March and May 1914, RIC, Belfast; *IN* 18 May 1914, p. 5; *BET* 18 May 1914, p. 3.

23 *IN* 25 May 1914, p. 5; CO 904/94: Monthly Report, July 1914, RIC, Belfast. See also Michael Wheatley, *Nationalism and the Irish Party, Provincial Ireland 1910–16* (Oxford, 2005), pp. 260–1.

24 *IN* 26 May 1914, p. 5; *BET* 8 June 1914, p. 3; *IN* 8 June 1914, p. 5.

25 *IN* 10 June 1914, p. 5, 13 June 1914, p. 5, 17 June 1914, p. 7 and 29 June 1914, p. 5; National Library of Ireland (NLI), Redmond MS 15,182/20: John Dillon to Redmond, 3 June 1914; Joseph Finnan, *John Redmond and Irish Unity* (Syracuse, 2004), pp. 136–9; Kelly, 'The Irish Volunteers', p. 77; Phoenix, *Northern Nationalism*, p. 14; A. C. Hepburn, *Catholic Belfast and Nationalist Ireland in the Era of Joe Devlin* (Oxford, 2008), p. 158.

26 *IN* 6 Jule 1914, p. 7, 13 July 1914, p. 8, 20 July 1914, p. 5 and 27 July 1914, p. 8.

27 Phoenix, *Northern Nationalism*, p. 12.

Notes to Chapter 2: Volunteers and Reserves

1 *BET* 4 June 1915, p. 6 and 21 February 1918, p. 3.

2 CO 904/94: Monthly Report, August 1914, RIC, Belfast.

3 *BNL* 7 August 1914, p. 8.

4 *BET* 10 August 1914, pp. 3 and 4.

5 *IN* 4 August 1914, p. 6, 6 August 1914, p. 5 and 28 August 1914, p. 6.

6 *BNL* 3 August 1914, p. 7, 5 August 1914, p. 5 and 6 August 1914, p. 5.

7 *Northern Whig* (*NW*) 10 August 1914, p. 8 and *BNL* 7 August 1914, p. 5.

8 Jeffery, *Ireland and the Great War*, p. 30.

9 *IN* 19 September 14, p. 4.

10 *BNL* 12 August 1914, p. 5.

11 Jonathan Bardon, *A History of Ulster* (Belfast, 1992; 2001 repr.), pp. 449–51.

12 F. P. Crozier, *A Brass Hat in No Man's Land* (London, 1930), p. 45.

3 *BNL* 4 September 1914, p. 8.

14 *BNL* 5 September 1914, p. 3.

15 *BET* 5 September 1914, p. 3; *BNL* 5 September 1914, p. 3.

16 *BNL* 10 September 1914, p. 8; *NW* 10 September 1914, p. 8.

17 *NW* 11 September 1914, p. 8; *BNL* 12 September 1914, p. 3.

18 CO 904/94: Monthly Report for September 1914, Commissioner's Office, RIC, Belfast, p. 2; *BET* 9 October 1914, p. 3; Falls, *History of the 36th (Ulster) Division*, p. 11; *BET* 3 October 1914, p. 3.

19 Crozier wrote about one nationalist soldier in the 9th RIRifles (*Brass Hat*, p. 107). Of 287 West Belfast men on the 14th RIRifles nominal roll, only five were Catholics and that battalion's YCV rather than UVF origins (in contrast to other battalions) made Catholic membership more likely.

20 NLI, Moore MS 10,572: Evidence for Rebellion Commission 1916.

21 *IN* 7 September 1914, p. 4.

22 *IN* 8 September 1914, p. 4 and 14 September 1914, p. 4.

23 *IN* 16 September 1914, p. 5.

24 Charles Hannon, 'The Irish Volunteers and the Concepts of Military Service and Defence 1913–24' (University College Dublin, unpublished PhD thesis, 1989), pp. 82–101; *IN* 21 September 1914, p. 5.

25 University College Dublin, Eoin MacNeill Papers, LA1/P/2; *BET* 25 September 1914, p. 6. See also reservations expressed by Redmond supporters: National Library of Ireland (hereafter NLI), Moore MS 10561(8): Moore to Devlin, 28 September 1914.

26 Hannon, *The Irish Volunteers*, p. 105.

27 CO 904/94: Monthly Report for September 1914, Commissioner's Office, RIC, Belfast, p. 2; NLI, Redmond MS 15258 Irish National Volunteers' Strength on 31 October 1914; *IN* 28 September 1914, p. 6, 30 September 1914, p. 6, 1 October 1914, p. 5, 9 October 1914, p. 6, 10 October 1914, p. 6. The police believed 300 were against Redmond, whereas INV figures stated 200.

28 Denman, *Ireland's Unknown*, p. 38.

29 *IN* 26 October 1914, p. 5.

30 *National Volunteer* 31 October 1914, p. 1.

31 David Fitzpatrick, 'The Logic of Collective Sacrifice: Ireland and the British Army, 1914–18', *Historical Journal*, 38, 4 (195), pp. 1017–30 (see pp. 1025 and 1030).

32 E-mail to author from Michael Brennan's granddaughter, Siobhán Deane, 16 September 2007.

33 *IN* 10 September 14, p. 4. See also *BET* 12 November 1914, p. 6; *NW* 13 November 1914, p. 8; *IN* 13 November 1914, p. 5; NLI, Redmond MS 15,258; CO 904/95: Monthly Report, October 1914, RIC, Belfast.

34 *IN* 26 February 1915, p. 4.

35 *BNL* 19 November 1914, p. 6; *IN* 19 November 1914, p. 5.

36 *IN* 17 November 1914, p. 4.

37 *BNL* 12 August 1914, p. 5 and 21 December 1914, p. 7; *IN* 1 October 1914, p. 6.

38 *IN* 20 November 1914, p. 5.

39 Imperial War Museum (IWM) 67/41/1: 'Kitchener's Soldier, 1914–18: The Letters of John H. M. Staniforth': letters to parents, 24 October 1914, 23 May 1915 and 10 November 1915.

40 This figure was reached by reducing the overall estimate of the strength of the city's INV to the more widely accepted 3,000 mark (rather than the newspaper's occasional 4,000 figure). It then said that about 1,000 had been reservists, 600 had joined up individually, with another 1,100 joining together as INV members, making 2,700 in total. See *IN* 25 November 1914, p. 5 and 26 November 1914, p. 5.

41 NLI, Redmond MS 15,220/3 Parsons to Redmond, 29 November 1914.

42 *IN* 12 February 15, p. 4.

43 *Battle Lines* 4 (1991) pp. 30–1.

44 WO 97/5345: John McManus (1396); CWGC record; e-mail from great-grandson, Máirtín Ó Muilleoir, 12 July 2008.

45 WO 364 pensions record and personal papers provided by Marie Toner Moore.

46 E-mail from grandson, Ed McCann, 4 July 2006.

47 E-mail from, Siobhán Deane, 16 September 2007.

48 WO 364 individual files.

49 IWM 67/41/1: 'Kitchener's Soldier': letter to parents, 1 November 1914, p. 23.

50 IWM 79/35/1: David Starrett, 'Batman', pp. 2 and 52–3.

51 *Battle Lines* 11 (1996), pp. 8–9.

52 WO 364 individual files.

53 Ibid.

54 Ibid.

55 Ibid.

56 Patrick Callan, 'Recruiting for the British Army in Ireland during the First World War', *Irish Sword* 17.66 (1987), pp. 42–56 (see esp. p. 56).

57 *NW* 14 November 1914, p. 6; *BET* 30 November 1914, p. 8 and 22 October 1914, p. 6.

58 William Stewart, Mayo Street, *Belfast Weekly Telegraph (BWT)* 13 February 1915, p. 3 and William McKinstry, Snugville Street, *BWT* 20 February 1915, p. 2.

59 Royal Ulster Rifles Museum, AC 878: photo album of 9th RIRifles.

60 *BNL* 10 May 1915, pp. 5–8.

61 *IN* 10 May 1915, p. 8.

Notes to Chapter 3: The British Expeditionary Force, 1914–15

1 *BET* 13 April 1916, p. 5, 23 May 1916, p. 3 and 14 August 1916, p. 3; *BNL* 15 August 1916, p. 8.

2 WO 95/1505: 2nd Royal Inniskilling Fusiliers' War Diary, August–December 1914.

3 *BNL* 3 September 1915, p. 10; *BET* 18 June 1915, p. 6 and 12 September 1918, p. 4.

4 Fox, *Inniskillings*, p. 41.

5 WO 95/1343: 5 Brigade War Diary, August 1914–December 1915.

6 *BNL* 24 September 1915, p. 10 and 25 July 1916, p. 8; 1911 census.

7 For Templeton, see: *BNL* 9 September 1915, p. 10; *BET* 22 September 1915, p. 6; for McGrogan see WO 363.

8 *BET* 18 November 1914, p. 4.

9 Fox, *Inniskillings*, p. 49.

10 *BET* 28 September 1914, p. 3; *IN* 30 September 14, p. 5; St Michael's memorial roll.

11 In the newspaper the date was given as 18 September 1914. Although it was unusual for reports to appear in the newspapers so quickly (it was published on 28 September) for other ranks, it is not impossible. However, *Soldiers Died in the Great War (SDGW)* gives 15 September, and the Commonwealth War Graves Commission (CWGC) website opts for 27 August. Meanwhile, Taylor, *2nd RIRifles*, p. 137, goes for 26 August. The difference between 26 and 27 August might matter little, especially as the operations so often took place over night, and it might be unclear what day it actually was, but the battalion war diary suggests the battalion was not in action on 27 August, which rules out the CWGC date. *SDGW* was not compiled in 1914, and it pieced together deaths in that year from a range of sources. Clearly, newspapers are the most contemporary source, but they could make mistakes and it is not difficult to imagine typographical errors (on the part of either *SDGW* or the newspaper) explaining the difference between 15 and 18 September. Given the pattern for time taken to report casualties, 26 August would appear to be the more accurate estimate.

12 For details of Catholic chaplains see Jane Leonard, 'The Catholic Chaplaincy', in David Fitzpatrick (ed.), *Ireland and the First World War* (Dublin, 1988), pp. 1–14.

13 Papers of Fr Henry Gill, Irish Jesuit Archives, Dublin: CHP1/28 *1914–18 As seen by a Chaplain with the 2nd Battalion RIRifles* (unpublished MS, 1933), pp. 7, 84 and 152.

14 John F. Lucy, *There's a Devil in the Drum* (Uckfield, 1993), p. 75.

15 WO 95/1415: 2nd Battalion RIRifles' War Diary, August 1914–October 1915.

16 Lucy, *Devil in the Drum*, p. 114.

17 WO 95/1413: 7 Brigade War Diary, August 1914–October 1915.

18 WO 95/1375: 3rd Division General Staff War Diary: 'Report on the Operations of the 3rd Division from 11th to 30 October 1914'.

19 Lucy, *Devil in the Drum*, p. 211.

20 *BET* 25 May 1915, p. 6; *BNL* 19 January 1916, p. 10.

21 WO 95/1413.
22 Gordon Corrigan, *Mud, Blood and Poppycock* (London, 2003), pp. 89–91.
23 Charles Brett, *Charles Brett MC: An Irish Soldier with the Connaught Rangers in World War I* (Newtownards, 2007), p. 88.
24 Bowman, *Irish Regiments*, pp. 43 and 202.
25 *Belfast Weekly News* (*BWN*) 14 January 1915, p. 7; *BET* 11 January 1915, p. 5, 15 January 1915, p. 6 and 17 December 1915, p. 7; WO 372 Medal Roll.
26 Gerald Achilles Burgoyne, *The Burgoyne Diaries* (London, 1985), p. 25.
27 *BET* 13 December 1915, p. 8 and 14 December 1914, p. 8.
28 *BET* 5 January 1915, p. 3.
29 WO 95/1730: 1st RIRifles' War Diary, August 1914–January 1918.
30 *BWN* 8 April 1915, p. 7 and 15 April 1915, p. 7; *BET* 6 April 1915, p. 4 and 6 May 1915, p. 6.
31 NA WO 339/6822: A. O'H Wright.
32 IWM 85/28/1: J. Davey (Sapper 15495 2nd Field Coy RE) letter to IWM Curator, 20 July 1969.
33 WO 95/1671: 8th Division General Staff War Diary, September 1914–March 1915.
34 WO 95/1724: 25 Brigade War Diary, October 1914–August 1915.
35 Taylor, *1st RIRifles*, p. 37.
36 *BWN* 22 April 1915, p. 7; *BET* 26 April 1915, p. 6.
37 WO 95/1350: 2nd Royal Inniskilling Fusiliers' War Diary, January–December 1915.
38 *SDGW*.
39 In addition to the battalion war diary, see also Major V. Hinton Baker's report 'Capture of Neuve Chapelle', 17 March 1915.
40 *BWN* 3 June 1915, p. 7.
41 Taylor, *1st Battalion RIRifles*, p. 56.
42 *BWN* 19 June 1915, p. 7.
43 *BNL* 8 July 1915, p. 7 and 7 September 1915, p. 10; *BET* 22 July 1915, p. 6.
44 *BNL* 27 September 1915, p. 10.
45 *BNL* 13 September 1915, p. 10 and 11 April 1916, p. 8; *BET* 3 November 1915, p. 6.
46 *SDGW*.
47 *BWN* 1 July 1915, p. 7; *BNL* 16 June 1916, p. 3.
48 *BNL* 14 September 1915, p. 10; *BET* 13 September 1915, p. 3.
49 All references to statements made during the trial are from WO 71/432: Peter Sands. See also, Walker, *Forgotten Soldiers,* pp. 114–18.
50 Julian Putowski and Julian Sykes, *Shot at Dawn: Executions in World War One by Authority of the British Army Act* (Barnsley, 1996), p. 52.
51 WO 95/1413: 'Report on Trenches from 16th March to 23rd'.
52 Johnstone: *BNL* 17 July 1915, p. 6; *BET* 29 March 1915, p. 6. Hall: *BNL* 13 August 1915, p. 10.
53 *BWN* 1 July 1915, p. 7; *BET* 16 July 1917, p. 6.
54 *Supplement to London Gazette*, 1 April 1915, p. 3217.
55 *BWT* 23 October 1915, p. 2.
56 William Corkey, *Glad did I Live* (Belfast, 1963), pp. 116 and 174–6.
57 James Brewster (Bedeque Street), *BNL* 6 December 1915, p. 10, *BET* 24 December 1915, p. 6; Samuel Saulters (Weir Street), CWGC website.
58 Joseph Finnan, '"Let Irishmen Come Together in the Trenches": John Redmond and Irish Party Policy in the Great War, 1914–18', *Irish Sword* 22.88 (2000–1), pp. 174–92.
59 Irish Jesuit Archives, Gill, *1914–18 As Seen by a Chaplain*, p. 63.

Notes to Chapter 4: The Nature of War

1 *BET* 23 January 1915, p. 6.
2 WO 364 individual file.
3 *BNL* 21 October 1915, p. 10.
4 *BET* 4 February 15, p. 3.
5 Somme Heritage Centre (SHC) SOM 1994/512–14.
6 *BET* 17 October 1914, p. 6 and 22 October 1914, p. 4.
7 *BNL* 15 June 1916, p. 7, *BET* 17 June 1916, p. 4. See also Nigel Steel and Peter Hart, *Jutland 1916* (London, 2003), pp. 200–2, 228–32 and 436–9.
8 *BWN* 31 December 1914, p. 7; *BET* 2 January 1915, p. 6.
9 *BET* 29 November 1915, p. 6.
10 WO 161/99/4, no. 864; WO 161/98/137, no. 98; WO 161/98/119, no. 98.
11 *BET* 21 October 1915, p. 6 and 16 May 1916, p. 4.
12 *BET* 12 March 1915, p. 3.
13 *BNL* 31 October 1916, p. 8.
14 *BET* 28 October 1914, p. 3, 30 October 1914, p. 6, 31 October 1914, p. 6 and 20 November 1914, p. 6.
15 *BWT* 26 December 1914, p. 6.
16 *BWN* 24 June 1915, p. 7; *BET* 13 May 1915, p. 6 and 18 June 1915, p. 6.
17 *BET* 13 January 1915, p. 6.
18 *BET* 9 March 1915, p. 6.
19 *BNL* 9 May 1917, p. 8.
20 St Michael's Memorial Roll.
21 *IN* 6 November 1914, p. 6, 6 September 1915, p. 2; *BNL* 17 December 1915, p. 12, 31 December 1915, p. 8 and 24 July 1916, p. 8.
22 *BET* 28 October 1914, p. 6.
23 *BET* 9 December 1914, p. 3.
24 *IN* 19 January 1915, p. 5, 9 December 1915, p. 5, 22 March 1916, p. 5 and 15 April 1916, p. 5.
25 *IN* 1 May 1915, p. 5, 9 September 1915, p. 3, 30 September 1916, p. 6 and 28 August 1918, p. 4.
26 *BNL* 9 June 1917, p. 6 and *IN* 29 April 1916, p. 6. Corkey, *Glad did I Live*, pp. 176–95.
27 *BNL* 27 May 1916, p. 8, 12 June 1916, p. 8 and 28 June 1916, p. 8.

Notes to Chapter 5: Gallipoli and the Eastern Front

1 The 4th, 5th and 6th Inniskillings; the 5th and 6th Royal Irish Fusiliers; the 5th Royal Irish Regiment; the 1st, 6th and 7th Royal Dublin Fusiliers and the 6th Royal Munster Fusiliers.
2 Stokers John Jones (Sugarfield St), John McAnally (Leopold St) and Private Alexander Harkness (Linen St) were lost on HMS *Goliath*. *BWN* 10 June 1915, p. 7; *BET* 2 June 1915, p. 5, 4 June 1915, p. 6 and 13 May 1916, p. 3.
3 Field Marshal Lord Carver, *The National Army Museum Book of the Turkish Front, 1914–18* (London, 2003), pp. 17–21.
4 Fox, *Royal Inniskilling Fusiliers*, p. 177.
5 WO 95/4311: 1st Royal Inniskilling Fusiliers' War Diary, January–October 1915.
6 *BET* 8 July 1916, p. 3.

7   WO 95/4304: 29th Division General Staff War Diary, January–June 1915.

8   *BWN* 27 May 1915, p. 7; *BET* 28 May 1915, p. 3.

9   Fox, *Royal Inniskilling Fusiliers*, p. 185.

10 *BWN* 1 July 1915, p. 7; *BET* 1 July 1915, p. 6. See pp. 46–7 and 147.

11 See 'Report on Operations on 18/19 June' in WO 95/4304.

12 A small trench dug out into No Man's Land to aid moving forward under fire, and sometimes joined with other saps to form a new front line.

13 Doherty and Truesdale, *Irish Winners*, pp. 112–13.

14 *BNL* 29 July 1915, p. 10; *BET* 15 September 1915, p. 6.

15 *BNL* 18 August 1915, p. 10; 1 September 1915, p. 6.

16 WO 95/4296: 6th RIRifles War Diary, July–September 1915.

17 WO 95/4296: 29 Brigade War Diary, letter from F. E. Eastwood, 7 January 1931.

18 *BNL* 8 September 1915, p. 10 and 30 September 1916, p. 8; *BET* 14 October 1916, p. 3.

19 *BNL* 7 September 1915, p. 10 and 16 October 1916, p. 8; *BET* 10 September 1915, p. 3 and 25 October 1916, p. 6.

20 Cathal Donaghy, 'The Conlon Family' in *6th Connaught Rangers Project, The 6th Connaught Rangers: Belfast Nationalists and the Great War* (Belfast, 2008), pp. 47–49.

21 *BNL* 23 November 1915, p. 10.

22 *BNL* 12 October 1915, p. 10.

23 *BNL* 7 December 1915, p. 10; *BET* 3 January 1916, p. 6.

24 *BNL* 8 September 1915, p. 10 and 27 September 1915, p. 10; *BET* 5 October 1915, p. 4 and 11 October 1915, p. 6.

25 WO 95/4296: 5th Royal Irish Fusiliers' War Diary.

26 WO 364 individual file.

27 Author's interview with Harry Donaghy, 12 September 2007; *BNL* 13 September 1915, p. 10 and 11 April 1916, p. 8; *BET* 3 November 1915, p. 6.

28 Fox, *Royal Inniskilling Fusiliers*, p. 196.

29 Ibid., p. 197.

30 *BNL* 4 October 1915, p. 10; *BET* 11 November 1915, p. 6.

31 Fox, *Royal Inniskilling Fusiliers*, p. 197.

32 *BNL* 31 December 1915, p. 10 and 20 November 1916, p. 8; *BET* 5 January 1916, p. 8.

33 Tim Travers, *Gallipoli 1915* (London, 2001), pp. 206–8.

34 Carver, *National Army Museum Book of the Turkish Front*, p. 101; Stephen Pope and Elizabeth-Anne Wheal, *The Macmillan Dictionary of the First World War* (London, 1995), p. 184.

35 For context see, Philip Orr, 'The Road to Belgrade: The Experiences of the 10th (Irish) Division in the Balkans, 1915–17', in Gregory and Pašeta (eds), *Ireland and the Great War*, pp. 171–89.

36 WO 95/4835: 6th RIRifles' War Diary, October 1915–August 1917. *BNL* 17 March 1916, p. 10; *BET* 16 March 1916, p. 5 and 28 March 1916, p. 6. The newspapers do not list a date of death. However, CWGC records show it as 24 February 1916. In usual circumstances, with many deaths in a battalion in one day, and the possibility of errors in the CWGC information, it would not be possible to be certain of the link with the reference in the war diary. However, *SDGW* lists only one fatality in the entire battalion between 10 December 1915 and 12 June 1916. That was Fitzgerald, listed as 'Died of wounds', so there is no other candidate for the machine-gun accident reference.

37 Johnstone, *Orange, Green and Khaki*, pp. 401–2.

38 Bryan Perrett and Anthony Lord, *The Czar's British Squadron* (London, 1981), p. 22.

39 Ibid., pp. 26–7. The National Archive, Kew, Admiralty Papers (hereafter ADM) 1/8403/428: O. Locker-Lampson to Admiralty, 3 November 1914; OL-L memorandum, 22 June 1915.

40 Perrett and Lord, *The Czar's British Squadron*, pp. 36–7 and 42.

41 Ibid., p. 43.

42 Ibid., p. 99.

43 He is listed variously as McFarland and MacFarlane, in newspapers and official records, but the CWGC memorial lists him as McFarland.

44 *BNL* 10 August 1917, p. 8; *BET* 23 August 1917, p. 6 and 30 July 1917, p. 5.

Notes to Chapter 6: Arrivals and Executions

1 WO 95/2503: 9th RIRifles' War Diary.

2 WO 374/16997: F. P. Crozier.

3 Bowman, *Irish Regiments*, p. 120.

4 Unless otherwise stated, quotations are from the battalion war diary.

5 Public Record Office, Northern Ireland (PRONI), D/2794/1/1/2: Montgomery to parents, 18 November 1915.

6 Bowman, *Irish Regiments*, p. 109 and 111; see also, Nicholas Perry, *Major General Oliver Nugent and the Ulster Division 1915–18* (Stroud, 2007).

7 Bowman, *Irish Regiments*, pp. 112–13, 114 and 116.

8 *Battle Lines* 17 (2000), pp. 9–11.

9 WO 95/2502: 107th Brigade War Diary.

10 *BNL* 6 December 1915, p. 10; *BET* 28 December 1915, p. 4 and 24 November 1916, p. 5.

11 *BNL* 22 December 1915, p. 10; *BET* 12 December 1916, p. 6 and 30 December 1915, p. 3. It is possible that this soldier (no. 294) is the same Private 12942, Daniel Crilly, who was discharged in October 1914 from the Royal Irish Fusiliers for absenteeism and drunkenness and then (as Driver 030944) from the Army Service Corps in April 1915 for theft of government property. The major reason for doubt is that the address of his wife varies in different records, but the wife of the twice-discharged Daniel Crilly was also called Martha. Meanwhile, his date of joining the 9th RIRifles (three months before his death, which was late to be joining that battalion) fits with being discharged from the ASC in April 1915. Moreover, the ASC records contain a reference to Crilly having been killed in the RIRifles. No other Daniel Crilly was killed in the British army in 1914–18, but given the different addresses we cannot be certain. See WO 364 Individual Files.

12 *BNL* 4 January 1916, p. 10; *BET* 5 January 1916, p. 8.

13 *BNL* 7 January 1916, p. 10; *BET* 11 January 1916, p. 6.

14 Orr, *Road to the Somme*, p. 131.

15 WO 95/2511: 14th RIRifles' War Diary.

16 Falls, *History of the 36th (Ulster) Division*, pp. 26–7.

17 *Battle Lines* 17 (2000), pp. 9–11.

18 *BNL* 27 January 1916, p. 10; *BET* 2 February 1916, p. 6.

19 *BNL* 10 January 16, p. 7 and 2 April 17, p. 8.

20 WO 339/14160: A. J. Annandale.

21 F. P. Crozier, *Brass Hat*, p. 81.

22 F. P. Crozier, *The Men I Killed* (London, 1937), p. 52.

23 WO 71/450: J. Crozier.

24 Crozier, *Men I Killed*, pp. 43–8 and *Brass Hat*, pp. 83–4.

25 Crozier has been an important cause for Loyalists. See www.freewebs.com/thewestbelfast volunteers, accessed 1 December 2008.

26 '300 WWI Soldiers Receive Pardon', online at http://news.bbc.co.uk/1/hi/uk/4796579.stm, accessed 1 December 2008.

27 Bowman, *Irish Regiments*, p. 131.

28 WO 71/454: James Templeton.

29 WO 71/453: J. F. McCracken.

30 WO 95/2491.

31 Crozier, *Brass Hat*, p. 92.

32 *BNL* 20 May 1916, p. 8; *BET* 19 May 1916, p. 3 and 30 May 1916, p. 4.

33 *BET* 10 May 1916, p. 3.

34 *BET* 5 June 1916, p. 4. *1916 Rebellion Handbook* (1916; repr. Dublin, 1998), p. 51.

35 E-mail from Siobhán Deane, 16 September 2007.

36 *IN* 29 April 15, p. 5.

37 *Irish Weekly* 18 December 1915, p. 7.

38 WO 95/1970: 6th Connaughts' and 7th Leinsters' war diaries.

39 Terence Denman, 'An Irish Battalion at War: From the Letters of Captain J. H. M. Staniforth 7th Leinsters 1914–18', *Irish Sword*, 17 (1989), pp. 165–217.

40 IWM 67/41/1: 'Kitchener's Soldier': Letters to parents, 29 December 1915.

41 WO 95/1969: 47th Brigade War Diary.

42 *IN* 10 February 16, p. 5.

43 *BNL* 25 February 1916, p. 10 and 3 April 1916, p. 8.

44 *IN* 23 March 16, p. 5, 1 April 1916, p. 4.

45 *BNL* 29 April 1916, p. 8.

Notes to Chapter 7: The Ulster Division on the Somme

1 WO 95/2511; *BNL* 12 May 1916, p. 8, 15 May 1916, p. 8, 16 May 1916, p. 3, 20 May 1916, p. 8; *BET* 17 May 1916, p. 4, 18 May 1916, p. 4 and 29 May 1916, p. 4.

 2 Addresses were: McKee, 44 Ashmore Street; Quinn, 27 Little Sackville Street; Todd, 26 Heather Street; Fowler, 30 Stanley Street; Gorman, 108 Tennent Street; Mooney, 11 Third Street; Barnes, 121 Lawnbrook Avenue. McIlwraith was at 15 Mawhinney Court in the Falls area. *BNL* 14 June 1916, p. 8, 15 June 1916, p. 8 and 17 July 1916, p. 8; *BET* 13 June 1916, p. 3, 15 June 1916, p. 3, 17 June 1916, p. 5, 21 June 1916, p. 3 and 4, 24 June 1916, p. 3 and 4, 30 June 1916, p. 4 and 13 June 1916, p. 3.

 3 *Battle Lines* 1 (1990), pp. 30–1.

 4 WO 95/2502.

 5 WO 95/2491.

 6 *Belfast Telegraph (BT)*, 30 June 1966, p. 11.

 7 WO 95/2491.

 8 WO 95/2502.

 9 WO 95/2491.

10 WO 95/2511.

11 Cited in Christopher Duffy, *Through German Eyes: The British and the Somme 1916* (London, 2006), p. 151.

12 WO 95/2503.

13 WO 95/2491.

14 WO 95/2491; Falls, pp. 56–7.

15 WO 95/2491.

16 *Battle Lines* 17 (2000), pp. 9–11.

17 Ibid.

18 WO 95/2502.

19 Ibid.

20 Cited in Jack Sheldon, *The German Army on the Somme 1914–16* (Barnsley, 2005), pp. 154–5.

21 WO 95/2502.

22 The figure of 107 for 1 and 2 July includes five men who are listed in *SDGW* as being in other units and three who are listed as 8th/9th Battalion even though that battalion did not yet exist. So the figure for other ranks ranges from 99 to 107. See p. 229n. 16 for further details.

23 Catherine Switzer, *Unionists and Great War Commemoration in the north of Ireland 1914–39: People, Places and Politics* (Dublin, 2007), pp. 30–1.

24 *BET* 1 July 1916, p. 3, 3 July 1916, p. 3 and 4, 4 July 1916, p. 3, 5 July 1916, p. 3, 6 July 1916, p. 3 and 7 July 1916, p. 2; *BNL*, 3 July 1916, p. 5, 7 July 1916, p. 10 and 10 July 1916, p. 7.

25 Letter to author from Brian Courtney, 27 September 2006.

26 Orr, *Road to the Somme*, p. 194. *BNL* 14 May 17, p. 6 and 24 May 17, p. 6.

27 *BNL* 17 July 1917, p. 6; *BET* 16 July 1917, p. 3 and 25 July 1917, p. 6.

28 *BNL* 8 November 1917, p. 6; *BET* 7 November 1917, p. 5.

29 *BNL* 28 July 1916, p. 8; *BET* 27 July 1916, p. 3.

30 *BET* 25 July 1916, p. 3.

31 *BNL* 21 February 1916, p. 10, 14 July 1916, p. 8, 15 August 1916, p. 8, 15 December 1916, p. 10 and 7 September 1917, p. 6; *BET* 18 July 1916, p. 4; WO 339/14325.

32 PRONI, D/2794/1/1/13: Captain Montgomery to his father, 24 July 1916.

33 PRONI, D/2794/1/1/20: Hill to Mr Montgomery, 5 December 1916.

34 Bowman, *Irish Regiments*, p. 22.

35 *BNL* 19 July 1916, p. 8; 15 August 1916, p. 8; *BET* 18 July 1916, p. 3 and 27 August 1919, p. 4.

36 *BNL* 4 October 1916, p. 8 and 4 September 1918, p. 6.

37 *BET* 7 July 1916, p. 3.

38 *BNL* 19 July 1916, p. 8; Crozier, *Brass Hat*, p. 105.

39 Dungan, *Irish Voices*, p. 109.

40 *BT*, 30 June 1966, p. 11.

Notes to Chapter 8: The Other Somme

1 WO 95/2305; *SDGW*; Fox, *Royal Inniskilling Fusiliers*, pp. 70–2.

2 *BNL* 17 March 1917, p. 8 and 17 April 1917, p. 8; *BET* 28 October 1917, p. 4, 20 March 1917, p. 6, 16 April 1917, p. 3 and 20 April 1917, p. 4.

3 Irish Jesuit Archives, Gill Papers, CHP1/28, p. 93.

4 *BET* 27 September 1916, p. 3 and 4 October 1916, p. 3.

5 WO 95/2247; Taylor, *2nd RIRifles*, pp. 85–7.

6 *BNL* 7 November 1916, p. 10.

7 *BNL* 15 July 1916, p. 8; WO 95/2397; Fox, *Royal Inniskilling Fusiliers*, pp. 73–4.

8 IWM 77/167/1 J. F. Blake O'Sullivan: 'At Rest in Philosophe'.

9 *BNL* 7 June 1916, p. 3; *IN* 7 June 1916, p. 5.

10 WO 95/1969.

11 Ibid.

12 *BET* 14 October 1916, p. 3.

13 *IN* 19 August 16, p. 5.

14 Names of 2 September fatalities were not recorded until the next day, and in the records that survive they are mixed up with the heavy losses of 3 September.

15 IWM 80/25/1: W. A. Lyon, *Memoirs*, p. 63.

16 IWM 77/167/1: J. F. Blake O'Sullivan, letter to his mother 10–13 September 1916.

17 *London Gazette*, 26 October 1916.

18 Denman, *Ireland's Unknown*, p. 82; Richard Doherty and David Truesdale, *Irish Winners of the Victoria Cross* (Dublin, 2000), p. 122.

19 IWM 80/25/1: W. A. Lyon, *Memoirs*, p. 64.

20 IWM 77/167/1: J. F. Blake O'Sullivan, letter to his mother 10–13 September 1916.

21 Addresses: John Sharkey (Lucknow Street), Breen (Bow Street), Doherty (Albert Street), Duffin (Varna Street), Campfield (Whitworth Street) and Edward Sharkey (Colligan Street). *IN* 6 October 1916, p. 1; *BNL* 19 September 1916, p. 8, 3 October 1916, p. 8, 4 October 1916, p. 8 and 30 November 1916, p. 8; *BET* 27 September 1916, p. 3, 4 October 1916, p. 3, 14 October 1916, p. 3, 14 November 1916, p. 4, and 29 November 1916, p. 5.

22 Addresses: Conway (Nail Street), Ferris (Silvio Street), and McGinney (Balkan Street). *BNL* 30 September 1916, p. 8, 3 October 1916, p. 8 and 24 April 1917, p. 8; *BET* 14 October 1916, p. 3, 4 November 1916, p. 6 and 28 April 1917, p. 4.

23 Rowland Feilding, *War Letters to a Wife: France and Flanders, 1915–19* (London, 2001), pp. x–xvi.

24 Denman, *Ireland's Unknown*, p. 117.

25 WO 95/1969.

26 Feilding, *War Letters to a Wife*, pp. 69 and 70. The precise sizes of the battalions following the capture of Guillemont are unclear. There appear to have been 1,147 casualties overall in 47th Brigade (WO 95/1969) of which 219 were in the 7th Leinsters, making it likely that there were similar figures for the 6th Connaughts and the other two battalions in the brigade.

27 Feilding, *War Letters to a Wife*, p. 70.

28 Ibid., p. 72.

29 WO 95/1955.

30 This figure was reached using *SDGW*. It includes all 12 infantry battalions in the division, plus the division's engineers, but information on specific RAMC and RFA units is rarely present.

31 *IN* 17 March 16, p. 6.

32 *IN* 31 October 1916, pp. 1 and 4, 1 November 1916, p. 6, 7 November 1916, p. 4, 8 November 1916, p. 1 and 9 November 1916, p. 6; *BNL* 31 October 1916, p. 8; *BET* 25 November 1916, p. 3.

33 E-mail from great-grandson, Máirtín Ó Muilleoir, 12 July 2008.

Notes to Chapter 9: On and On

1 *BNL* 12 April 1917, p. 8.

2 On steady learning by the military hierarchy see Paddy Griffith, *Battle Tactics of the Western Front: The British Army's Art of Attack, 1916–18* (New Haven, CT, 1994).

3 *BNL* 11 August 1916, p. 8 and 24 August 1916, p. 8.

4 *BNL* 25 October 1916, p. 10.

5 Nicholas Perry, 'Nationality in the Irish Regiments in the First World War', *War and Society*,

XII (1994), pp. 65–95 (see p. 69). See also Keith Grieves, *The Politics of Manpower, 1914–18* (Manchester, 1988), pp. 217–18.

6 Fitzpatrick, 'The Logic of Collective Sacrifice', p. 1024.

7 See below, pp. 195–6.

8 Denman, *Ireland's Unknown*, pp. 131–2; Callan, 'Recruiting for the British Army', pp. 49–50.

9 Bowman, *Irish Regiments*, pp. 142–3.

10 Perry, 'Nationality', p. 80 and 84.

11 Perry, 'Nationality', p. 69 and 89; Nicholas Perry, 'Politics and Command: General Nugent, the Ulster Division and Relations with Ulster Unionism, 1915–17', in Brian Bond (ed.), *'Look to your Front': Studies in the First World War* (Staplehurst, 1999), pp. 105–20 (see pp. 116–17).

12 IWM Sound Archive, 11214/2/3: F. W. S. Jourdain.

13 Feilding, *War Letters to a Wife*, pp. 75 and 87.

14 Ibid., p. 105. See also Terence Denman, 'The Catholic Irish Soldier in the First World War: The "Racial Environment"', *Irish Historical Studies*, 27.108 (1991), pp. 352–65.

15 Feilding, *War Letters to a Wife*, p. 107; Bowman, *Irish Regiments*, pp. 154–5; Denman, 'The Catholic Irish Soldier' p. 150.

16 IWM Sound Archive, 14142, Reel 3: Walter Collins.

17 *Battle Lines*, 4 (1991), pp. 30–1.

18 Denman, *Ireland's Unknown*, pp. 46–7; J. B. Lyons, *The Enigma of Tom Kettle* (Dublin, 1983); Terence Denman, *A Lonely Grave: The Life and Death of William Redmond* (Dublin, 1995).

19 Feilding, *War Letters to a Wife*, p. 80. For the effect of the Rising on nationalist officers see Jane Leonard, 'The Reaction of Irish Officers in the British Army to the Easter Rising of 1916', in Hugh Cecil and Peter H. Liddle (eds), *Facing Armageddon: The First World War Experienced* (London, 1996), pp. 256–68.

20 Feilding, *War Letters to a Wife*, pp. 76 and 78.

21 Bowman, *Irish Regiments*, p. 30.

22 *BET* 21 November 1916, p. 4; WO 339/91112: R. Moore.

23 WO 95/2491.

24 Crozier, *Brass Hat*, pp. 48, 50 and 127.

25 *BNL* 31 October 1916, p. 8; *BET* 1 November 1916, p. 3.

26 *BNL* 6 January 1917, p. 8 and 12 January 1917, p. 7; *BET* 15 January 1917, p. 4 and 18 January 1917, p. 6.

27 SHC, War Diary of Walter Collins.

28 Wendy Holden, *Shell Shock* (London, 1998), pp. 40–1.

29 WO 95/2503.

30 WO 364 individual files.

31 Ibid., individual file.

32 Ibid., individual file.

33 WO 95/2305: 1st Inniskillings War Diary; *BNL* 27 February 1917, p. 8, 5 April 1917, p. 8, 20 April 1917, p. 8; *BET* 26 February 1917, p. 5, 3 March 1917, p. 4, 7 April 1917, p. 4; CWGC.

34 Feilding, *War Letters to a Wife*, p. 97.

35 Ibid., pp. 98, 99 and 101.

36 WO 95/1955: 16th Division War Diary

37 Feilding, *War Letters to a Wife*, p. 103.

38 *BNL* 27 March 1917, p. 8.

39 *BET* 22 October 1917, p. 6.

40 *BNL* 9 March 1917, p. 8; *BET* 14 March 1917, p. 4.

41 WO 95/1969.

42 Feilding, *War Letters to a Wife*, p. 107.

Notes to Chapter 10: Messines

 1 WO 95/2502; *BNL* 1 December 1917, p. 5; *BET* 10 March 1917, p. 4 and 3 December 1917, p. 8.

 2 WO 339/91112: R. Moore.

 3 *BET* 5 May 1917, p. 4.

 4 Jim McDermott, *Northern Divisions: The Old IRA and the Belfast Pogroms 1920–2* (Belfast, 2001), p. 11; Hepburn, *Catholic Belfast*, pp. 165 and 173–4.

 5 Denman, *Ireland's Unknown*, p. 144.

 6 Bowman, *Irish Regiments*, pp. 128–9 and 196; IWM 67/41/1, Staniforth, 'Kitchener's Soldier, 1914–18', pp. 157–8.

 7 Irish Jesuit Archives, CHP1/28, Gill, *1914–18 As Seen by a Chaplain*, .

 8 Feilding, *War Letters to a Wife*, pp. 109–10.

 9 Ibid., pp. 108 and 147 n. 26.

10 WO 95/2502.

11 WO 95/2491.

12 WO 95/2511.

13 National Army Museum (NAM) 1956–03 December 4: H. F. N. Jourdain Diary, 7 June 1917.

14 WO 95/2491.

15 WO 95/1969.

16 WO 95/2491.

17 Ibid.

18 Feilding, *War Letters to a Wife*, p. 114.

19 IWM Sound Archive 14142, Reel 1: Walter Collins, interview.

20 WO 95/2491.

21 Ibid.

22 WO 95/2247.

23 WO 158/416: 16th Division, Narrative of Operations from 3.10 a.m., 7 June–4 p.m., 9 June 1917.

24 WO 158/416.

25 WO 95/2502.

26 WO 95/2511.

27 NAM 1956-03-12-4: H. F. N. Jourdain Diary, 8 June 1917.

28 *BET* 18 June 1917, p. 6.

29 *BNL* 19 June 1917, p. 6; *BET* 22 June 1917, p. 4.

30 Two were from West Belfast: Lance-Corporal George Frederick Henry Tiffin of Hazelfield Street and Corporal Robert Weir of Enfield Street. See *BNL* 26 June 1917, p. 8 and 30 June 1917, p. 8, and *BET* 3 July 1917, p. 6.

31 CWGC; *BNL* 15 June 1917, p. 8 and 29 June 1917, p. 8; *BET* 16 June 1917, p. 6, 30 June 1917, p. 7, 4 July 1917, p. 6 and 24 July 1917, p. 3.

32 SHC SOM 2004/125.

33 *BNL* 3 July 1917, p. 8; *BET* 2 July 1917, p. 7 and 7 July 1917, p. 6. The others were: Riflemen Robert Moore Adair (Elizabeth Street), James Gilliland (Crossland Street), John McConnell

(Ottawa Street), Charles Smith (Crimea Street), Isaac West (Fortingale Street) and Lance-Corporal John Hastings (Fifth Street). See *BNL* 18 June 1917, p. 6, 22 June 1917, p. 8, 3 July 1917, p. 8, 4 July 1917, p. 6, 6 July 1917, p. 8, 11 July 1917, p. 6, and 22 July 1917, p. 8; *BET* 21 June 1917, p. 5, 28 June 1917, p. 6, 30 June 1917, p. 5, 2 July 1917, p. 7, 3 July 1917, p. 5 and 7 July 1917, p. 6.

34 *BNL* 18 June 1917, p. 6, 4 July 1917, p. 6 and 9 July 1917, p. 8; *BET* 21 June 1917, p. 6, 16 July 1917, p. 6 and 20 July 1917, p. 6.

35 Denman, *Lonely Grave*, pp. 117–36.

Notes to Chapter 11: Mud

1   *BNL* 13 September 1917, p. 6.

2   *BET* 5 February 1918, p. 6.

3   *BET* 7 February 1918, p. 5.

4   *BET* 6 May 1918, p. 4.

5   *BET* 12 February 1918, p. 5. For details of the wreck see: www.mcga.gov.uk/c4mca/mcga-environmental/mcga-dops_row_receiver_of_wreck/mcga-dops-row-protected-wrecks/mcga-dops-sar-row.htm, accessed 17 July 2007.

6   Forty-one of these are listed only in the Presbyterian memorial roll. For Dunville see *BET* 7 September 1917, p. 3; *BNL* 7 September 1917, p. 6; *Grantham Journal* 8 September 1917, p. 8. The other air fatalities were Sergeants William Gray (Milltown) and Thomas Proctor (Lanark Street) on 15 August and 27 September 1918 (*BNL* 19 August 1918, p. 4 and 8 October 1918, p. 3; *BET* 2 November 1918, p. 4) and Air Mechanic 2nd Class Henry Hunt of Pernau Street on 27 October 1918 (CWGC).

7   *BNL* 5 October 1917, p. 5; *BET* 5 November 1917, p. 6.

8   Thomas Fegan, *The 'Baby Killers': German Air Raids on Britain in the First World War* (Barnsley, 2002), pp. 57 and 133; Robert Bedwell, 'The Chatham Air-Raid: Events of Monday 3 September 1917', *The Great War*, 23 (January 2006), pp. 23–32.

9   Feilding, *War Letters to a Wife*, p. 118.

10 *Battle Lines* 17 (2000), p. 10.

11 Ibid., 4 (1991), pp. 30–1.

12 Ibid., 17 (2000), pp. 9–11.

13 Falls, *History of the 36th (Ulster) Division*, pp. 110 and 112–13.

14 *BNL* 16 August 1916, p. 6, 22 August 1917, p. 6, 25 August 1917, p. 8; *BET* 21 September 1916, p. 4, 26 September 1916, p. 3, 27 August 1917, p. 4, 29 August 1917, p. 6.

15 WO 95/2247.

16 *BNL* 15 August 1917, p. 6; *BET* 23 August 1917, p. 3 and 28 November 1918, p. 4; CWGC; and Presbyterian roll.

17 WO 95/2511.

18 WO 95/1969.

19 Riflemen Robert Andrews (Crosby Street) Thomas Fleming (Mountcashel Street), George Wasson Hall (Old Lodge Road), Robert E. Lowry (Grosvenor Road), John McAteer (Blenheim Street), David McCullough (Meenan Street), John McGuiggan (Ceylon Street); Corporal Henry (Harry) Dorris (Bootle Street), Lance-Corporals William Keenan (Arundel Street) and David Hanley (Dagmar Street), Sergeant David Andrews (Grosvenor Road). *BNL* 1 September 1917, p. 5, 3 September 1917, p. 6; 15 September 1917, p. 5, 18 September 1917, p. 5, 8 December 1917, p. 6, *BET* 27 August 1917, p. 3, 19 September

1917, p. 6, 29 July 1918, p. 3, 16 August 1918, p. 3; Presbyterian roll; 14th RIRifles roll; CWGC.

20 McComb lived in North Howard Street. The others were Riflemen James McMordie (Lower Urney Street) and (William) Henry Gilmore (Andersonstown). *BNL* 29 August 1917, p. 6, 30 August 1917, p. 6 and 6 September 1917, p. 6.

21 1911 census; *BNL* 8 September 1917, p. 6; *BET* 7 September 1917, p. 5 and 8 September 1917, p. 6.

22 WO 95/2502.

23 Falls, *History of the 36th (Ulster) Division*, pp. 307–10.

24 Irish Jesuit Archives, Gill, p. 154.

25 Lucy, *Devil in the Drum*, pp. 378–9.

26 WO 95/2503.

27 Feilding, *War Letters to a Wife*, p. 124.

28 Ibid., pp. 127, 130–1 and 132.

29 Johnstone, *Orange, Green and Khaki*, pp. 303.

30 Jourdain and Fraser, *The Connaught Rangers*, p. 253.

31 Feilding, *War Letters to a Wife*, p. 139.

32 Falls, *History of the 36th (Ulster) Division*, p. 150; WO 95/2511.

33 WO 95/2502 and 2503.

34 See p. 109.

35 *BNL* 12 August 1916, p. 6 and 28 December 1917, p. 5; *BET* 28 January 1918, p. 6.

36 Falls, *History of the 36th (Ulster) Division*, p. 166.

37 Only five can be linked to West Belfast: Sergeant William James Reid (Aberdeen Street), Riflemen Thompson Bristow (Canmore Street), George Smith (Argyle Street), Edward Dawson (Magnetic Street) and Alexander Thompson (Woodvale Avenue). *BNL* 11 December 1917, p. 8, 21 December 1917, p. 8, and 22 December 1917, p. 6; *BET* 19 December 1917, p. 6 and 13 September 1918, p. 3.

38 *BNL* 4 October 1916, p. 8, 6 August 1917, p. 6 and 4 September 1918, p. 6. The other 11 were: Riflemen Frederick Bryans (Cambrai Street), Robert Carmichael (Glenvale Street), Joseph Cochrane (Palmer Street), Robert Stitt (Broom Street), Robert James Thompson (Hanover Street), David Bailie (Emerson Street), William McCormick (Leadbetter Street) and Ronald Walker (Salisbury Place); Corporal Kirker Gibson McBride (Upper Charleville Street); Lance-Corporal James Sanderson (Fairview Street) and Sergeant Thomas Wilkin (Hanover Street). See: *BNL* 8 December 1917, p. 5 and 6, 18 December 1917, p. 5, 21 December 1917, p. 6, 27 December 1917, p. 8 and 4 January 1918, p. 5; *BET* 14 December 1917, p. 6, 19 December 1917, p. 5, 26 December 1917, p. 4, 28 December 1917, p. 6, 15 January 1918, p. 6; 6 February 1918, p. 6, 9 September 1918, p. 3 and 27 September 1918, p. 3.

39 WO 95/2502.

40 Bowman, *Irish Regiments*, pp. 145–6.

41 With the limited information available it is not possible to see any patterns among men who went into different units, but it must be possible that the younger and/or fitter ones were moved to infantry units.

42 BET 9 January 1918, p. 5 and 28 January 1918, p. 6.

43 Irish Jesuit Archives, Gill, p. 177.

44 WO 95/2308: 2nd Leinsters' War Diary.

45 WO 95/905: 19th Entrenching Battalion War Diary.

Notes to Chapter 12: Retreat

1 *IN* 10 April 18, p. 10 and 1 May 18, p. 3. Jérôme Aan de Wiel, *The Catholic Church in Ireland, 1914–18: War and Politics* (Dublin, 2003), pp. 203–55. Grieves, *Politics of Manpower*, pp. 188–91.

2 Yvonne McEwen, 'What Have You Done for Ireland? The 36th (Ulster) Division in the Great War: Politics, propaganda and the demography of deaths', *Irish Sword* 24.96 (2004), pp. 194–218. See Table 5: in 1916, Ulster-born deaths in the division were 80.85 per cent of the total, with those of soldiers from Great Britain amounting to 10.5 per cent. The percentages in 1917 were 54.23 and 31.18, while in 1918 they were 43.54 and 29.49 (with the number of 'unknown' origin rising). See also Denman, 'Nationality', pp. 79 and 86, which shows that a majority of deaths in the Ulster Division were only from outside Ulster towards the end of the war.

3 Assessing relative numbers by looking at West Belfast men killed in the different battalions in 1917 shows that the largest numbers were in the 9th RIRifles (27, plus four in the 8th/9th), and the 15th RIRifles (21). There were 20 in one regular battalion (1st Inniskillings), 16 in the 1st Royal Irish Fusiliers, 16 in the 2nd RIRifles, and 14 in the 2nd Inniskillings, but in other volunteer battalions of the RIRifles there were 16 in the 8th and 18 in the 14th. In 1918, 33 died in the 2nd RIRifles, but the next highest number was 22 in the 15th RIRifles.

4 Quoted in Jourdain and Fraser, *The Connaught Rangers*, p. 263.

5 Feilding, *War Letters to a Wife*, p. 158.

6 The 6th Connaughts and 47th Brigade war diaries for this time were lost or never made, but there are details of 47th Brigade's movements in the 2nd Leinsters' diary, and soon after the retreat Feilding made a detailed note in WO 95/1956.

7 NAM 1977-7-12: Desmond McWeeney note on 21 March 1918, May 1977.

8 Taylor, *2nd RIRifles*, p. 116.

9 Ibid., p. 117.

10 WO 339/94802: R. Sprott.

11 Bowman, *Irish Regiments*, pp. 169–70 and 172; Terence Denman, 'The 16th (Irish) Division on 21 March 1918: Fight or Flight?' *Irish Sword*, 69 (1999), pp. 273–87; Lynn Speer Lemisko, 'Morale in the 16th (Irish) Division, 1916–18', *Irish Sword*, 20.81 (1997), pp. 217–33.

12 WO 95/828: 21st Entrenching Battalion.

13 Falls, *History of the 36th (Ulster) Division*, pp. 215–16; SDGW.

14 Sergeants Thomas Crowe (Courtrai Street) and Andrew McCormick (Glenbank Place), Lance-Corporal John Wilson (Scotch Street), Riflemen Henry Bell (Lawnbrook Avenue), John Best (Brussels Street), Edward Magee (Malvern Street), Robert McCoy (Greenland Street), Frank McTier (Crumlin Road), Edward Redmond (Canmore Street), Samuel Young (Sugarfield Street), Hugh McGinn (Campbell's Row) and Albert Staunton (Heather Street); Bugler Samuel Vogan (Vistula Street). See *BET* 9 May 1918, p. 4, 10 May 1918, p. 4, 14 May 1918, p. 4, 19 April 1919, p. 3 and 14 August 1919, p. 3; Presbyterian roll; CWGC.

15 NA WO 95/2503: 15th RIRifles' War Diary.

16 Corporal Richard McVeigh (Crumlin Road); Riflemen James Smeeth (Malvern Street), John Crossan (Legnavea Street), William Colquhoun (Broadbent Street), James Clare (Coniston Street), Nicholas Orr (Crimea Street) and Robert Mills (Joseph Street). *BNL* 5 November 1918, p. 6; *BET* 7 May 1918, p. 4, 15 May 1918, p. 3, 4 November 191, p. 3, 15 May 1919, p. 3, 12 September 1919, p. 8; Presbyterian Roll; CWGC.

17 Feilding, *War Letters to a Wife*, p. xvi. After the war, Feilding pursued various business interests before retiring and publishing his war letters in 1929. He died in 1945, three weeks after the end of the Second World War.

18 This figure includes 61 listed on *SDGW* as 2nd, and eight listed as 7th.

19 *IN* 5 July 1918, p. 1

20 *BET* 10 May 1918, p. 4.

21 See www.lennonwylie.co.uk/ww1_soldiers_database.htm, accessed 1 December 2008; e-mail to author from granddaughter, Carole Zandvliet, 28 August 2008.

22 *BET* 6 April 1918, p. 3; World War I Irish Soldiers' Wills.

23 Martin Gilbert, *First World War* (1994), pp. 409–10.

24 Alexander Watson, *Enduring the Great War: Combat, Morale and Collapse in the German and British Armies, 1914–18* (Cambridge, 2008), pp. 179–83.

25 *Battle Lines* 17 (2000), pp. 9–11.

26 *BET* 7 May 1918, p. 4.

27 *BET* 4 May 1918, p. 4, 4 September 1918, p. 4 and 9 September 1918, p. 4; SHC SOM 2008/033.

28 SHC SOM 1994/512–14.

29 *BET* 19 April 1919, p. 4.

30 *BET* 19 April 1918, p. 3.

31 WO 95/2506.

32 Riflemen William Collins (Disraeli Street), William McCormick (Oakley Street), Henry Purdy (Thames Street), George Alexander Scott (Argyle Street), William John Scott (Crimea Street) and Samuel Taylor (Ligoniel Road). *BET* 12 April 1918, p. 3, 27 April 1918, p. 4, 11 May 1918, p. 3 and 14 May 1918, p. 4; CWGC.

33 Falls, *History of the 36th (Ulster) Division*, pp. 238–9.

34 *BNL* 29 May 1918, p. 3; *BET* 30 May 1918, p. 3, 9 September 1918, p. 3, 11 September 1918, p. 3 and 28 September 1918, p. 3.

Notes to Chapter 13: Victory

1 Watson, *Enduring the Great War*, pp. 234–5.

2 Dan Todman, *The Great War: Myth and Memory* (London, 2005).

3 Gary Sheffield, 'Military Revisionism: The Case of the British Army on the Western Front', in Michael Howard, *A Part of History: Aspects of the British Experience of the First World War* (London, 2008), pp. 1–7.

4 *IN* 2 May 1918, p. 1.

5 *BET* 17 September 1918, pp. 3 and 4.

6 *BET* 4 December 1918, p. 4 and 18 January 1919, p. 4.

7 Falls, *History of the 36th (Ulster) Division*, pp. 251–2; Bowman, *Irish Regiments*, p. 180.

8 WO 95/2492; Falls, *History of the 36th (Ulster) Division*, pp. 256–7.

9 In the 1st RIRifles they were Riflemen Joseph Adams (Gardiner Street), Henry Dornan (Cambrai Street) and Alexander Dougan (Roden Street); in the 2nd they were Riflemen Matthew Andrews (Harrison Street), David Crothers (Disraeli Street), Thomas Maxwell (Crosby Street), Aubrey Patterson (Ambleside Street), Alexander Scott (Dundee Street) and Robert Stewart (English Street). See *BNL* 1 October 1918, p. 3; *BET* 30 September 1918, p. 3, 9 October 1918, p. 3, 17 October 1918, p. 3 and 12 September 1918, p. 8; CGWC; Presbyterian roll.

10 For Irish units, see Bowman, *Irish Regiments*, p. 180.

11 Postwar address of wife from CWGC.

12 *BNL* 9 October 1918, p. 4 and 5 November 1918, p. 6; *BET* 9 October 1918, p. 4, 28 November 1918, p. 4 and 20 February 1919, p. 4.

13 The others two West Belfast losses were Riflemen James Glencross (1st RIRifles, Brookmount Street) and James Gabriel Murdock (2nd RIRifles, Upper Charleville Street). See *BNL* 9 August 1916, p. 8, 4 November 1918, p. 3, 1 November 1918, p. 7, 11 November 1918, p. 4 and 12 November 1918, p. 6; *BET* 7 November 1918, p. 4, 9 November 1918, p. 3 and 14 December 1918, p. 4.

14 WO 95/2502.

15 1st Royal Irish Fusiliers: Privates John Lewis (Harrison Street) and Matthew Wilson (Hopeton Street); 12th RIRifles: Rifleman Alexander Kerr (Linview Street); 15th RIRifles: Rifleman Humphrey Griffith Duggan (Seventh Street). *BNL* 16 November 1918, p. 6 and 22 November 1918, p. 6; *BET* 15 November 1918, p. 3, 30 November 1918, p. 4 and 17 December 1918, p. 4.

16 *BNL* 1 September 1917, p. 5 and 5 November 1918, p. 6; *BET* 8 September 1917, p. 6 and 28 November 1917, p. 4. For an account of various actions see Canning, *Wheen of Medals*, pp. 201–13.

17 *BNL* 8 November 1918, p. 6.

18 Official medal citations provided by Dickson's daughter, Mrs M. Close, June 2008.

19 *BET* 2 November 1918, p. 4.

20 Email from great-nephew, Brian Reid, to author, 5 February 2009.

21 *BNL* 2 December 1918, p. 7; *BET* 28 December 1918, p. 4, 30 November 1918, p. 3 and 17 December 1918, p. 4.

22 Falls, *History of the 36th (Ulster) Division*, p. 292.

23 *SDGW.*

24 *BET* 1 January 1919, p. 4.

25 *IN* 26 February 1919, p. 3. Tom Hartley, *Written in Stone: The History of Belfast City Cemetery* (Belfast, 2006), pp. 86–7.

26 *BNL* 12 November 1918, p. 4; 13 November 1918, p. 3; *IN* 12 November 1918, p. 2.

27 *BNL* 11 November 1918, p. 4; *BET* 9 November 1918, p. 3.

28 www.irishregiments.com/r-past/sterling.html, accessed 1 December 2008.

Notes to Chapter 14: Peace and Partition

1 See pp. 46–7 and 147.

2 SHC SOM 1994/512–14; Presbyterian memorial roll.

3 *IN* 10 June 1918, p. 1; Clonard Historical Society. The family are clear that Owen Senior was not killed in service and that he was in the Connaughts. The reason for believing that he also served in the Leinsters is that a family photograph shows him wearing that cap badge.

4 Corrigan, *Mud, Blood and Poppycock*, pp. 52–76.

5 Patrick J. Casey, 'Irish Casualties in the First World War', *Irish Sword*, 20.81 (1997), pp. 193–206 (see p. 195).

6 J. M. Winter, *The Great War and the British People* (London, 2003), pp. 73 and 82. Jeffery, *Ireland and the Great War*, p. 35.

7 The records of the Ulster Special Constabulary are not yet open, which limits research into membership by ex-soldiers.

8 *BNL* 3 December 1918, p. 8.

9 *IN* 30 December 1918, p. 3.

10 Some had joined after the war, serving in Mesopotamia, but others were war veterans. Royal Irish Fusiliers Attestation Books, Royal Irish Fusiliers Museum, Armagh.

11 Hartley, p. 191.
12 *BT* 14 October 1919, p. 8.
13 *BNL* 19 December 1918, p. 7.
14 *BET* 6 January 1919, p. 4.
15 *BET* 27 February 1919, p. 3 and 11 March 1919, p. 4.
16 *BET* 7 March 1919, p. 4; Hartley, *Written in Stone*, p. 251.
17 *BT* 27 August 1919, p. 6.
18 *BET* 27 December 1916, p. 4 and CWGC.
19 E-mail from great-nephew, Brian Reid, to author, 5 February 2009; *BT* 4 November 1919, p. 3.
20 WO 364 individual file.
21 *IN* 4 January 1919, p. 3.
22 *BNL* 15 April 1918, p. 3 and 9 December 1918, p. 3; NA WO 339/94802: R. Sprott.
23 WO 339/91112.
24 *BT* 14 June 1919, p. 4.
25 Jeffery, *Ireland and the Great War*, p. 117.
26 Letter to author from Mrs M. Close, 9 June 2008.
27 Edgar Jones, *et al.* , 'Post-combat Syndromes from the Boer War to the Gulf War: A Cluster Analysis of their Nature and Attribution', *British Medical Journal* 324 (9 February 2002), pp. 1–7.
28 WO 364 individual file.
29 Personal papers provided by Marie Toner Moore.
30 Notes sent to author and prepared by Marie Toner Moore, 28 June 2007.
31 *BNL* 6 October 1916, p. 10; *BET* 11 November 1916, p. 6.
32 SHC, Patriotic Fund papers.
33 Ibid.
34 Author's interview with Jackie Hewitt, 25 June 2008; *Ireland's Saturday Night* 1 August 1925, p. 3; *BNL* 23 July 1925, p. 5 and 28 July 1925, p. 2.
35 *Battle Lines* 17 (2000), pp. 9–11. Helga Woggon, *Silent Radical – Winifred Carney, 1887–1943: A Reconstruction of her Biography* (Dublin, 2000), pp. 27–31.
36 *IN* 11 November 1919, p. 2.
37 Author's interview with Desy Brennan, 8 September 2007.
38 *IN* 4 January 1919, p. 4 and 30 March 1919, p. 3.
39 *IN* 25 June 18, p. 4 and 29 June 18, p. 4.
40 *BNL* 29 March 1919, p. 6; *IN* 18 October 1919, p. 6.
41 *IN* 29 June 18, p. 4 and 23 May 19, p. 5.
42 *IN* 24 July 1919, p. 5.
43 *IN* 31 July 1919, p. 5, 18 October 1919, p. 6, 22 December 1919, p. 5, 1 January 1920, p. 4 and 27 January 1920, p. 6; *BNL* 31 July 1919, p. 7.
44 Peter Barberis, John McHugh, Mike Tyldesley, *Encyclopedia of British and Irish Political Organizations: Parties, Groups and Movements of the 20th Century* (London, 2003), p. 254; *BNL* 9 May 1921, p. 6.
45 *IN* 28 April 1920, p. 6 and 3 May 1920, p. 5.
46 The National Archive, Kew, Ministry of Pensions and National Insurance (PIN) 15/139: Belfast War Pensions Committee to Ministry of Pensions, 26 June 1919.
47 *IN* 24 March 1920, p. 6 and 7 April 1920, p. 6.
48 *IN* 12 July 1915, p. 4, 13 July 1915, p. 4, 14 July 1915, p. 4, 16 July 1915, p. 5 and 4 August 1915, p. 6.

49 Peter Hart, *The IRA at War 1916–23* (Oxford, 2003), pp. 33, 34, 247 and 248.

50 Alan F. Parkinson, *Belfast's Unholy War: The Troubles of the 1920s* (Dublin, 2004), pp. 12, 15 and 326 nn. 19 and 20.

51 *IN* 14 July 1919, p. 6.

52 Bowman, *Carson's Army*, pp. 190–3 and 196.

53 *IN* 27 May 1919, p. 6.

54 *IN* 5 July 1919, p. 5.

55 *BNL* 31 July 1920, p. 7. On the general situation in the Belfast shipyards, see Kevin Johnston, *In the Shadows of Giants: A Social History of the Belfast Shipyards* (Dublin, 2008), pp. 198–232.

56 *IN* 22 July 1920, p. 5 and 24 July 1920, pp. 1 and 5.

57 *BT* 23 July 1920, p. 3.

58 *BT* 24 July 1920, p. 3.

59 *BT* 26 July 1920, p. 3.

60 *IN* 18 June 1921, p. 5, 12 July 1921, p. 5. In the newspaper coverage, the *Belfast Telegraph* focused on the actions of gunmen, while the *Irish News* focused on nationalist districts being under 'siege' due to sweeping of streets by gunfire from 'Crown forces'.

61 *IN* 12 November 1920, p. 5; *Irish Times* 12 November 1920, p. 6.

62 Parkinson, *Belfast's Unholy War*, p. 286.

63 Ibid., p. 154. The other two Catholics were Hugh McAree (Sackville Street, 14 June 1921) and Benedict Leith (Regent Street, 9 March 1922). See ibid., pp. 140 and 243; *BT* 11 July 1921, p. 5; 13 July 1921, p. 5; *IN* 14 July 1915, p. 5 and 10 March 1922.

64 Parkinson, *Belfast's Unholy War*, pp. 95–6 and 244.

65 *BT* 11 June 1921, p. 5.

66 Parkinson, *Belfast's Unholy War*, p. 106, 116, 137 and 338 n. 39. Others of unknown religion were George Walker (Eighth Street, 17 May 1921) and Robert Dudgeon (Westland Street, 17 May 1922). See ibid., p. 128 and 266. On Nixon, see Chris Ryder, *The Fateful Split: Catholics and the Royal Ulster Constabulary* (London, 2004), pp. 73–85.

67 *BNL* 3 April 1922, p. 5. Reports list him as Walsh, but the gravestone (thanks to Tom Hartley for a photo) has Walshe.

68 NA, Dublin: S/1801/A Memo for Mr Michael Collins, March 1922: Extracts from Statutory Declarations Re: Arnon Street and Stanhope Massacres; Parkinson, *Belfast's Unholy War*, p. 246 and nn. 13–15; Robert Lynch, *The Northern IRA and the Early Years of Partition, 1920–2* (Dublin, 2006), pp. 122–3.

69 NAM 2006-11-14 Enlistment Books of the Connaught Rangers; National Archives WWI Medal Rolls online; WO 95/1690. O'Hare's number in the Leinsters was 7986 and 32626, although he is listed as O'Hara in WO 329/2479 the 1914 Star Roll for the Leinsters.

70 *IN* 21 June 1921, p. 5.

71 Author's interview with Seán O'Hare, 15 November 2007.

72 Denise Kleinrichert, *Republican Internment and the Prison Ship* Argenta *1922* (Dublin, 2001).

73 PRONI HA5/2181: Patrick Barnes.

74 Letter from Kate McNeill to author, September 2007; PRONI HA/5/1995: Peter Murray.

75 PRONI HA5/1904 2045 2191 and 2311: Henry McIlhone (Baker Street), Malachy Trainor (Cinnamond Street, ex-Leinsters and PoW), James Walsh (Lady Street, former 2nd Inniskillings) and Patrick Burden (McDonnell Street).

76 E-mails from Ed McCann, 4 July 2006 and 10 July 2008.

77 NA, medal roll; *BNL* 9 September 1915, p. 10. His lawyer claimed service in France in 1914–17, but this does not match military records.

78 PRONI HA5/1878: James Davey.

79 PRONI HA5/1938: Thomas McCrory.

80 Jane Leonard, 'Getting them at Last: The IRA and Ex-Servicemen', in David Fitzpatrick (ed.), *Revolution? Ireland 1917–23* (Dublin, 1990), pp. 118–29 and 'Facing the "Finger of Scorn": Veterans' Memories of Ireland after the Great War', in Eoin Magennis and Cronan O'Doibhlin, *World War One and its Impacts* (Armagh, 2005), pp. 87–107; Paul Taylor, 'Heroes or Traitors? Public Reaction to Returning Irish Soldiers from World War One' (MA dissertation, University College London, 2008), pp. 22–4.

81 PRONI HA 5/2024 and 2026: George Hamill and Hugh Harper; McDermott, *Northern Divisions*, pp. 146–7.

82 PRONI HA 5/2477: David McKinstry.

83 PRONI HA 5/2181: Patrick Barnes; McDermott, *Northern Divisions*, pp. 139–40 and 269–70.

84 Parkinson, *Belfast's Unholy War*, pp. 237–9.

85 PRONI HA5/2261: Samuel Ditty.

86 McDermott, *Northern Divisions*, p. 213; author's conversation with Desmond Cassidy (son of James Cassidy), 28 June 2007.

87 E-mail from Siobhán Deane, 16 September 2007; HA/5/1819: Mary Brennan.

88 PRONI HA/32/1/271: Disappearance of A. J. P. Stapleton.

89 In British military records in Ireland, Seán was Anglicized as John. A search of the UK-wide medal roll suggests that only three men with Seán/Sean as a first or middle name served in the war. None of these was from Ireland, which shows the extent of Anglicization of enlistment papers.

90 I am grateful to Pól Wilson of the Irish Republican History Museum for obtaining copies from private possession of Cunningham's IV enlistment record, an unnamed newspaper cutting and other papers. Details of military service are taken from PRONI Cunningham Papers: D/1625/4, Certificate of Military Service, 21 August 1928; D/1625/12, Certificate of Discharge from Garda Síochána (this shows his date of birth as 17 August 1889, which would mean he was 15 years old in September 1904); and D/1625/18, Replacement of Discharge Certificate, 20 October 1936; D/1625/18, *IN* 2 March 1963.

91 Orr, *Field of Bones*, pp. 228–229.

92 Author's interview with Harry Donaghy, 12 September 2007 and e-mail to author 22 August 2008.

Notes to Chapter 15: Remembrance

1 Robert Greacen, *Selected and New Poems* (Cliffs of Moher, 2006), p. 154.

2 For an excellent broad view, see James Loughlin, 'Mobilising the Sacred Dead: Ulster Unionism, the Great War and the Politics of Remembrance', in Gregory and Pašeta (eds), *Ireland and the Great War*, pp. 133–54.

3 *BET* 5 February 1916, p. 5.

4 *BET* 7 June 1915, p. 3.

5 *BET* 25 July 1916, p. 3.

6 *BET* 15 October 1915, p. 7.

7 *BET* 30 June 1917.

8 *BNL* 6 June 1917, p. 6 and 29 June 1917, p. 8.

9 *BNL* 2 July 1917, p. 8.

10 *BNL* 1 July 1916, p. 3, 2 July 1916, p. 2 and 14 July 1919, pp. 7–9; *BT* 2 July 1919, p. 6.

11 *IN* 24 December 1918, p. 6.

12 *BT* 30 July 1919, p. 3; *IN* 30 July 1915, p. 5.

13 For detailed accounts see Nuala C. Johnson, *Ireland, the Great War and the Geography of Remembrance* (Cambridge, 2007), pp. 72–7 and Nuala C. Johnson, 'Memorialising and Marking the Great War: Belfast Remembers', in Frederick W. Boal and Stephen A. Royle, *Enduring City: Belfast in the Twentieth Century* (Belfast, 2006), pp. 207–20.

14 *IN* 21 July 1919, p. 5.

15 *BNL* 11 August 1919, p. 5; *IN* 11 August 1919, p. 5.

16 *BT* 3 August 1919, p. 6.

17 Catherine Switzer, *Unionists and Great War Commemoration in the North of Ireland 1914–39: People, Places and Politics* (Dublin, 2007), pp. 18 and 22; *IN* 10 October 1916, p. 4.

18 *IN* 19 July 1919, p. 4.

19 *IN* 12 August 1919, p. 6.

20 It is unclear how many attended. A photograph in the *BT* showed no more than 20 men, while the *IN* spoke of the parade's 'large dimensions'. The curate, Fr Lagan, conducted the service, but as Robert McKillen said to me, for major occasions, it would have been usual for the parish priest (Fr Thomas McDonald) to have said Mass. *BT* 13 October 1919, p. 8; *IN* 13 October 1919, p. 6.

21 *IN* 12 November 1919, p. 5.

22 See for example, *BT* 1 July 1926, p. 9 and 2 July 1926, p. 3.

23 Adrian Gregory, *The Silence of Memory: Armistice Day 1919–46* (Oxford, 1994), pp. 11, 24, 99 and 241.

24 Jeffery, *Ireland and the Great War*, pp. 108–9.

25 List provided by Billy Ervine.

26 Jeffery, *Ireland and the Great War*, p. 111; Moore, pp. 261–4.

27 See, for example, *Shankill Mirror* November 1999, pp. 13–15 and *The Irish on the Somme*, December 1999, p. 15.

28 Jane Leonard, 'The Twinge of Memory: Armistice Day and Remembrance Sunday in Dublin since 1919', in Richard English and Graham Walker (eds), *Unionism in Modern Ireland: New Perspectives on Politics and Culture* (London, 1996), pp. 99–114 (see pp. 109–11), and 'Lest we Forget', in David Fitzpatrick (ed.), *Ireland and the First World War* (Dublin, 1988), pp. 59–68 (see pp. 64–7).

29 Switzer, *Unionists and the Great War Commemoration*, pp. 88–9, 119, 151–2 and 156.

30 Gillian McIntosh, *The Force of Culture: Unionist Identities in Twentieth-Century Ireland* (Cork, 1999), pp. 15–16.

31 Jeffery, *Ireland and the Great War*, p. 132; *BNL* 12 November 1929, pp. 7–9.

32 *IW*, 22 September 1934, p. 8 and 29 September 1934, p. 14.

33 Jim Gibney, 'Fresh Eyes Revisit Battle of the Somme', *IN* 6 July 2006, p. 2.

34 WO 95/1970: undated and anonymous note in War Diary addressed to the battalion's officers and men.

35 Orr, *Road to the Somme*, p. 222.

36 Lieutenant-Colonel V. Unsworth, Captain R. P. MacGregor, Mr R. Spence, Mr J. Hanlon, Mr J. Atcheson, Mr J. Lavery, Mr J. McAteer.

37 *Battle Lines*, 11 (1996), pp. 8–9; *Quis Separabit* VII, 2 (1936), pp. 181–4, XXVI (1956), pp. 125–33, XXXVIII (1966), pp. 5 and 39–49. *BT* 30 June 1966, pp. 1 and 8.

38 Royal Ulster Rifles Museum MU97; 9 RIRifles Old Comrades Association (OCA) Minute Books 1951–76. Names and addresses are covered by government rules on personal records and cannot be released, although the individuals are now all deceased.

39 *Battle Lines*, 12 (1996), p. 4.

40 *Battle Lines*, 11 (1996), pp. 8–9 and 12 (1996), p. 2.

41 *Shankill Mirror* June 1999, p. 18 and November 2002, p. 12.

42 Jeffery, *Ireland and the Great War*, p. 133.

43 B. Graham and P. Shirlow, 'The Battle of the Somme in Ulster Memory and Identity', *Political Geography* 21 (2002), pp. 881–904; Kris Brown, '"Our Father Organization": The Cult of the Somme and the Unionist "Golden Age" in Modern Ulster Loyalist Commemoration', *The Round Table*, 96.393 (2007), pp. 707–23. See also Jeffery, *Ireland and the Great War*, pp. 133–4 and Jane McGaughey, 'Ulster Masculinity and Militarisation, 1912–23' (unpublished PhD thesis, University of London, 2008), pp. 258–366.

44 Brown, 'Our Father Organization'.

45 *Shankill Mirror* June 1999, p. 17.

46 See http://www.beyondconflict.net/, accessed 1 December 2008. See the news and photo sections of this site for April 2007.

47 Interviews with Ian Adamson 23 June 2008; Michael Hall and Jackie Hewitt 25 June 2008. Farset minute-book and papers in possession of Ian Adamson. Michael Hall, *A Shared Sacrifice for Peace* (Belfast, 2007), pp. 14–15.

48 Michael Hall, *Sacrifice on the Somme* (Belfast, 1993).

49 Hall, *Shared Sacrifice*, p. 26.

50 Ibid., p. 32.

51 *IN* 10 November 1987, p. 1 and 14 November 1987, p. 4.

52 *BT* 14 November 1988, p. 4; Alban Maginness, interview with author, 31 March 2009.

53 *BT* 9 November 1992, p. 3 and 15 November 1993, p. 3.

54 *BNL* 12 November 1990, p. 12; *IN* 14 November 1994, p. 3; *BT* 4 January 2005, p. 6.

55 *BT* 14 November 1994, pp. 3 and 4.

56 *BT* (North West Edition) 13 November 1995, p. 1; *BNL* 13 November 1995, p. 14; *IN* 10 November 1995, p. 8.

57 *IN* 2 July 1997, p. 4; Alban Maginness, interview with author, 31 March 2009.

58 *IN* 10 November 1997, p. 1; Alban Maginness, interview with author, 31 March 2009.

59 *BNL* 3 July 2006, p. 4.

60 *BNL* 11 November 2002, p. 27.

61 Author's interview with Tom Hartley, 26 June 2008.

62 WO 372 Medal Roll.

63 Speech by Alex Maskey, 'The Memory of the Dead: Seeking Common Ground' 26 June 2002: www.info-nordirland.de/new_234_e.htm, accessed 1 December 2008.

64 Barry McCaffrey, *Alex Maskey: Man and Mayor* (Belfast, 2003), pp. 159–64; 'Maskey marks Somme with wreath', BBC News Online, 1 July 2002: http://news.bbc.co.uk/1/hi/northern_ireland/2076528.stm, accessed 1 December 2008.

65 See http://news.bbc.co.uk/1/hi/northern_ireland/74647th95.stm, accessed 18 June 2008 and http://news.bbc.co.uk/1/hi/northern_ireland/7483338.stm, accessed 1 December 2008; *BNL* 3 July 2006, p. 4.

66 E-mail from Máirtín Ó Muilleoir, 12 July 2008.

67 E-mail from Ed McCann, 10 July 2008.

68 See www.connaughtrangersassoc.com/r_past.htm and http://www.irishregiments.com/r-past/, accessed 1 December 2008.

69 Author's interview with Seán O'Hare, 15 Nov 2007.

70 *IN* 26 April 2006, p. 9; www.connaughtrangers.blogspot.com, accessed 1December 2008.

71 John Morrissey, 'A Lost Heritage: The Connaught Rangers and Multivocal Irishness', in Mark McCarthy (ed.), *Ireland's Heritage: Critical Perspectives on Memory and Identity* (Aldershot,

2005), pp. 71–87; 6th Connaught Rangers' Research Project, *The 6th Connaught Rangers: Belfast Nationalists and the Great War* (Belfast, 2008); Roy Garland, 'Liberating Memory from Tribal Loyalties', *IN*, 1 December 2008.

72 Author's interview with Harry Donaghy, 12 September 2007.
73 Gregory and Pašeta, *Ireland and the Great War,* p. 2.

Notes to Appendix: Methods and Patterns of 'Military History from the Street'

1 A soldier's own address is used wherever it is given, otherwise, next-of-kin address is used, which will often be own address in any case.

2 The records were originally due out by the end of November 2008: www.nationalarchives. gov.uk/news/stories/166.htm?homepage=news, accessed 3 November 2008. Consequently, publication of this book, which had been otherwise completed in September 2008, was delayed to allow their use. However, they have been further delayed by a year, and may not be available even to begin research on until late 2009.

3 The 421 and 319 figures have been reached as follows. First of all, the percentage of surnames in Belfast for each letter of the alphabet can be determined from the pensions records. These reveal that 24 per cent of surnames in Belfast begin with letters O to Z. On that basis, if the 7,325 service records used so far constitute 76 per cent of the total, then we would expect there to be 2,313 in the O-Z category. From the 7,325 A-N service records, 18.2 per cent were for West Belfast, and 13.8 per cent were individuals who were not found in any other source. Applying these percentages to the 2,313 predicted O-Z service records results in 421 individuals, of whom 319 would be unique to the service records.

4 These figures cover the combined total for Court, Falls, Shankill, Smithfield and Woodvale wards for which the 1911 Census recorded 110,799, plus an estimate for St Anne's of which about one-third has been included. Because the area covered only part of St Anne's ward, it has been more difficult to assess that accurately. Source: Command Paper, Cd. 6051-I, *Census of Ireland, 1911, Province of Ulster, City of Belfast*, pp. 40–41.

5 For example, Short Strand is transcribed as 'Shurkhard' in one place and Crumlin Road as 'Greenlees Road'.

6 These figures include searches for Belfast, Shankill, Shankhill, Falls, Ballysillan, Ligoniel, Andersonstown, St Anne's Belfast, and St Peter's Antrim. St Peter's Belfast found no West Belfast records. Approximately 98 per cent of records are for three terms: Belfast, Shankill and Shankhill, so although the other terms are important in order to build up as full a list as possible, they, and other small areas or spelling mistakes which may have been missed, cannot be seen to have a significant impact on overall figures or patterns. Meanwhile, it should be noted that even though 'Shankhill' is a spelling mistake for the Belfast parish, and correctly refers to a parish in County Armagh, over 91 per cent relate to Belfast.

7 Eric Mercer, 'For King, Country and a Shilling a Day: Belfast Recruiting Patterns in the Great War', *History Ireland* 11, 4 (2003), pp. 29–33 and 'For King, Country and a Shilling a Day: Recruitment in Belfast during the Great War, 1914 – 18' (MA Dissertation, The Queen's University Belfast. 1998), p. 9.

8 It should be possible to establish the percentages of Protestants and Catholics whose records have survived, and then compare those to the known population of West Belfast. If one takes the five wards which are entirely contained in West Belfast, then one finds a Catholic population of 35.9 per cent in the 1911 Census, with 28.2 per cent Church of Ireland, 27.7 per cent Presbyterian, 5 per cent Methodist, and 3.2 per cent 'All Other Denominations', the vast

majority of which were other Protestants. The five wards which have been used are Court, Falls, Shankill, Smithfield and Woodvale. The section of St Anne's Ward which is included in West Belfast has not been used because accurate figures for the precise make-up of the streets included would involve an extremely time-consuming analysis of each street as figures for whole wards are the only ones published. In filling gaps in the pensions and service records, it is essential to use material that is not biased against one or more denominations. So, for example, although there is plenty of information about Presbyterians and Anglicans from relevant memorial rolls, there is no such roll for Catholics, which means that rolls cannot be used. The only useful source is therefore the 1911 Census. This has been used by the author to add religion for men who were at the same address in 1911 as when they enlisted. Using only the data in the pensions and service records, we find that in 2,539 individuals' records, 1,738 (68.5 per cent) have a known denomination. Among the latter, Catholics comprise 29.3 per cent. However, adding Census data provides information on another 4.2 per cent of the soldiers. Among these, Catholics are disproportionately high, and their overall percentage rises to 30.8 per cent. Yet, that figure remains problematic because it excludes over one quarter of the volunteers. Consequently, one can try to estimate denomination among those for whom it remains unknown. Two methods have been used for this, and they lead to figures which show Catholic recruitment as either slightly lower (at 33.5 per cent) than their share of the population (35.9 per cent), or slightly higher (at 37.6 per cent). The higher figure comes from assuming that all those whose religion is not recorded can be attributed a denomination in the same percentages as the 4.2 per cent who could be found in the Census, across all five wards. With this *uniform estimate*, 55.6 per cent of those whose religion is unknown would be recorded as Catholics, leading to the total of 37.6 per cent. However, the lower total of 33.5 per cent is based on different patterns for how the 4.2 per cent broke down in each ward, which is a more sophisticated approach. This *ward estimate* means, for example, that because 84 per cent of those found in the 1911 Census in Falls Ward were Catholics, and only 6.4 per cent of those in the Shankill, those figures are applied to the 'unknown' in these wards, rather than a uniform 55.6 per cent. This figure is likely to be more reliable than the *uniform estimate*.

9   The different Protestant populations of the five wards in the 1911 Census were: Church of Ireland 28.2 per cent, Presbyterian 27.7 per cent, Methodist 5 per cent, and the vast majority of the 3.2 per cent for 'All Other Denominations'. The pensions/service records reveal: Church of Ireland 37.7 per cent, Presbyterian 29.6 per cent, Methodist 2.8 per cent. Adding in 1911 Census data alters those to: Church of Ireland 37.0 per cent, Presbyterian 28.9 per cent, Methodist 2.6 per cent. The *uniform estimate* results in: Church of Ireland 34.0 per cent, Presbyterian 25.5 per cent, Methodist 1.9 per cent. The *ward estimate* leads to Church of Ireland 34.7 per cent, Presbyterian 28.6 per cent, Methodist 1.9 per cent. Presbyterians only fall below their percentage of the population using the less sophisticated *uniform estimate*. Only two Jewish volunteers (Louis Cohen and Morris Glover) were found among the 2,573 with pensions/service records, both in Court Ward. One further (Louis Goldwater) was identified in the 1911 Census. The *uniform estimate* results in a total of nine, while the *ward estimate* suggests 13, but with such small numbers, estimates are extremely unreliable.

10 Available data shows, for example, the 9th RIRifles to have been 100 per cent Protestant, the 6th Connaughts 98 per cent Catholic (and two per cent Protestant) and the 7th Leinsters 97 per cent Catholic (and three per cent Protestant). In contrast, the Protestant/Catholic divide in regular battalions appears to have been 72/28 in the 1st RIRifles, 68/32 in the 2nd RIRifles, 67/33 in the 1st Inniskillings, and 75/25 in the 2nd Inniskillings. Meanwhile, among the non-political volunteers of the 6th RIRifles, the divide looks like 65/35. However, for

reasons already stated, these figures are likely to heavily underestimate the Catholic recruits, and Father Gill of the 2nd RIRifles was earlier cited as believing the battalion to have been 70 per cent Catholic. Moreover, figures are not large enough to show how the composition changed over time.

11 'War' deaths officially ran to 1921, and 72 of the confirmed 1,990 were after 11 November 1918, with 54 of those within one year of the war's end.

12 The estimate of around 4,000 has been reached on the basis that we know that there are service records for 1,016 men from West Belfast (with surnames beginning A-N) who cannot be found elsewhere. This has led, as already explained, to an estimate of another 319 in records for 319. If these 1,335 are 25 percent of the total records which were made, then there could well be 4,005 which were destroyed.

13 Command Paper, Cd. 6051-I, *Census of Ireland, 1911, Province of Ulster, City of Belfast*, p. 37.

14 http://news.bbc.co.uk/1/hi/uk/7940540.stm, accessed 13 March 2009.

15 Adrian Gregory, *The Last Great War: British Society and the First World War* (Cambridge, 2008), pp. 122–131.

16 Of the 99 whom we can be sure were in the 9th RIRifles, sixty-one had a West Belfast address, nine had an address elsewhere in Belfast (five East, two North and two South), and five had an address elsewhere in Ulster. Of the 24 without an address, seven were Shankill-born, two have no information attached, and the rest had some kind of Ulster connection. Of the eight who *might* have been in the 9th RIRifles, different sources give different battalions, covering the 8th, 8th/9th (which did not exist at that point) and 11th. No address has been found for any of these men. Among the officers, two were from Dublin, one from North Belfast, one Ardglass, and the other had no address.

17 Of the other six, *Soldiers Died* says that two were born in Belfast, one enlisted in Belfast (but was from Galway), and three were born elsewhere in Ulster.

18 www.shankilltourism.com/page/default.asp?cmsid=3_62_72&cms=history_Shankill+History_World+War+One, accessed 13 July 2008.

19 Crozier, *Brass Hat*, p. 60 & 112–116. Crozier's batman, David Starrett also wrote that 'six hundred good men and true had gone west' in his unpublished memoirs: IWM 79/35/1: 'Batman' by David Starrett, p. 67.

20 1,836 can be identified through *SDGW*. This covers all the division's infantry battalions, plus the engineers, but information on specific RAMC and RFA units is rarely present.

Bibliography

ARCHIVE COLLECTIONS

IMPERIAL WAR MUSEUM, LONDON

J. F. Blake O'Sullivan, Papers
J. Davey, Papers
R. A. E. Edis, Papers
W. A. Lyon, Papers
J. H. M. Staniforth, 'Kitchener's Soldier, 1914–18: The Letters of John H. M. Staniforth'
   (unpublished MS)
David Starrett, 'Batman' (unpublished MS)
C. J. Wintour, Papers

IMPERIAL WAR MUSEUM SOUND ARCHIVE, LONDON

Walter Collins, interview
F. W. S. Jourdain, interview

IRISH JESUIT ARCHIVES, DUBLIN

Fr Henry Gill, Papers

LINENHALL LIBRARY, BELFAST

1914–18 Belfast Street Directory
Irish Volunteers Papers

THE NATIONAL ARCHIVE, KEW

ADM 1/8403/428: Royal Naval Air Service (RNAS) Papers
CO 904/88–95: Monthly Reports, Royal Irish Constabulary, 1912–14
PIN 15/139 and 2488: Veterans' Pensions Papers
WO 71/ Courts Martial files
——432: Peter Sands
——14160: A. J. Annandale
——450: James Crozier
——454: James Templeton
——453: J. F. McCracken
WO 95/ War Diaries

——828: 21st Entrenching Battalion
——905: 19th Entrenching Battalion
——1350 and 1505: 2nd Royal Inniskilling Fusiliers
——1375: 3rd Division
——1413: 7th Brigade
——1415 and 2247: 2nd RIRifles
——1671: 8th Division
——1724: 25th Brigade
——1730: 1st RIRifles
——1955 and 1956: 16th Division
——1969: 47th Brigade
——1970: 6th Connaught Rangers and 7th Leinster Regiment
——2305: 1st Royal Inniskilling Fusiliers
——2308: 2nd Leinster Regiment
——2491 and 2492: 36th Division
——2502: 107th Brigade
——2503: 9th, 15th and 8th/9th RIRifles
——2511: 14th RIRifles
——4296: 6th RIRifles and 29 Brigade and 5th Royal Irish Fusilisers
——4304: 29th Division
——4311: 1st Royal Inniskilling Fusiliers
——4835: 6th RIRifles
WO 158/416: 16th Division, Narrative of Operations 7 June 1917
WO 161/98 and 99: Committe on the Treatment of British Prisoners of War, Interviews and
    Reports.
WO 339/ Officers' Records
——14325: J. H. Berry
——48941: R. Feilding
——91112: R. Moore
——94802: R. Sprott
——6822: A O'Halloran Wright
WO 363: Soldiers' Service Records 1914–20 (www.ancestry.co.uk)
WO 364: Soldiers' Pensions Records 1914–20 (www.ancestry.co.uk)
WO 372: Medal Rolls 1914–20 (www.ancestry.co.uk)
WO 374/16997: F. P. Crozier

NATIONAL ARCHIVES, DUBLIN

1911 census (www.census.nationalarchives.ie)
S/1801/A Memos for Mr Michael Collins
Hibernian Journal

NATIONAL ARMY MUSEUM, LONDON

Charles A. Brett, Papers
Enlistment Books of the Connaught Rangers, Leinster Regiment, Royal Dublin Fusiliers and
    Royal Munster Fusiliers
H. F. N. Jourdain, Papers

Desmond McWeeney, Papers
Quis Separabit

NATIONAL LIBRARY OF IRELAND, DUBLIN

George F.-H. Berkeley, Papers
Maurice Moore, Papers
Lawrence Parsons, Papers
John Redmond, Papers

PUBLIC RECORD OFFICE OF NORTHERN IRELAND

D1327/4, 14 and 15: Ulster Volunteer Force
D/1625: Seán Cunningham
D/2794/1/1: William A. Montgomery
HA/5/ Internment Files
——1878: James Davey
——1904: Henry McIlhone
——1938: Thomas McCrory
——2024: George Hamill
——2026: Hugh Harper
——2045: Malachy Trainor
——2181: Patrick Barnes
——2191: James Walsh
——2261: Samuel Ditty
——2311: Patrick Burden
——2477: David McKinstry
HA/32/1/271: Disappearance of A. J. P. Stapleton.
Online 1912 Covenant database: www.proni.gov.uk

ROYAL INNISKILLING FUSILIERS MUSEUM, ENNISKILLEN

A Sprig of Shillelagh

ROYAL IRISH FUSILIERS MUSEUM, ARMAGH

Royal Irish Fusiliers Attestation Books

ROYAL ULSTER RIFLES MUSEUM, LONDON

9th RIRifles Photographs
9th RIRifles Old Comrades Association minute-books 1951–76
George and Jeremiah Mabin

SOMME HERITAGE CENTRE

Walter Collins, Papers
David, George and William Tully, Papers

Bertie Holohan, Papers
Ashley Milne, Papers
Patriotic Fund, Papers
Samuel Matier, Papers

UNIVERSITY COLLEGE, DUBLIN

Mary Sheehy Kettle, Papers
Thomas Kettle, Papers
Eoin MacNeill Papers
Belfast Irish National Volunteers minute-book

NEWSPAPERS

Andersonstown News
Belfast Evening Telegraph (*Evening* dropped from title in April 1918)
Belfast News Letter
Belfast Weekly News
Belfast Weekly Telegraph
Freeman's Journal
Irish News
Irish Weekly
National Volunteer
Northern Whig
Shankill Mirror

CD-ROMS

Ireland's National War Memorial Records (Eneclann)
Officers Died in the Great War (Naval and Military Press)
Soldier's Wills (Eneclann)
Soldiers Died in the Great War (Naval and Military Press)
World War I Irish Soldiers: The Final Testament, compiled and edited by Kiara Gregory (Eneclann)

WEBSITES

Commonwealth War Graves Commission: www.cwgc.org
The Long, Long Trail: www.1914–18.net

MEMORIAL ROLLS

Presbyterian Church of Ireland
St Michael's Parish Church, Belfast

JOURNALS

Battle Lines
The New Ranger

MEMOIRS

(Place of publication London unless otherwise stated.)

Brett, Charles, *Charles Brett MC: An Irish Soldier with the Connaught Rangers in World War I* (Newtownards, 2007).

Burgoyne, Gerald Achilles, *The Burgoyne Diaries* (1985).

Corkey, William, *Glad did I Live* (Belfast, 1963).

Crozier, F. P., *A Brass Hat in No Man's Land* (1930).

Crozier, F. P., *The Men I Killed* (1937).

Feilding, Rowland, *War Letters to a Wife: France and Flanders, 1915–19*.

Lucy, John F., *There's a Devil in the Drum* (Uckfield, 1993).

BOOKS, CHAPTERS, ARTICLES AND THESES

(Place of publication London unless otherwise stated.)

1916 Rebellion Handbook (Dublin, 1998).

6th Connaught Rangers Research Project, *The 6th Connaught Rangers: Belfast Nationalists and the Great War* (Belfast, 2008).

Bardon, Jonathan, *A History of Ulster* (Belfast, 2001).

Bartlett, Thomas and Jeffery, Keith (eds), *A Military History of Ireland* (Cambridge, 1996).

Bedwell, Robert, 'The Chatham Air-Raid: Events of Monday 3 September 1917', *The Great War*, 23 (January 2006), pp. 23–32.

Belfast Book of Honour Commitee, *Journey of Remembering: Belfast Book of Honour* (Belfast, 2009).

Bowman, Timothy, 'The Ulster Volunteers 1913–14: Force or Farce?' *History Ireland* 10.1 (2002), pp. 43–7.

—— *Irish Regiments in the Great War: Discipline and Morale* (Manchester, 2003).

—— 'The Ulster Volunteer Force, 1910–20: New Perspectives', in D. George Boyce and Alan O'Day (eds), *The Ulster Crisis 1885–1921* (2006), pp. 247–58.

—— *Carson's Army: The Ulster Volunteer Force, 1910–22* (Manchester, 2007).

Brown, Kris, '"Our Father Organization": The Cult of the Somme and the Unionist "Golden Age" in Modern Ulster Loyalist Commemoration', *The Round Table* 96.393 (2007), pp. 707–23.

Burke, Tom, *The 16th (Irish) and 36th (Ulster) Divisions at the Battle of Wijtschate – Messines Ridge, 7 June 1917* (Dublin, 2007).

Callan, Patrick, 'Recruiting for the British Army in Ireland during the First World War', *Irish Sword* 17.66 (1987), pp. 42–56.

Canning, W. J., *A Wheen of Medals: The History of the 9th (Service) Bn. The Royal Inniskilling Fusiliers (The Tyrones) in World War One* (Antrim, 2006).

Carver, Field Marshal Lord, *The National Army Museum Book of the Turkish Front, 1914–18* (2003).

Casey, Patrick J., 'Irish Casualties in the First World War', *Irish Sword* 20.81 (1997), pp. 193–206.

Cooper, Bryan, *The Tenth (Irish) Division in Gallipoli* (Dublin, 1993).

Corrigan, Gordon, *Mud, Blood and Poppycock* (2003).

de Wiel, Jérôme Aan, *The Catholic Church in Ireland, 1914–18: War and Politics* (Dublin, 2003).

Denman, Terence, 'The 10th (Irish) Division 1914–15: A Study in Military and Political Interaction', *Irish Sword* 17, 66 (1987), pp. 16–25.

—— 'An Irish Battalion at War: From the Letters of Captain J. H. M. Staniforth, 17 Leinsters 1914–18', *Irish Sword*, 17 (1989), pp. 165–217.

—— 'The Catholic Irish Soldier in the First World War: the "Racial Environment"', *Irish Historical Studies*, XXVII, 27. (1991), pp. 352–65.

—— *Ireland's Unknown Soldiers: The 16th (Irish) Division in the Great War* (Dublin, 1992).

—— *A Lonely Grave: The Life and Death of William Redmond* (Dublin, 1995).

—— 'The 16th (Irish) Division on 21 March 1918: Fight or Flight?' *Irish Sword*, 69 (1999), pp. 273–87.

Doherty, Richard and David Truesdale, *Irish Winners of the Victoria Cross* (Dublin, 2000).

Duffy, Christopher, *Through German Eyes: The British and the Somme 1916* (2006).

Dungan, Myles, *Irish Voices from the Great War* (Dublin, 1995).

—— *They Shall Grow Not Old: Irish Soldiers and the Great War* (Dublin, 1997).

Falls, Cyril, *The History of the 36th (Ulster) Division* (Belfast, 1922).

Fegan, Thomas, *The 'Baby Killers': German Air Raids on Britain in the First World War* (Barnsley, 2002).

Finnan, Joseph, *John Redmond and Irish Unity* (Syracuse, WY, 2004).

—— '"Let Irishmen Come Together in the Trenches": John Redmond and Irish Party Policy in the Great War, 1914–18', *Irish Sword* 22.88 (2000–1), pp. 174–92.

Fitzpatrick, David, 'The Logic of Collective Sacrifice: Ireland and the British Army, 1914–18', *Historical Journal* 38.4 (1995), pp. 1017–30.

Fox, Frank, *The Royal Inniskilling Fusiliers in the World War* (1928).

Gilbert, Martin, *The First World War* (1994).

Graham, B. and P. Shirlow, 'The Battle of the Somme in Ulster Memory and Identity', *Political Geography* 21 (2002), pp. 881–904.

Gregory, Adrian, *The Silence of Memory: Armistice Day 1919–46* (Oxford, 1994).

—— *The Last Great War: British Society and the First World War* (Cambridge, 2008).

Gregory, Adrian and Senia Pašeta (eds), *Ireland and the Great War: 'A War to Unite Us All'?* (Manchester, 2002).

Grieves, Keith, *The Politics of Manpower, 1914–18* (Manchester, 1988).

Griffith, Paddy, *Battle Tactics of the Western Front: The British Army's Art of Attack, 1916–18* (New Haven, CT, 1994).

Hall, Michael, *A Shared Sacrifice for Peace* (Belfast, 2007).

—— *Sacrifice on the Somme* (Belfast, 1993).

Hannon, Charles, 'The Irish Volunteers and the Concepts of Military Service and Defence 1913–24' (University College Dublin, unpublished PhD thesis, 1989).

Harris, Henry, *Irish Regiments in the First World War* (Cork, 1968).

Hart, Peter, *The IRA at War 1916–23* (Oxford, 2003).

Hartley, Tom, *Written in Stone: The History of Belfast City Cemetery* (Belfast, 2006).

Hepburn, A. C., *Catholic Belfast and Nationalist Ireland in the Era of Joe Devlin* (Oxford, 2008).

Jackson, Alvin, *Home Rule: An Irish History, 1800–2000* (Oxford, 2003).

Jeffery, Keith, *Ireland and the Great War* (Cambridge, 2000).

Johnson, Nuala C., 'Memorialising and Marking the Great War: Belfast Remembers', in Frederick W. Boal and Stephen A. Royle, *Enduring City: Belfast in the Twentieth Century* (Belfast, 2006), pp. 207–20.

—— *Ireland, the Great War and the Geography of Remembrance* (Cambridge, 2007).

Johnstone, Kevin, *In the Shadows of Giants: A Social History of the Belfast Shipyards* (Belfast, 2008).

Johnstone, Tom, *Orange, Green and Khaki: The Story of the Irish Regiments in the Great War, 1914–18* (Dublin, 1992).

Jones, Edgar *et al.*, 'Post-Combat Syndromes from the Boer War to the Gulf War: A Cluster Analysis of their Nature and Attribution', *British Medical Journal* 2002 9 February, pp. 324–21.

Jourdain, H. F. N. and Edward Fraser, *The Connaught Rangers: Vol. III* (1928).

Kipling, Rudyard, *The Irish Guards in the Great War, Volume 1: The 1st Battalion* and *Volume 2: The 2nd Battalion* (1923).

Kleinrichert, Denise, *Republican Internment and the Prison Ship* Argenta *1922* (Dublin, 2001).

Lemisko, Lynn Speer, 'Morale in the 16th (Irish) Division, 1916–18', *Irish Sword* 20.81 (1997), pp. 217–33.

Leonard, Jane, 'The Catholic Chaplaincy', in David Fitzpatrick (ed.), *Ireland and the First World War* (Dublin, 1988), pp. 1–14.

—— '"Lest we Forget"', in David Fitzpatrick (ed.), *Ireland and the First World War* (Dublin, 1988), pp. 59–68.

—— 'Getting them at Last: The IRA and Ex-Servicemen', in David Fitzpatrick (ed.), *Revolution? Ireland 1917–23* (Dublin, 1990), pp. 118–29.

—— 'The Reaction of Irish Officers in the British Army to the Easter Rising of 1916', in Hugh Cecil and Peter H. Liddle (eds), *Facing Armageddon: the First World War Experienced* (1996), pp. 256–68.

—— 'The Twinge of Memory: Armistice Day and Remembrance Sunday in Dublin since 1919', in Richard English and Graham Walker (eds), *Unionism in Modern Ireland: New Perspectives on Politics and Culture* (1996), pp. 99–114.

—— 'Facing the "Finger of Scorn": Veterans' Memories of Ireland after the Great War', in Eoin Magennis and Cronan O'Doibhlin, *World War One and its Impacts* (Armagh, 2005), pp. 87–107.

Loughlin, James, 'Mobilising the Sacred Dead: Ulster Unionism, the Great War and the Politics of Remembrance', in Gregory and Pašeta (eds), *Ireland and the Great War*, pp. 133–54.

Lynch, Robert, *The Northern IRA and the Early Years of Partition, 1920–2* (Dublin, 2006).

Lyons, J. B., *The Enigma of Tom Kettle* (Dublin, 1983).

Maume, Patrick, 'The *Irish Independent* and the Ulster Crisis, 1912–21', in G. George Boyce and Alan O'Day (eds), *The Ulster Crisis, 1885–1921* (Basingstoke, 2006), pp. 202–28.

McCaffrey, Barry, *Alex Maskey: Man and Mayor* (Belfast, 2003).

McDermott, Jim, *Northern Divisions: The Old IRA and the Belfast Pogroms 1920–2* (Belfast, 2001).

McGaughey, Jane, 'Ulster Masculinity and Militarisation, 1912–23' (unpublished PhD thesis, University of London, 2008).

McIntosh, Gillian, *The Force of Culture: Unionist Identities in Twentieth-Century Ireland* (Cork, 1999).

Mercer, Eric, 'For King, Country and a Shilling a Day: Recruitment in Belfast during the Great War, 1914–18' (MA dissertation, Queen's University Belfast, 1998).

—— 'For King, Country and a Shilling a Day: Belfast Recruiting Patterns in the Great War', *History Ireland* 11.4 (2003), pp. 29–33.

Moore, Steven, *The Irish on the Somme: A Battlefield Guide to the Irish Regiments in the Great War and the Monuments in their Memory* (Belfast, 2005).

Morrissey, John, 'A Lost Heritage: The Connaught Rangers and Multivocal Irishness', in Mark McCarthy (ed.), *Ireland's Heritage: Critical Perspectives on Memory and Identity* (Aldershot, 2005), pp. 71–87.

Orr, Philip, *The Road to the Somme: Men of the Ulster Division Tell their Story* (Belfast, 1987).

—— 'The Road to Belgrade: the Experiences of the 10th (Irish) Division in the Balkans, 1915–17', in Gregory and Pašeta (eds), *Ireland and the Great War*, pp. 171–89.

—— *Field of Bones: An Irish Division at Gallipoli* (Dublin, 2006).

Parkinson, Alan F., *Belfast's Unholy War: The Troubles of the 1920s* (Dublin, 2004).

Patterson, Henry, 'Industrial Labour and the Labour Movement, 1820–1914', in Líam Kennedy and Philip Ollerenshaw (eds), *An Economic History of Ulster, 1820–1940* (Manchester, 1985).

Perrett, Bryan and Anthony Lord, *The Czar's British Squadron* (1981).

Perry, Nicholas, 'Politics and Command: General Nugent, the Ulster Division and Relations with Ulster Unionism, 1915–17', in Brian Bond (ed.), *'Look to your Front': Studies in the First World War* (Staplehurst, 1999), pp. 105–20.

—— 'Nationality in the Irish Regiments in the First World War', *War and Society*, 12 (1994), pp. 65–95.

—— *Major General Oliver Nugent and the Ulster Division 1915–18* (Stroud, 2007).

Phoenix, Eamon, *Northern Nationalism: Nationalist Politics, Partition and the Catholic Minority in Northern Ireland, 1890–1940* (Belfast, 1994).

Putowski, Julian and Julian Sykes, *Shot at Dawn: Executions in World War One by Authority of the British Army Act* (Barnsley, 1996).

Ryder, Chris, *The Fateful Split: Catholics and the Royal Ulster Constabulary* (2004).

Sheffield, Gary, 'Military Revisionism: The Case of the British Army on the Western Front', in Michael Howard, *A Part of History: Aspects of the British Experience of the First World War* (2008), pp. 1–7.

Sheldon, Jack, *The German Army on the Somme 1914–16* (Barnsley, 2005).

Stanley, Jeremy, *Ireland's Forgotten 10th: A Brief History of the 10th (Irish) Division 1914–18, Turkey, Macedonia and Palestine* (Ballycastle, 2003).

Steel, Nigel and Peter Hart, *Jutland 1916* (2003).

Stewart, A. T. Q., *The Ulster Crisis: Resistance to Home Rule 1914–14* (Belfast, 1967).

Switzer, Catherine, *Unionists and Great War Commemoration in the North of Ireland 1914–39: People, Places and Politics* (Dublin, 2007).

Taylor, James W., *The 1st RIRifles in the Great War* (Dublin, 2002).

—— *The 2nd RIRifles in the Great War* (Dublin, 2005).

Taylor, Paul, 'Heroes or Traitors? Public Reaction to Returning Irish Soldiers from World War One' (MA dissertation, University College London, 2008).

Todman, Dan, *The Great War: Myth and Memory* (2005).

Travers, Tim, *Gallipoli 1915* (2001).

Walker, Stephen, *Forgotten Soldiers: The Irishmen Shot at Dawn* (Dublin, 2007).

Watson, Alexander, *Enduring the Great War: Combat, Morale and Collapse in the German and British Armies, 1914–18* (Cambridge, 2008).

Wheatley, Michael, *Nationalism and the Irish Party, Provincial Ireland 1910–16* (Oxford, 2005).

White, Stuart N., *The Terrors: 16th (Pioneer) Battalion RIRifles* (Belfast, 1996).

Whitton, Frederick Ernest, *A History of the Prince of Wales's Leinster Regiment (Royal Canadians), Volume II* (Aldershot, 1924).

Winter, J. M., *The Great War and the British People* (2003).

Woggon, Helga, *Silent Radical – Winifred Carney, 1887–1943: A Reconstruction of her Biography* (Dublin, 2000).

INTERVIEWS

Ian Adamson
Desy Brennan
Harry Donaghy
Michael Hall
Tom Hartley
Jackie Hewitt
Alban Maginness
Seán O'Hare

EMAILS

Siobhán Deane
Harry Donaghy
Ed McCann
Márirtín ó Muilleoir
Carole Zandvliet

Index